Letters of Horace Walpole, V2

Horace Walpole

Table of Contents

Letters of Horace Walpole, V2 1
  Horace Walpole 1
  MADAME DE BOUFFLERS AT STRAWBERRY—THE FRENCH OPINION OF THE ENGLISH CHARACTER—RICHARDSON'S NOVELS—MADAME DE BEAUMONT 13
  DEBATE ON AMERICAN TAXES—PETITION OF THE PERIWIG-MAKERS—FEMALE HEAD-DRESSES—LORD BYRON'S DUEL—OPENING OF ALMACK'S—NO. 45 15
  HIS "CASTLE OF OTRANTO"—BISHOP PERCY'S COLLECTION OF OLD BALLADS 18
  ILLNESS OF THE KING—FRENCH AND ENGLISH ACTORS AND ACTRESSES: CLAIRON, GARRICK, QUIN, MRS. CLIVE 20
  RIOTS OF WEAVERS—MINISTERIAL CHANGES—FACTIOUS CONDUCT OF MR. PITT 23
  PROSPECTS OF OLD AGE WHEN JOINED TO GOUT 25
  HAS REACHED PARIS—THE FRENCH OPERA—ILLNESS OF THE DAUPHIN—POPULARITY OF MR. HUME 26
  IS MAKING NEW FRIENDS IN PARIS—DECAY OF THE FRENCH STAGE—LE KAIN—DUMENIL—NEW FRENCH INCLINATION FOR PHILOSOPHY AND FREE-THINKING—GENERAL ADMIRATION OF HUME'S HISTORY AND RICHARDSON'S NOVELS 28
  HIS PRESENTATION AT COURT—ILLNESS OF THE DAUPHIN—DESCRIPTION OF HIS THREE SONS 31
  SUPPER PARTIES AT PARIS—WALPOLE WRITES A LETTER FROM LE ROI DE PRUSSE A MONSIEUR ROUSSEAU 33
  A CONSTANT ROUND OF AMUSEMENTS—A GALLERY OF FEMALE PORTRAITS—MADAME GEOFFRIN—MADAME DU DEFFAND—MADAME DE MIREPOIX—MADAME DE BOUFFLERS—MADAME DE ROCHFORT—THE MARECHALE DE LUXEMBURG—THE DUCHESSE DE CHOISEUL—AN OLD FRENCH DANDY—M. DE MAUREPAS—POPULARITY OF HIS LETTER TO ROUSSEAU 35
  SITUATION OF AFFAIRS IN ENGLAND—CARDINAL YORK—DEATH OF STANILAUS LECZINSKI, EX-KING OF POLAND 42

Table of Contents

Letters of Horace Walpole, V2

SINGULAR RIOT IN MADRID—CHANGES IN THE FRENCH MINISTRY—INSURRECTIONS IN THE PROVINCES.................46
THE BATH GUIDE—SWIFT'S CORRESPONDENCE.................48
BATH—WESLEY.................50
MINISTERIAL DIFFICULTIES—RETURN OF LORD CLIVE.................51
DEATH OF CHARLES TOWNSHEND AND OF THE DUKE OF YORK—WHIST THE NEW FASHION IN FRANCE.................53
SOME NEW POEMS OF GRAY—WALPOLE'S "HISTORIC DOUBTS"—BOSWELL'S "CORSICA.".................58
WILKES IS RETURNED M.P. FOR MIDDLESEX—RIOTS IN LONDON—VIOLENCE OF THE MOB.................62
FLEETING FAME OF WITTICISMS—"THE MYSTERIOUS MOTHER.".................65
CASE OF WILKES.................67
THE ENGLISH CLIMATE.................70
VOLTAIRE'S CRITICISMS ON SHAKESPEARE—PARNELL'S "HERMIT.".................71
ARRIVAL OF THE KING OF DENMARK—HIS POPULARITY WITH THE MOB.................73
WILKES'S ELECTION—THE COMTESSE DE BARRI—THE DUC DE CHOISEUL'S INDISCRETION.................75
A GARDEN PARTY AT STRAWBERRY—A RIDOTTO AT VAUXHALL.................77
PAOLI—AMBASSADORIAL ETIQUETTE.................79
HIS RETURN TO PARIS—MADAME DEFFAND—A TRANSLATION OF "HAMLET"—MADAME DUMENIL—VOLTAIRE'S "MEROPE" AND "LES GUEBRES.".................81
THE FRENCH COURT—THE YOUNG PRINCES—ST. CYR—MADAME DE MAILLY.................83
A MASQUERADE—STATE OF RUSSIA.................87
WILKES—BURKE'S PAMPHLET—PREDICTION OF AMERICAN REPUBLICS—EXTRAVAGANCE IN ENGLAND.................89
MASQUERADES IN FASHION—A LADY'S CLUB.................92
THE PRINCESS OF WALES IS GONE TO GERMANY—TERRIBLE ACCIDENT IN PARIS.................93

Table of Contents

Letters of Horace Walpole, V2

- FALL OF THE DUC DE CHOISEUL'S MINISTRY ... 95
- PEACE WITH SPAIN—BANISHMENT OF THE FRENCH PARLIAMENT—MRS. CORNELYS'S ESTABLISHMENT—THE QUEEN OF DENMARK ... 98
- QUARREL OF THE HOUSE OF COMMONS WITH THE CITY—DISSENSIONS IN THE FRENCH COURT AND ROYAL FAMILY—EXTRAVAGANCE IN ENGLAND ... 101
- GREAT DISTRESS AT THE FRENCH COURT ... 103
- ENGLISH GARDENING IN FRANCE—ANGLOMANIE—HE IS WEARY OF PARIS—DEATH OF GRAY ... 105
- SCANTINESS OF THE RELICS OF GRAY—GARRICK'S PROLOGUES, ETC.—WILKES'S SQUINT ... 108
- MARRIAGE OF THE PRETENDER—THE PRINCESS LOUISE, AND HER PROTECTION OF THE CLERGY—FOX'S ELOQUENCE ... 109
- AN ANSWER TO HIS "HISTORIC DOUBTS"—HIS EDITION OF GRAMMONT ... 111
- POPULARITY OF LOUIS XVI—DEATH OF LORD HOLLAND—BRUCE'S "TRAVELS." ... 113
- DISCONTENT IN AMERICA—MR. GRENVILLE'S ACT FOR THE TRIAL OF ELECTION PETITIONS—HIGHWAY ROBBERIES ... 115
- THE POPE'S DEATH—WILKES IS RETURNED FOR MIDDLESEX—A QUAKER AT VERSAILLES ... 118
- BURKE'S ELECTION AT BRISTOL—RESEMBLANCE OF ONE HOUSE OF COMMONS TO ANOTHER—COMFORT OF OLD AGE ... 120
- DEATH OF LORD CLIVE—RESTORATION OF THE FRENCH PARLIAMENT—PREDICTION OF GREAT MEN TO ARISE IN AMERICA—THE KING'S SPEECH ... 122
- RIOTS AT BOSTON—A LITERARY COTERIE AT BATH—EASTON ... 124
- OPPOSITION OF THE FRENCH PARLIAMENTS TO TURGOT'S MEASURES ... 127
- HIS DECORATIONS AT "STRAWBERRY"—HIS ESTIMATE OF HIMSELF, AND HIS ADMIRATION OF CONWAY ... 130
- ANGLOMANIE IN PARIS—HORSE-RACING ... 131
- OSSIAN—CHATTERTON ... 133

Table of Contents

Letters of Horace Walpole, V2

- AFFAIRS IN AMERICA—THE CZARINA AND THE EMPEROR OF CHINA...................134
- DEATH OF LORD CHATHAM—THURLOW BECOMES LORD CHANCELLOR...................136
- EXULTATION OF FRANCE AT OUR DISASTERS IN AMERICA—FRANKLIN—NECKER—CHATTERTON...................138
- ADMIRAL KEPPEL'S SUCCESS—THREATS OF INVASION—FUNERAL OF LORD CHATHAM...................141
- SUGGESTION OF NEGOTIATIONS WITH FRANCE—PARTITION OF POLAND...................143
- UNSUCCESSFUL CRUISE OF KEPPEL—CHARACTER OF LORD CHATHAM...................146
- CAPTURE OF PONDICHERRY—CHANGES IN THE MINISTRY—LA FAYETTE IN AMERICA...................148
- DIVISIONS IN THE MINISTRY—CHARACTER OF THE ITALIANS AND OF THE FRENCH...................150
- ERUPTION OF VESUVIUS—DEATH OF LORD TEMPLE...................152
- CHANCES OF WAR WITH HOLLAND—HIS FATHER'S POLICY—POPE—CHARACTER OF BOLINGBROKE...................154
- POLITICAL EXCITEMENT—LORD G. GORDON—EXTRAORDINARY GAMBLING AFFAIRS IN INDIA...................156
- RODNEY'S VICTORY—WALPOLE INCLINES TO WITHDRAW FROM AMUSEMENTS...................159
- THE GORDON RIOTS...................161
- HOGARTH—COLONEL CHARTERIS—ARCHBISHOP BLACKBURNE—JERVAS—RICHARDSON'S POETRY...................165
- THE PRINCE OF WALES—HURRICANE AT BARBADOES—A "VOICE FROM ST. HELENA."...................167
- NAVAL MOVEMENTS—SIEGE OF GIBRALTAR—FEMALE FASHIONS...................169
- CAPITULATION OF LORD CORNWALLIS—PITT AND FOX...................171
- THE LANGUAGE PROPER FOR INSCRIPTIONS IN ENGLAND—FALL OF LORD NORTH'S MINISTRY—BRYANT...................174
- HIGHWAYMEN AND FOOTPADS...................176

Table of Contents

Letters of Horace Walpole, V2

FOX'S INDIA BILL—BALLOONS 177
BALLOONS 180
HIS LETTERS ON LITERATURE—DISADVANTAGE OF MODERN WRITERS—COMPARISON OF LADY MARY WORTLEY WITH MADAME DE SEVIGNE 181
CRITICISM ON VARIOUS AUTHORS: GREEK, LATIN, FRENCH, AND ENGLISH—HUMOUR OF ADDISON, AND OF FIELDING—WALLER—MILTON—BOILEAU'S "LUTRIN"—"THE RAPE OF THE LOCK"—MADAME DE SEVIGNE 184
MINISTERIAL DIFFICULTIES—THE AFFAIR OF THE NECKLACE IN PARIS—FLUCTUATING UNPOPULARITY OF STATESMEN—FALLACIES OF HISTORY 189
BREVITY OF MODERN ADDRESSES—THE OLD DUCHESS OF MARLBOROUGH 193
LADY CRAVEN—MADAME PIOZZI—"THE ROLLIAD"—HERSCHEL'S ASTRONOMICAL DISCOVERY 196
MRS. YEARSLEY—MADAME PIOZZI—GIBBON—"LE MARIAGE DE FIGARO." 199
GENTLEMEN WRITERS—HIS OWN REASONS FOR WRITING WHEN YOUNG—VOLTAIRE—"EVELINA"—MISS SEWARD—HAYLEY 202
DIVISIONS IN THE ROYAL FAMILY—THE REGENCY—THE IRISH PARLIAMENT 205
"THE ARABIAN NIGHTS"—THE AENEID—BOCCALINI—ORPHEUS AND EURYDICE 209
DISMISSAL OF NECKER—BARON DE BRETEUIL—THE DUC D'ORLEANS—MIRABEAU 211
BRUCE'S "TRAVELS"—VIOLENCE OF THE FRENCH JACOBINS—NECKER 213
THE PRINCE OF WALES—GROWTH OF LONDON AND OTHER TOWNS 215
SIR W. AND LADY HAMILTON—A BOAT-RACE—THE MARGRAVINE OF ANSPACH 218
ARREST OF THE DUCHESSE DE BIRON—THE QUEEN OF

Table of Contents

Letters of Horace Walpole, V2
    FRANCE—PYTHAGORAS 220
    EXPECTATIONS OF A VISIT TO STRAWBERRY BY THE QUEEN 222
    REPORT OF THE VISIT 223

Letters of Horace Walpole, V2

Horace Walpole

Kessinger Publishing reprints thousands of hard-to-find books!

Visit us at http://www.kessinger.net

- MADAME DE BOUFFLERS AT STRAWBERRY—THE FRENCH OPINION OF THE ENGLISH CHARACTER—RICHARDSON'S NOVELS—MADAME DE BEAUMONT.
- DEBATE ON AMERICAN TAXES—PETITION OF THE PERIWIG-MAKERS—FEMALE HEAD-DRESSES—LORD BYRON'S DUEL—OPENING OF ALMACK'S—NO. 45.
- HIS "CASTLE OF OTRANTO"—BISHOP PERCY'S COLLECTION OF OLD BALLADS.
- ILLNESS OF THE KING—FRENCH AND ENGLISH ACTORS AND ACTRESSES: CLAIRON, GARRICK, QUIN, MRS. CLIVE.
- RIOTS OF WEAVERS—MINISTERIAL CHANGES—FACTIOUS CONDUCT OF MR. PITT.
- PROSPECTS OF OLD AGE WHEN JOINED TO GOUT.
- HAS REACHED PARIS—THE FRENCH OPERA—ILLNESS OF THE DAUPHIN—POPULARITY OF MR. HUME.
- IS MAKING NEW FRIENDS IN PARIS—DECAY OF THE FRENCH STAGE—LE KAIN—DUMENIL—NEW FRENCH INCLINATION FOR PHILOSOPHY AND FREE-THINKING—GENERAL ADMIRATION OF HUME'S HISTORY AND RICHARDSON'S NOVELS.
- HIS PRESENTATION AT COURT—ILLNESS OF THE DAUPHIN—DESCRIPTION OF HIS THREE SONS.
- SUPPER PARTIES AT PARIS—WALPOLE WRITES A LETTER FROM LE ROI DE PRUSSE A MONSIEUR ROUSSEAU.
- A CONSTANT ROUND OF AMUSEMENTS—A GALLERY OF FEMALE PORTRAITS—MADAME GEOFFRIN—MADAME DU DEFFAND—MADAME DE MIREPOIX—MADAME DE BOUFFLERS—MADAME DE ROCHFORT—THE MARECHALE DE LUXEMBURG—THE DUCHESSE DE

- CHOISEUL—AN OLD FRENCH DANDY—M. DE MAUREPAS—POPULARITY OF HIS LETTER TO ROUSSEAU.
- SITUATION OF AFFAIRS IN ENGLAND—CARDINAL YORK—DEATH OF STANILAUS LECZINSKI, EX-KING OF POLAND.
- SINGULAR RIOT IN MADRID—CHANGES IN THE FRENCH MINISTRY—INSURRECTIONS IN THE PROVINCES.
- THE BATH GUIDE—SWIFT'S CORRESPONDENCE.
- BATH—WESLEY.
- MINISTERIAL DIFFICULTIES—RETURN OF LORD CLIVE.
- DEATH OF CHARLES TOWNSHEND AND OF THE DUKE OF YORK—WHIST THE NEW FASHION IN FRANCE.
- SOME NEW POEMS OF GRAY—WALPOLE'S "HISTORIC DOUBTS"—BOSWELL'S "CORSICA."
- WILKES IS RETURNED M.P. FOR MIDDLESEX—RIOTS IN LONDON—VIOLENCE OF THE MOB.
- FLEETING FAME OF WITTICISMS—"THE MYSTERIOUS MOTHER."
- CASE OF WILKES.
- THE ENGLISH CLIMATE.
- VOLTAIRE'S CRITICISMS ON SHAKESPEARE—PARNELL'S "HERMIT."
- ARRIVAL OF THE KING OF DENMARK—HIS POPULARITY WITH THE MOB.
- WILKES'S ELECTION—THE COMTESSE DE BARRI—THE DUC DE CHOISEUL'S INDISCRETION.
- A GARDEN PARTY AT STRAWBERRY—A RIDOTTO AT VAUXHALL.
- PAOLI—AMBASSADORIAL ETIQUETTE.
- HIS RETURN TO PARIS—MADAME DEFFAND—A TRANSLATION OF "HAMLET"—MADAME DUMENIL—VOLTAIRE'S "MEROPE" AND "LES GUEBRES."
- THE FRENCH COURT—THE YOUNG PRINCES—ST. CYR—MADAME DE MAILLY.
- A MASQUERADE—STATE OF RUSSIA.
- WILKES—BURKE'S PAMPHLET—PREDICTION OF AMERICAN REPUBLICS—EXTRAVAGANCE IN ENGLAND.
- MASQUERADES IN FASHION—A LADY'S CLUB.
- THE PRINCESS OF WALES IS GONE TO GERMANY—TERRIBLE ACCIDENT IN PARIS.
- FALL OF THE DUC DE CHOISEUL'S MINISTRY.

- PEACE WITH SPAIN—BANISHMENT OF THE FRENCH PARLIAMENT—MRS. CORNELYS'S ESTABLISHMENT—THE QUEEN OF DENMARK.
- QUARREL OF THE HOUSE OF COMMONS WITH THE CITY—DISSENSIONS IN THE FRENCH COURT AND ROYAL FAMILY—EXTRAVAGANCE IN ENGLAND.
- GREAT DISTRESS AT THE FRENCH COURT.
- ENGLISH GARDENING IN FRANCE—ANGLOMANIE—HE IS WEARY OF PARIS—DEATH OF GRAY.
- SCANTINESS OF THE RELICS OF GRAY—GARRICK'S PROLOGUES, ETC.—WILKES'S SQUINT.
- MARRIAGE OF THE PRETENDER—THE PRINCESS LOUISE, AND HER PROTECTION OF THE CLERGY—FOX'S ELOQUENCE.
- AN ANSWER TO HIS "HISTORIC DOUBTS"—HIS EDITION OF GRAMMONT.
- POPULARITY OF LOUIS XVI—DEATH OF LORD HOLLAND—BRUCE'S "TRAVELS."
- DISCONTENT IN AMERICA—MR. GRENVILLE'S ACT FOR THE TRIAL OF ELECTION PETITIONS—HIGHWAY ROBBERIES.
- THE POPE'S DEATH—WILKES IS RETURNED FOR MIDDLESEX—A QUAKER AT VERSAILLES.
- BURKE'S ELECTION AT BRISTOL—RESEMBLANCE OF ONE HOUSE OF COMMONS TO ANOTHER—COMFORT OF OLD AGE.
- DEATH OF LORD CLIVE—RESTORATION OF THE FRENCH PARLIAMENT—PREDICTION OF GREAT MEN TO ARISE IN AMERICA—THE KING'S SPEECH.
- RIOTS AT BOSTON—A LITERARY COTERIE AT BATH—EASTON.
- OPPOSITION OF THE FRENCH PARLIAMENTS TO TURGOT'S MEASURES.
- HIS DECORATIONS AT "STRAWBERRY"—HIS ESTIMATE OF HIMSELF, AND HIS ADMIRATION OF CONWAY.
- ANGLOMANIE IN PARIS—HORSE-RACING.
- OSSIAN—CHATTERTON.
- AFFAIRS IN AMERICA—THE CZARINA AND THE EMPEROR OF CHINA.
- DEATH OF LORD CHATHAM—THURLOW BECOMES LORD CHANCELLOR.
- EXULTATION OF FRANCE AT OUR DISASTERS IN AMERICA—FRANKLIN—NECKER—CHATTERTON.
- ADMIRAL KEPPEL'S SUCCESS—THREATS OF INVASION—FUNERAL OF LORD CHATHAM.

- SUGGESTION OF NEGOTIATIONS WITH FRANCE—PARTITION OF POLAND.
- UNSUCCESSFUL CRUISE OF KEPPEL—CHARACTER OF LORD CHATHAM.
- CAPTURE OF PONDICHERRY—CHANGES IN THE MINISTRY—LA FAYETTE IN AMERICA.
- DIVISIONS IN THE MINISTRY—CHARACTER OF THE ITALIANS AND OF THE FRENCH.
- ERUPTION OF VESUVIUS—DEATH OF LORD TEMPLE.
- CHANCES OF WAR WITH HOLLAND—HIS FATHER'S POLICY—POPE—CHARACTER OF BOLINGBROKE.
- POLITICAL EXCITEMENT—LORD G. GORDON—EXTRAORDINARY GAMBLING AFFAIRS IN INDIA.
- RODNEY'S VICTORY—WALPOLE INCLINES TO WITHDRAW FROM AMUSEMENTS.
- THE GORDON RIOTS.
- HOGARTH—COLONEL CHARTERIS—ARCHBISHOP BLACKBURNE—JERVAS—RICHARDSON'S POETRY.
- THE PRINCE OF WALES—HURRICANE AT BARBADOES—A "VOICE FROM ST. HELENA."
- NAVAL MOVEMENTS—SIEGE OF GIBRALTAR—FEMALE FASHIONS.
- CAPITULATION OF LORD CORNWALLIS—PITT AND FOX.
- THE LANGUAGE PROPER FOR INSCRIPTIONS IN ENGLAND—FALL OF LORD NORTH'S MINISTRY—BRYANT.
- HIGHWAYMEN AND FOOTPADS.
- FOX'S INDIA BILL—BALLOONS.
- BALLOONS.
- HIS LETTERS ON LITERATURE—DISADVANTAGE OF MODERN WRITERS—COMPARISON OF LADY MARY WORTLEY WITH MADAME DE SEVIGNE.
- CRITICISM ON VARIOUS AUTHORS: GREEK, LATIN, FRENCH, AND ENGLISH—HUMOUR OF ADDISON, AND OF FIELDING—WALLER—MILTON—BOILEAU'S "LUTRIN"—"THE RAPE OF THE LOCK"—MADAME DE SEVIGNE.
- MINISTERIAL DIFFICULTIES—THE AFFAIR OF THE NECKLACE IN PARIS—FLUCTUATING UNPOPULARITY OF STATESMEN—FALLACIES OF HISTORY.

- BREVITY OF MODERN ADDRESSES—THE OLD DUCHESS OF MARLBOROUGH.
- LADY CRAVEN—MADAME PIOZZI—"THE ROLLIAD"—HERSCHEL'S ASTRONOMICAL DISCOVERY.
- MRS. YEARSLEY—MADAME PIOZZI—GIBBON—"LE MARIAGE DE FIGARO."
- GENTLEMEN WRITERS—HIS OWN REASONS FOR WRITING WHEN YOUNG—VOLTAIRE—"EVELINA"—MISS SEWARD—HAYLEY.
- DIVISIONS IN THE ROYAL FAMILY—THE REGENCY—THE IRISH PARLIAMENT.
- "THE ARABIAN NIGHTS"—THE AENEID—BOCCALINI—ORPHEUS AND EURYDICE.
- DISMISSAL OF NECKER—BARON DE BRETEUIL—THE DUC D'ORLEANS—MIRABEAU.
- BRUCE'S "TRAVELS"—VIOLENCE OF THE FRENCH JACOBINS—NECKER.
- THE PRINCE OF WALES—GROWTH OF LONDON AND OTHER TOWNS.
- SIR W. AND LADY HAMILTON—A BOAT-RACE—THE MARGRAVINE OF ANSPACH.
- ARREST OF THE DUCHESSE DE BIRON—THE QUEEN OF FRANCE—PYTHAGORAS.
- EXPECTATIONS OF A VISIT TO STRAWBERRY BY THE QUEEN.
- REPORT OF THE VISIT.

[Illustration]

LETTERS

OF

HORACE WALPOLE

SELECTED AND EDITED BY

Letters of Horace Walpole, V2

CHARLES DUKE YONGE, M.A.

AUTHOR OF "THE HISTORY OF FRANCE UNDER THE BOURBONS," "A LIFE OF MARIE ANTOINETTE," ETC., ETC.

WITH PORTRAITS AND ILLUSTRATIONS

VOLUME II

London

T. FISHER UNWIN

PATERNOSTER SQUARE

NEW YORK: G.P. PUTNAM'S SONS

MDCCCXC

CONTENTS.

1764–1795.

81. TO MANN, *Dec.* 20, 1764.—Madame de Boufflers at Strawberry—The French Opinion of the English Character—Richardson's Novels—Madame de Beaumont

82. TO THE EARL OF HERTFORD, *Feb.* 12, 1765.—Debate on American Taxes—Petition of the Periwig-Makers—Female Head-dresses—Lord Byron's Duel—Opening of Almack's—No. 45

83. TO COLE, *March* 9, 1765.—His "Castle of Otranto"—Bishop Percy's Collection of Old Ballads

84. TO THE EARL OF HERTFORD, *March* 26, 1765.—Illness of the King—French and English Actors and Actresses: Clairon, Garrick, Quin, Mrs. Clive

85. TO MANN, *May* 25, 1765.—Riots of Weavers—Ministerial Changes—Factious Conduct of Mr. Pitt

86. TO MONTAGU, *July* 28, 1765.—Prospects of Old Age when joined to Gout

87. TO LADY HERVEY, *Sept.* 14, 1765.—Has reached Paris—The French Opera—Illness of the Dauphin—Popularity of Mr. Hume

88. TO MONTAGU, *Sept.* 22, 1765.—Is Making New Friends in Paris—Decay of the French Stage—Le Kain—Dumenil—New French inclination for Philosophy and Free-Thinking—General Admiration of Hume's History and Richardson's Novels

89. TO CHUTE, *Oct.* 3, 1765.—His Presentation at Court—Illness of the Dauphin—Description of his Three Sons

90. TO CONWAY, *Jan.* 12, 1766.—Supper Parties at Paris—Walpole Writes a Letter from Le Roi de Prusse a Monsieur Rousseau

91. TO GRAY, *Jan.* 25, 1766.—A Constant Round of Amusements—A Gallery of Female Portraits—Madame Geoffrin—Madame du Deffand—Madame de Mirepoix—Madame de Boufflers—Madame de Rochfort—The Marechale de Luxemburg—The Duchesse de Choiseul—An old French Dandy—M. de Maurepas—Popularity of his Letter to Rousseau

92. TO MANN, *Feb.* 29, 1766.—Situation of Affairs in England—Cardinal York—Death of Stanilaus Leczinski, Ex-King of Poland

93. TO CONWAY, *April* 8, 1766.—Singular Riot in Madrid—Changes in the French Ministry—Insurrections in the Provinces

94. TO MONTAGU, *June 20*, 1766.—The Bath Guide—Swift's Correspondence

95. TO CHUTE, *Oct.* 10, 1766.—Bath—Wesley

96. TO MANN, *July* 20, 1767.—Ministerial Difficulties—Return of Lord Clive

97. TO THE SAME, *Sept.* 27, 1767.—Death of Charles Townshend and of the Duke of York—Whist the New Fashion in France

98. TO GRAY, *Feb.* 18, 1768.—Some New Poems of Gray—Walpole's "Historic Doubts"—Boswell's "Corsica"

99. TO MANN, *March* 31, 1768.—Wilkes is returned M.P. for Middlesex—Riots in London—Violence of the Mob

100. TO MONTAGU, *April* 15, 1768.—Fleeting Fame of Witticisms—"The Mysterious Mother"

101. TO MANN, *June* 9, 1768.—Case of Wilkes

102. TO MONTAGU, *June* 15, 1768.—The English Climate

103. TO VOLTAIRE, *July* 27, 1768.—Voltaire's Criticisms on Shakespeare—Parnell's "Hermit"

104. TO THE EARL OF STRAFFORD, *Aug.* 16, 1768.—Arrival of the King of Denmark—His Popularity with the Mob

105. TO MANN, *Jan.* 31, 1769.—Wilkes's Election—The Comtesse de Barri—The Duc de Choiseul's Indiscretion

106. TO MONTAGU, *May* 11, 1769.—A Garden Party at Strawberry—A Ridotto at Vauxhall

107. TO MANN, *June* 14, 1769.—Paoli—Ambassadorial Etiquette

108. TO CHUTE, *Aug.* 30, 1765.—His Return to Paris—Madame Deffand—A Translation of "Hamlet"—Madame Dumenil—Voltaire's "Merope" and "Les Guebres"

109. TO MONTAGU, *Sept.* 17, 1769.—The French Court—The Young Princes—St. Cyr—Madame de Mailly

Letters of Horace Walpole, V2

110. TO MANN, *Feb.* 27, 1770.—A Masquerade—State of Russia

111. TO THE SAME, *May* 6, 1770.—Wilkes—Burke's Pamphlet—Prediction of American Republics—Extravagance in England

112. TO MONTAGU, *May* 6, 1770.—Masquerades in Fashion—A Lady's Club

113. TO MANN, *June* 15, 1770,—The Princess of Wales is gone to Germany—Terrible Accident in Paris

114. TO THE SAME, *Dec.* 29, 1770.—Fall of the Duc de Choiseul's Ministry

115. TO THE SAME, *Feb.* 22, 1771.—Peace with Spain—Banishment of the French Parliament—Mrs. Cornelys's Establishment—The Queen of Denmark 116. TO THE SAME, *April* 26, 1771.—Quarrel of the House of Commons with the City—Dissensions in the French Court and Royal Family—Extravagance in England

117. TO CONWAY, *July* 30, 1771.—Great Distress at the French Court

118. TO CHUTE, *August* 5, 1771.—English Gardening in France—Anglomanie—He is weary of Paris—Death of Gray

119. TO COLE, *Jan.* 28, 1772.—Scantiness of the Relics of Gray—Garrick's Prologues, &c.—Wilkes's Squint

120. TO MANN, *April* 9, 1772.—Marriage of the Pretender—The Princess Louise, and her Protection of the Clergy—Fox's Eloquence

121. TO COLE, *Jan.* 8, 1773.—An Answer to his "Historic Doubts"—His Edition of Grammont

122. TO MANN, *July_10, 1774.—Popularity of Louis XVI.—Death of Lord Holland—Bruce's "Travels"*

123. TO THE SAME, *Oct.* 6, 1774.—Discontent in America—Mr. Grenville's Act for the Trial of Election Petitions—Highway Robberies

124. TO THE SAME, *Oct.* 22, 1774.—The Pope's Death—Wilkes is returned for Middlesex—A Quaker at Versailles

125. TO THE COUNTESS OF AILESBURY, *Nov.* 7, 1774.—Burke's Election at Bristol—Resemblance of one House of Commons to Another—Comfort of Old Age

126. TO MANN, *Nov.* 24, 1774.—Death of Lord Clive—Restoration of the French Parliament—Prediction of Great Men to arise in America—The King's Speech

127. TO CONWAY AND LADY AYLESBURY, *Jan.* 15, 1775.—Riots at Boston—A Literary Coterie at Bath–Easton

128. TO GEM, *April* 4, 1776.—Opposition of the French Parliaments to Turgot's Measures

129. TO CONWAY, *June* 20, 1776.—His Decorations at "Strawberry"—His Estimate of himself, and his Admiration of Conway

130. TO MANN, *Dec.* 1, 1776.—Anglomanie in Paris—Horse-Racing

131. TO COLE, *June* 19, 1777.—Ossian—Chatterton

132. TO MANN, *Oct.* 26, 1777.—Affairs in America—The Czarina and the Emperor of China

133. TO THE SAME, *May* 31, 1778.—Death of Lord Chatham—Thurlow becomes Lord Chancellor

134. TO COLE, *June* 3, 1778.—Exultation of France at our Disasters in America—Franklin—Necker—Chatterton

135. TO MANN, *July* 7, 1778.—Admiral Keppel's Success—Threats of Invasion—Funeral of Lord Chatham

136. TO CONWAY, *July* 8, 1778.—Suggestion of Negotiations with France—Partition of Poland

137. TO MANN, *Oct.* 8, 1778.—Unsuccessful Cruise of Keppel—Character of Lord Chatham

138. TO THE SAME, *March* 22, 1779.—Capture of Pondicherry—Changes in the Ministry—La Fayette in America

139. TO THE SAME, *July* 7, 1779.—Divisions in the Ministry—Character of the Italians and of the French

140. TO THE SAME, *Sept.* 16, 1779.—Eruption of Vesuvius—Death of Lord Temple

141. TO THE SAME, *Jan.* 13, 1780.—Chances of War with Holland—His Father's Policy—Pope—Character of Bolingbroke

142. TO THE SAME, *Feb.* 6, 1780.—Political Excitement—Lord G. Gordon—Extraordinary Gambling Affairs in India

143. TO THE SAME, *March* 3, 1780.—Rodney's Victory—Walpole inclines to Withdraw from Amusements

144. TO THE SAME, *June* 5, 1780.—The Gordon Riots

145. TO DALRYMPLE, *Dec.* 11, 1780.—Hogarth—Colonel Charteris—Archbishop Blackburne—Jervas—Richardson's Poetry

146. TO MANN, *Dec.* 31, 1780.—The Prince of Wales—Hurricane at Barbadoes—A "Voice from St. Helena"

147. TO THE SAME, *Sept.* 7, 1781.—Naval Movements—Siege of Gibraltar—Female Fashions

148. TO THE SAME, *Nov.* 29, 1781.—Capitulation of Lord Cornwallis—Pitt and Fox

149. TO COLE, *April* 13, 1782.—The Language proper for Inscriptions in England—Fall of Lord North's Ministry—Bryant

Letters of Horace Walpole, V2

150. TO MANN, *Sept.* 8, 1782.—Highwaymen and Footpads

151. TO THE SAME, *Dec.* 2, 1783.—Fox's India Bill—Balloons

152. TO CONWAY, *Oct.* 15, 1784.—Balloons

153. TO PINKERTON, *June* 22, 1785.—His Letters on Literature—Disadvantage of Modern Writers—Comparison of Lady Mary Wortley with Madame de Sevigne

154. TO THE SAME, *June* 26, 1785.—Criticism on various Authors: Greek, Latin, French, and English—Humour of Addison, and of Fielding—Waller—Milton—Boileau's "Lutrin"—"The Rape of the Lock"—Madame de Sevigne

155. TO MANN, *Aug.* 26, 1785.—Ministerial Difficulties—The Affair of the Necklace in Paris—Fluctuating Unpopularity of Statesmen—Fallacies of History

156. TO THE SAME, *Oct.* 4, 1785.—Brevity of Modern Addresses—The old Duchess of Marlborough

157. TO THE SAME, *Oct.* 30, 1785.—Lady Craven—Madame Piozzi—"The Rolliad"—Herschel's Astronomical Discovery

158. TO MISS MORE, *Oct.* 14, 1787.—Mrs. Yearsley—Madame Piozzi—Gibbon—"Le Mariage de Figaro"

159. TO THE SAME, *July* 12, 1788.—Gentlemen Writers—His own Reasons for Writing when Young—Voltaire—"Evelina"—Miss Seward—Hayley

160. TO MANN, *Feb.* 12, 1789.—Divisions in the Royal Family—The Regency—The Irish Parliament

161. TO MISS BERRY, *June* 30, 1789.—"The Arabian Nights"—The Aeneid—Boccalini—Orpheus and Eurydice

162. TO CONWAY, *July* 15, 1789.—Dismissal of Necker—Baron de Breteuil—The Duc D'Orleans—Mirabeau

163. TO THE SAME, *July* 1, 1790.—Bruce's "Travels"—Violence of the French Jacobins—Necker

164. TO MISS BERRYS, *June* 8, 1791.—The Prince of Wales—Growth of London and other Towns

165. TO THE SAME, *Aug.* 23, 1791.—Sir W. and Lady Hamilton—A Boat-race—The Margravine of Anspach

166. TO THE SAME, *Oct.* 15, 1793.—Arrest of the Duchesse de Biron—The Queen of France—Pythagoras

167. TO CONWAY, *July 2*, 1795.—Expectations of a Visit to Strawberry by the Queen

168. TO THE SAME, *July* 7, 1795.—Report of the Visit

A SELECTION

FROM THE

LETTERS OF HORACE WALPOLE.

VOLUME II.

MADAME DE BOUFFLERS AT STRAWBERRY—THE FRENCH OPINION OF THE ENGLISH CHARACTER—RICHARDSON'S NOVELS—MADAME DE BEAUMONT.

TO SIR HORACE MANN.

ARLINGTON STREET, *Dec.* 20, 1764.

... My journey to Paris is fixed for some time in February, where I hear I may expect to find Madame de Boufflers, Princess of Conti. Her husband is just dead; and you know the

House of Bourbon have an alacrity at marrying their old mistresses. She was here last year, being extremely infected with the *Anglomanie*, though I believe pretty well cured by her journey. She is past forty, and does not appear ever to have been handsome, but is one of the most agreeable and sensible women I ever saw; yet I must tell you a trait of her that will not prove my assertion. Lady Holland asked her how she liked Strawberry Hill? She owned that she did not approve of it, and that it was not *digne de la solidite Angloise.* It made me laugh for a quarter of an hour. They allot us a character we have not, and then draw consequences from that idea, which would be absurd, even if the idea were just. One must not build a Gothic house because the nation is *solide.* Perhaps, as everything now in France must be *a la Grecque*, she would have liked a hovel if it pretended to be built after Epictetus's—but Heaven forbid that I should be taken for a philosopher! Is it not amazing that the most sensible people in France can never help being domineered by sounds and general ideas? Now everybody must be a *geometre*, now a *philosophe*, and the moment they are either, they are to take up a character and advertise it: as if one could not study geometry for one's amusement or for its utility, but one must be a geometrician at table, or at a visit! So the moment it is settled at Paris that the English are solid, every Englishman must be wise, and, if he has a good understanding, he must not be allowed to play the fool. As I happen to like both sense and nonsense, and the latter better than what generally passes for the former, I shall disclaim, even at Paris, the *profondeur*, for which they admire us; and I shall nonsense to admire Madame de Boufflers, though her nonsense is not the result of nonsense, but of sense, and consequently not the genuine nonsense that I honour. When she was here, she read a tragedy in prose to me, of her own composition, taken from "The Spectator:" the language is beautiful and so are the sentiments.

There is a Madame de Beaumont who has lately written a very pretty novel, called "Lettres du Marquis du Roselle." It is imitated, too, from an English standard, and in my opinion a most woful one; I mean the works of Richardson, who wrote those deplorably tedious lamentations, "Clarissa" and "Sir Charles Grandison," which are pictures of high life as conceived by a bookseller, and romances as they would be spiritualized by a Methodist teacher: but Madame de Beaumont has almost avoided sermons, and almost reconciled sentiments and common sense. Read her novel—you will like it.

DEBATE ON AMERICAN TAXES—PETITION OF THE PERIWIG-MAKERS—FEMALE HEAD-DRESSES—LORD BYRON'S DUEL—OPENING OF ALMACK'S—NO. 45.

TO THE EARL OF HERTFORD.

ARLINGTON STREET, *Feb.* 12, 1765.

A great many letters pass between us, my dear lord, but I think they are almost all of my writing. I have not heard from you this age. I sent you two packets together by Mr. Freeman, with an account of our chief debates. Since the long day, I have been much out of order with a cold and cough, that turned to a fever: I am now taking James's powder, not without apprehensions of the gout, which it gave me two or three years ago.

There has been nothing of note in Parliament but one slight day on the American taxes,[1] which, Charles Townshend supporting, received a pretty heavy thump from Barre, who is the present Pitt, and the dread of all the vociferous Norths and Rigbys, on whose lungs depended so much of Mr. Grenville's power. Do you never hear them to Paris?

[Footnote 1: Mr. Grenville's taxation of stamps and other articles in our American colonies, which caused great discontent, and was repealed by Lord Rockingham's Ministry.]

The operations of the Opposition are suspended in compliment to Mr. Pitt, who has declared himself so warmly for the question on the Dismission of officers, that that motion waits for his recovery. A call of the House is appointed for next Wednesday, but as he has had a relapse, the motion will probably be deferred. I should be very glad if it was to be dropped entirely for this session, but the young men are warm and not easily bridled.

If it was not too long to transcribe, I would send you an entertaining petition of the periwig-makers to the King, in which they complain that men will wear their own hair. Should one almost wonder if carpenters were to remonstrate, that since the peace their trade decays, and that there is no demand for wooden legs? *Apropos* my Lady Hertford's friend, Lady Harriot Vernon, has quarrelled with me for smiling at the enormous head-gear of her daughter, Lady Grosvenor. She came one night to Northumberland House with such display of friz, that it literally spread beyond her shoulders. I happened to say it looked as if her parents had stinted her in hair before marriage, and that she was determined to indulge her fancy now. This, among ten thousand things said by all the world, was reported to Lady Harriot, and has occasioned my disgrace. As she never found fault with anybody herself, I excuse her. You will be less surprised to hear that the Duchess of Queensberry has not yet done dressing herself marvellously: she was at Court on Sunday in a gown and petticoat of red flannel....

We have not a new book, play, intrigue, marriage, elopement, or quarrel; in short, we are very dull. For politics, unless the ministers wantonly thrust their hands into some fire, I think there will not even be a smoke. I am glad of it, for my heart is set on my journey to Paris, and I hate everything that stops me. Lord Byron's[1] foolish trial is likely to protract the session a little; but unless there is any particular business, I shall not stay for a puppet-show. Indeed, I can defend my staying here by nothing but my ties to your brother. My health, I am sure, would be better in another climate in winter. Long days in the House kill me, and weary me into the bargain. The individuals of each party are alike indifferent to me; nor can I at this time of day grow to love men whom I have laughed at all my lifetime—no, I cannot alter;—Charles Yorke or a Charles Townshend are alike to me, whether ministers or patriots. Men do not change in my eyes, because they quit a black livery for a white one. When one has seen the whole scene shifted round and round so often, one only smiles, whoever is the present Polonius or the Gravedigger, whether they jeer the Prince, or flatter his phrenzy.

[Footnote 1: In a previous letter Walpole mentions the duel caused by a dispute at cards, in which Lord Byron was so unfortunate as to kill his cousin, Mr. Chaworth.]

Thursday night, 14th.

The new Assembly Room at Almack's[1] was opened the night before last, and they say is very magnificent, but it was empty; half the town is ill with colds, and many were afraid to go, as the house is scarcely built yet. Almack advertized that it was built with hot bricks and boiling water—think what a rage there must be for public places, if this notice, instead of terrifying, could draw anybody thither. They tell me the ceilings were dropping with wet—but can you believe me, when I assure you the Duke of Cumberland was there?—Nay, had had a levee in the morning, and went to the Opera before the assembly! There is a vast flight of steps, and he was forced to rest two or three times. If he dies of it,—and how should he not?—it will sound very silly when Hercules or Theseus ask him what he died of, to reply, "I caught my death on a damp staircase at a new club-room."

[Footnote 1: Almack was a Scotchman, who got up a sort of female club in King Street, St. James's, at the place since known as Willis's Rooms. In the first half of the present century the balls of Almack's were the most fashionable and exclusive in London, under the government of six lady patronesses, without a voucher from one of whom no one could obtain admittance. For a long time after trousers had become the ordinary wear they were proscribed at Almack's, and gentlemen were required to adhere to the more ancient and showy attire of knee-breeches; and it was said that in consequence of one having attempted unsuccessfully to obtain admission in trousers the tickets for the next ball were headed with a notice that "gentlemen would not be admitted without breeches and stockings."]

Williams, the reprinter of the *North Briton*, stood in the pillory to-day in Palace Yard.[1] He went in a hackney-coach, the number of which was 45. The mob erected a gallows opposite him, on which they hung a boot[2] with a bonnet of straw. Then a collection was made for Williams, which amounted to near L200. In short, every public event informs the Administration how thoroughly they are detested, and that they have not a friend whom they do not buy. Who can wonder, when every man of virtue is proscribed, and they have neither parts nor characters to impose even upon the mob! Think to what a government is sunk, when a Secretary of State is called in Parliament to his face "the most profligate sad dog in the kingdom," and not a man can open his lips in his defence. Sure power must have some strange unknown charm, when it can compensate for such contempt! I see many who triumph in these bitter pills which the ministry are so often forced to swallow; I own I do not; it is more mortifying to me to reflect how great and respectable we were three years ago, than satisfactory to see those insulted who have brought such shame upon us. 'Tis poor amends to national honour to know, that if a printer is set in the pillory, his country wishes it was my Lord This, or Mr. That. They will be gathered to the Oxfords, and Bolingbrokes, and ignominious of former days; but the wound they have inflicted is perhaps indelible. That goes to *my* heart, who had felt all the Roman pride of being one of the first nations upon earth!—Good night!—I will go to bed, and dream of Kings drawn in triumph; and then I will go to Paris, and dream I am pro-consul there: pray, take care not to let me be awakened with an account of an invasion having taken place from Dunkirk![3] Yours ever, H.W.

[Footnote 1: This was the last occasion on which the punishment of the pillory was inflicted.]

[Footnote 2: A scandal, for which there was no foundation, imputed to the Princess of Wales an undue intimacy with John Earl of Bute; and with a practical pun on his name the mob in some of the riots which were common in the first years of his reign showed their belief in the lie by fastening a *jack-boot* and a petticoat together and feeding a bonfire with them.]

[Footnote 3: One article in the late treaty of peace had stipulated for the demolition of Dunkirk.]

HIS "CASTLE OF OTRANTO"—BISHOP PERCY'S COLLECTION OF OLD BALLADS.

TO THE REV. WILLIAM COLE.

STRAWBERRY HILL, *March* 9, 1765.

Dear Sir,—I had time to write but a short note with the "Castle of Otranto," as your messenger called on me at four o'clock, as I was going to dine abroad. Your partiality to me and Strawberry have, I hope, inclined you to excuse the wildness of the story. You will even have found some traits to put you in mind of this place. When you read of the picture quitting its panel, did not you recollect the portrait of Lord Falkland, all in white, in my Gallery? Shall I even confess to you, what was the origin of this romance! I waked one morning, in the beginning of last June, from a dream, of which, all I could recover was, that I had thought myself in an ancient castle (a very natural dream for a head filled like mine with Gothic story), and that on the uppermost banister of a great staircase I saw a gigantic hand in armour. In the evening I sat down, and began to write, without knowing in the least what I intended to say or relate. The work grew on my hands, and I grew fond of it—add, that I was very glad to think of anything, rather than politics. In short, I was so engrossed with my tale, which I completed in less than two months, that one evening, I wrote from the time I had drunk my tea, about six o'clock, till half an hour after one in the morning, when my hand and fingers were so weary, that I could not hold the pen to finish the sentence, but left Matilda and Isabella talking, in the middle of a paragraph. You will laugh at my earnestness; but if I have amused you, by retracing with any fidelity the manners of ancient days, I am content, and give you leave to think me idle as you please....

Lord Essex's trial is printed with the State Trials. In return for your obliging offer, I can acquaint you with a delightful publication of this winter, "A Collection of Old Ballads and Poetry," in three volumes, many from Pepys's Collection at Cambridge. There were three such published between thirty and forty years ago, but very carelessly, and wanting many in this set: indeed, there were others, of a looser sort, which the present editor [Dr. Percy[1]], who is a clergyman, thought it decent to omit....

[Footnote 1: Dr. Percy, Bishop of Dromore, in Ireland, was the heir male of the ancient Earls of Northumberland, and the title of his collection was "Reliques of English Poetry." He was also himself the author of more than one imitation of the old ballads, one of which is mentioned by Johnson in a letter to Mr. Langton: "Dr. Percy has written a long ballad in many *fits* [fyttes]. It is pretty enough: he has printed and will soon publish it" (Boswell, iii., ann. 1771).]

My bower is determined, but not at all what it is to be. Though I write romances, I cannot tell how to build all that belongs to them. Madame Danois, in the Fairy Tales, used to *tapestry* them with *jonquils*; but as that furniture will not last above a fortnight in the year, I shall prefer something more huckaback. I have decided that the outside shall be of *treillage*, which, however, I shall not commence, till I have again seen some of old Louis's old-fashioned *Galanteries* at Versailles. Rosamond's bower, you, and I, and Tom Hearne know, was a labyrinth: but as my territory will admit of a very short clew, I lay aside all thoughts of a mazy habitation: though a bower is very different from an arbour, and must have more chambers than one. In short, I both know, and don't know what it should be. I am almost afraid I must go and read Spenser, and wade through his allegories, and drawling stanzas, to get at a picture. But, good night! you see how one gossips, when one is alone, and at quiet on one's own dunghill!—Well! it may be trifling; yet it is such trifling as Ambition never is happy enough to know! Ambition orders palaces, but it is Content that chats for a page or two over a bower.

ILLNESS OF THE KING—FRENCH AND ENGLISH ACTORS AND ACTRESSES: CLAIRON, GARRICK, QUIN, MRS. CLIVE.

TO THE EARL OF HERTFORD.

ARLINGTON STREET, *March* 26, 1765.

Three weeks are a great while, my dear lord, for me to have been without writing to you; but besides that I have passed many days at Strawberry, to cure my cold (which it has done), there has nothing happened worth sending across the sea. Politics have dozed, and common events been fast asleep. Of Guerchy's affair, you probably know more than I do; it is now forgotten. I told him I had absolute proof of his innocence, for I was sure, that if he had offered money for assassination, the men who swear against him would have taken it.

The King has been very seriously ill, and in great danger. I would not alarm you, as there were hopes when he was at the worst. I doubt he is not free yet from his complaint, as the humour fallen on his breast still oppresses him. They talk of his having a levee next week, but he has not appeared in public, and the bills are passed by commission; but he rides out. The Royal Family have suffered like us mortals; the Duke of Gloucester has had a fever, but I believe his chief complaint is of a youthful kind. Prince Frederick is thought to be in a deep consumption; and for the Duke of Cumberland, next post will probably certify you of his death, as he is relapsed, and there are no hopes of him. He fell into his lethargy again, and when they waked him, he said he did not know whether he could call himself obliged to them.

I dined two days ago at Monsieur de Guerchy's, with the Count de Caraman, who brought me your letter. He seems a very agreeable man, and you may be sure, for your sake, and Madame de Mirepoix's, no civilities in my power shall be wanting. I have not yet seen Schouvaloff,[1] about whom one has more curiosity—it is an opportunity of gratifying that passion which one can so seldom do in personages of his historic nature, especially remote foreigners. I wish M. de Caraman had brought the "Siege of Calais," which he tells me is printed, though your account has a little abated my impatience. They tell us the French comedians are to act at Calais this summer—is it possible they can be so absurd, or think us so absurd as to go thither, if we would not go further? I remember, at Rheims, they believed that English ladies went to Calais to drink champagne—is this the suite of that belief? I was mightily pleased with the Duc de Choiseul's answer to the Clairon;[2] but when I hear of the French admiration of Garrick, it takes off something of my wonder at the prodigious adoration of him at home. I never could conceive the marvellous merit of repeating the works of others in one's own language with propriety, however well delivered. Shakespeare is not more admired for writing his plays, than Garrick for acting them. I think him a very good and very various player—but several have pleased me more, though I allow not in so many parts. Quin[3] in Falstaff, was as excellent as Garrick[4] in Lear. Old Johnson far more natural in everything he attempted. Mrs. Porter and your Dumesnil surpassed him in passionate tragedy; Cibber and O'Brien were what Garrick could never reach, coxcombs, and men of fashion. Mrs. Clive is at least as perfect in low comedy—and yet to me, Ranger was the part that suited Garrick the best of all he ever performed. He was a poor Lothario, a ridiculous Othello, inferior to Quin in Sir John Brute and Macbeth, and to Cibber in Bayes, and a woful Lord Hastings and Lord Townley. Indeed, his Bayes was original, but not the true part: Cibber was the burlesque of a great poet, as the part was designed, but Garrick made it a Garretteer. The town did not like him in Hotspur, and yet I don't know whether he did not succeed in it beyond all the rest. Sir Charles Williams and Lord Holland thought so too, and they were no bad judges. I am impatient to see the Clairon, and certainly will, as I have promised, though I have not fixed my day. But do you know you alarm me! There was a time when I was a match for Madame de Mirepoix at pharaoh, to any hour of the night, and I believe did play with her five nights in a week till three and four in the morning—but till eleven o'clock to-morrow morning—Oh! that is a little too much, even at loo. Besides, I shall not go to Paris for pharaoh—if I play all night, how shall I see everything all day?

[Footnote 1: Schouvaloff was notorious as a favourite of the Empress Catharine.]

[Footnote 2: Mdlle. Clairon had been for some years the most admired tragic actress in France. In that age actors and actresses in France were exposed to singular insults. M. Lacroix, in his "France in the Eighteenth Century," tells us: "They were considered as inferior beings in the social scale; excommunicated by the Church, and banished from society, they were compelled to endure all the humiliations and affronts which the public chose to inflict on them in the theatre; and, if any of them had the courage to make head against the storm, and to resist the violence and cruelty of the pit, they were sent to prison, and not released but on condition of apologising to the tyrants who had so cruelly insulted them. Many had a sufficient sense of their own dignity to withdraw themselves from this odious despotism after having been in prison in Fort l'Evecque, their ordinary place of confinement, by the order of the gentlemen of the chamber or the lieutenant of police; and it was in this way that Mdlle. Clairon bade farewell to the Comedie Francaise and gave up acting in 1765, when at the very height of her talent, and in the middle of her greatest dramatic triumphs." The incident here alluded to by Walpole was that "a critic named Freron had libelled her in a journal to which he contributed; and, as she could not obtain justice, she applied to the Duc de Choiseul, the Prime Minister. Even he was unable to put her in the way of obtaining redress, and sought to pacify her by comparing her position to his own. 'I am,' said he, 'mademoiselle, like yourself, a public performer; with this difference in your favour, that you choose what parts you please, and are sure to be crowned with the applause of the public; for I reckon as nothing the bad taste of one or two wretched individuals who have the misfortune of not adoring you. I, on the other hand, am obliged to act the parts imposed on me by necessity. I am sure to please nobody; I am satirised, criticised, libelled, hissed; yet I continue to do my best. Let us both, then, sacrifice our little resentments and enmities to the public service, and serve our country, each in our own station. Besides, the Queen has condescended to forgive Freron, and you may therefore, without compromising your dignity, imitate Her Majesty's clemency'" ("Mem. de Bachaumont," i. 61). But Mdlle. was not to be pacified, nor to be persuaded to expose herself to a repetition of insult; but, though only forty-one, she retired from the stage for ever.]

[Footnote 3: Quin was employed by the Princess of Wales to teach her son elocution, and when he heard how generally his young sovereign was praised for the grace and dignity of his delivery of his speech to his Parliament, he boasted, "Ah, it was I taught the boy to speak."]

[Footnote 4: Garrick was not only a great actor, but also a great reformer of the stage. He seems to have excelled equally both in tragedy and comedy, which makes it natural to suppose that in some parts he may have been excelled by other actors; though he had no equal (and perhaps never has had) in both lines. He was also himself the author of several farces of more than average merit.]

Lady Sophia Thomas has received the Baume de vie, for which she gives you a thousand thanks, and I ten thousand.

We are extremely amused with the wonderful histories of your hyena[1] in the Gevaudan; but our fox-hunters despise you: it is exactly the enchanted monster of old romances. If I had known its history a few months ago, I believe it would have appeared in the "Castle of Otranto,"—the success of which has, at last, brought me to own it, though the wildness of it made me terribly afraid; but it was comfortable to have it please so much, before any mortal suspected the author: indeed, it met with too much honour far, for at first it was universally believed to be Mr. Gray's. As all the first impression is sold, I am hurrying out another, with a new preface, which I will send you.

[Footnote 1: A wolf of enormous size, and, in some respects, irregular conformation, which for a long time ravaged the Gevaudan; it was, soon after the date of this letter, killed, and Mr. Walpole saw it in Paris.]

RIOTS OF WEAVERS—MINISTERIAL CHANGES—FACTIOUS CONDUCT OF MR. PITT.

TO SIR HORACE MANN.

ARLINGTON STREET, *May* 25, 1765, *sent by way of Paris.*

My last I think was of the 16th. Since that we have had events of almost every sort. A whole administration dismissed, taken again, suspended, confirmed; an insurrection; and we have been at the eve of a civil war. Many thousand Weavers rose, on a bill for their relief being thrown out of the House of Lords by the Duke of Bedford. For four days they were suffered to march about the town with colours displayed, petitioning the King, surrounding the House of Lords, mobbing and wounding the Duke of Bedford, and at last besieging his house, which, with his family, was narrowly saved from destruction. At last it grew a regular siege and blockade; but by garrisoning it with horse and foot literally, and calling in several regiments, the tumult is appeased. Lord Bute rashly taking advantage of this unpopularity of his enemies, advised the King to notify to his Ministers that he intended to dismiss them,—and by this step, no *succedaneum* being prepared, reduced his Majesty to the alternative of laying his crown at the foot of Mr. Pitt, or of the Duke of Bedford; and as it proved at last, of both. The Duke of Cumberland was sent for, and was sent to Mr. Pitt, from whom, though offering almost *carte blanche*, he received a peremptory refusal. The next measure was to form a Ministry from the Opposition.

Willing were they, but timid. Without Mr. Pitt nobody would engage. The King was forced to desire his old Ministers to stay where they were. They, who had rallied their very dejected courage, demanded terms, and hard ones indeed—*promise* of never consulting Lord Bute, dismission of his brother, and the appointment of Lord Granby to be Captain-General—so soon did those tools of prerogative talk to their exalted sovereign in the language of the Parliament to Charles I.

The King, rather than resign his sceptre on the first summons, determined to name his uncle Captain-General. Thus the commanders at least were ready on each side; but the Ministers, who by the Treaty of Paris showed how little military glory was the object of their ambition, having contented themselves with seizing St. James's without bloodshed. They gave up their General, upon condition Mr. Mackenzie and Lord Holland were sacrificed to them, and, tacitly, Lord Northumberland, whose government they bestow on Lord Weymouth without furnishing another place to the earl, as was intended for him. All this is granted. Still there are inexplicable riddles. In the height of negotiation, Lord Temple was reconciled to his brother George, and declares himself a fast friend to the late and present Ministry. What part Mr. Pitt will act is not yet known—probably not a hostile one; but here are fine seeds of division and animosity sown!

I have thus in six words told you the matter of volumes. You must analyse them yourself, unless you have patience to wait till the consequences are the comment. Don't you recollect very similar passages in the time of Mr. Pelham, the Duke of Newcastle, Lord Granville, and Mr. Fox? But those wounds did not penetrate so deep as these! Here are all the great, and opulent noble families engaged on one side or the other. Here is the King insulted and prisoner, his Mother stigmatised, his Uncle affronted, his Favourite persecuted. It is again a scene of Bohuns, Montforts, and Plantagenets.

While I am writing, I received yours of the 4th, containing the revolutions in the fabric and pictures of the palace Pitti. My dear sir, make no excuse; we each write what we have to write; and if our letters remain, posterity will read the catastrophes of St. James's and the Palace Pitti with equal indifference, however differently they affect you and me now. For my part, though agitated like Ludlow or my Lord Clarendon on the events of the day, I have more curiosity about Havering in the Bower, the jointure house of ancient royal dowagers, than about Queen Isabella herself. Mr. Wilkes, whom you mention, will be still more interested, when he hears that his friend Lord Temple has shaken hands with his foes Halifax and Sandwich; and I don't believe that any amnesty is stipulated for the exile. Churchill, Wilkes's poet, used to wish that he was at liberty to attack Mr. Pitt and Charles Townshend,—the moment is come, but Churchill is gone! Charles Townshend has got Lord Holland's place—and yet the people will again and again believe that nothing is intended but their interest.

When I recollect all I have seen and known, I seem to be as old as Methuselah: indeed I was born in politics,—but I hope not to die in them. With all my experience, these last five weeks have taught me more than any other ten years; accordingly, a retreat is the whole scope of my wishes; but not yet arrived.

Your amiable sister, Mrs. Foote, is settled in town; I saw her last night at the Opera with Lady Ailesbury. She is enchanted with Manzuoli—and you know her approbation is a test, who has heard all the great singers, learnt of all, and sings with as much taste as any of them. Adieu!

PROSPECTS OF OLD AGE WHEN JOINED TO GOUT.

TO GEORGE MONTAGU, ESQ.

STRAWBERRY HILL, *July* 28, 1765.

The less one is disposed, if one has any sense, to talk of oneself to people that inquire only out of compliment, and do not listen to the answer, the more satisfaction one feels in indulging a self-complacency, by sighing to those that really sympathise with our griefs. Do not think it is pain that makes me give this low-spirited air to my letter. No, it is the prospect of what is to come, not the sensation of what is passing, that affects me. The loss of youth is melancholy enough; but to enter into old age through the gate of infirmity most disheartening. My health and spirits make me take but slight notice of the transition, and, under the persuasion of temperance being a talisman, I marched boldly on towards the descent of the hill, knowing I must fall at last, but not suspecting that I should stumble by the way. This confession explains the mortification I feel. A month's confinement to one who never kept his bed a day is a stinging lesson, and has humbled my insolence to almost indifference. Judge, then, how little I interest myself about public events. I know nothing of them since I came hither, where I had not only the disappointment of not growing better, but a bad return in one of my feet, so that I am still wrapped up and upon a couch. It was the more unlucky as Lord Hertford is come to England for a very few days. He has offered to come to me; but as I then should see him only for some minutes, I propose being carried to town to-morrow. It will be so long before I can expect to be able to travel, that my French journey will certainly not take place so soon as I intended, and if Lord Hertford goes to Ireland, I shall be still more fluctuating; for though the Duke and Duchess of Richmond will replace them at Paris, and are as eager to have me with them, I have had so many more years heaped upon me within this month, that I have not the conscience to trouble young people, when I can no longer be as juvenile as they are. Indeed I shall think myself decrepit, till I again saunter into the garden in my slippers and without my hat in all weathers,—a point I am determined to regain if possible; for even this experience cannot make me resign my temperance and my hardiness. I am tired of the world, its politics, its pursuits, and its pleasures; but it will cost me some struggles before I submit to be tender and careful. Christ! Can I ever stoop to the regimen of old age? I do not wish to dress up a withered person, nor drag it about to public places; but to sit in one's room, clothed warmly, expecting visits from folks I don't wish to see, and tended and nattered by relations impatient for one's death! Let the gout do its worse as expeditiously as it can; it would be more welcome in my stomach than in my limbs. I am not made to bear a course of nonsense and advice, but must play the fool in my own way to the last, alone with all my heart, if I cannot be with the very few I wished to see: but, to depend for comfort on others, who would be no comfort to me; this surely is not a state to be preferred to death: and nobody can have truly enjoyed the advantages of youth, health, and spirits, who is content to exist without the two last, which alone bear any resemblance to the first.

You see how difficult it is to conquer my proud spirit: low and weak as I am, I think my resolution and perseverance will get the better, and that I shall still be a gay shadow; at least, I will impose any severity upon myself, rather than humour the gout, and sink into that indulgence with which most people treat it. Bodily liberty is as dear to me as mental, and I would as soon flatter any other tyrant as the gout, my Whiggism extending as much to my health as to my principles, and being as willing to part with life, when I cannot preserve it, as your uncle Algernon when his freedom was at stake. Adieu!

HAS REACHED PARIS—THE FRENCH OPERA—ILLNESS OF THE DAUPHIN—POPULARITY OF MR. HUME.

TO THE RIGHT HON. LADY HERVEY.

PARIS, *Sept.* 14, 1765.

I am but two days old here, Madam, and I doubt I wish I was really so, and had my life to begin, to live it here. You see how just I am, and ready to make *amende honorable* to your ladyship. Yet I have seen very little. My Lady Hertford has cut me to pieces, and thrown me into a caldron with tailors, periwig-makers, snuff-box-wrights, milliners, &c., which really took up but little time; and I am come out quite new, with everything but youth. The journey recovered me with magic expedition. My strength, if mine could ever be called strength, is returned; and the gout going off in a minuet step. I will say nothing of my spirits, which are indecently juvenile, and not less improper for my age than for the country where I am; which, if you will give me leave to say it, has a thought too much gravity. I don't venture to laugh or talk nonsense, but in English.

Madame Geoffrin came to town but last night, and is not visible on Sundays; but I hope to deliver your ladyship's letter and packet to-morrow. Mesdames d'Aiguillon, d'Egmont, and Chabot, and the Duc de Nivernois are all in the country. Madame de Boufflers is at l'Isle Adam, whither my Lady Hertford is gone to-night to sup, for the first time, being no longer chained down to the incivility of an ambassadress. She returns after supper; an irregularity that frightens me, who have not yet got rid of all my barbarisms. There is one, alas! I never shall get over—the dirt of this country: it is melancholy, after the purity of Strawberry! The narrowness of the streets, trees clipped to resemble brooms, and planted on pedestals of chalk, and a few other points, do not edify me. The French Opera, which I have heard to-night, disgusted me as much as ever; and the more for being followed by the Devin de Village, which shows that they can sing without cracking the drum of one's ear. The scenes and dances are delightful: the Italian comedy charming. Then I am in love with *treillage* and fountains, and will prove it at Strawberry. Chantilly is so exactly what it was when I saw it above twenty years ago, that I recollected the very position of Monsieur le Duc's chair and the gallery. The latter gave me the first idea of mine; but, presumption apart, mine is a thousand times prettier. I gave my Lord Herbert's compliments to the statue of his friend the Constable; and, waiting some time for the concierge, I called out, *Ou est Vatel*?

In short, Madam, being as tired as one can be of one's own country,—I don't say whether this is much or little,—I find myself wonderfully disposed to like this. Indeed I wish I could wash it. Madame de Guerchy is all goodness to me; but that is not new. I have already been prevented by great civilities from Madame de Brentheim and my old friend Madame de Mirepoix; but am not likely to see the latter much, who is grown a most particular favourite of the King, and seldom from him. The Dauphin is ill, and thought in a very bad way. I hope he will live, lest the theatres should be shut up. Your ladyship knows I never trouble my head about royalties, farther than it affects my interest. In truth, the way that princes affect my interest is not the common way.

I have not yet tapped the chapter of baubles, being desirous of making my revenues maintain me here as long as possible. It will be time enough to return to my Parliament when I want money.

Mr. Hume, that is *the Mode*, asked much about your ladyship. I have seen Madame de Monaco, and think her very handsome, and extremely pleasing. The younger Madame d'Egmont, I hear, disputes the palm with her; and Madame de Brionne is not left without partisans. The nymphs of the theatres are *laides a faire peur*, which at my age is a piece of luck, like going into a shop of curiosities, and finding nothing to tempt one to throw away one's money.

There are several English here, whether I will or not. I certainly did not come for them, and shall connect with them as little as possible. The few I value, I hope sometimes to hear of. Your ladyship guesses how far that wish extends. Consider, too, Madam, that one of my unworthinesses is washed and done away, by the confession I made in the beginning of my letter.

IS MAKING NEW FRIENDS IN PARIS—DECAY OF THE FRENCH STAGE—LE KAIN—DUMENIL—NEW FRENCH INCLINATION FOR PHILOSOPHY AND FREE-THINKING—GENERAL ADMIRATION OF HUME'S HISTORY AND RICHARDSON'S NOVELS.

TO GEORGE MONTAGU, ESQ.

PARIS, *Sept.* 22, 1765.

The concern I felt at not seeing you before I left England, might make me express myself warmly, but I assure you it was nothing but concern, nor was mixed with a grain of pouting. I knew some of your reasons, and guessed others. The latter grieve me heartily; but I advise you to do as I do: when I meet with ingratitude, I take a short leave both of it and its host. Formerly I used to look out for indemnification somewhere else; but having lived long enough to learn that the reparation generally proved a second evil of the same sort, I am content now to skin over such wounds with amusements, which at least leave no scars. It is true, amusements do not always amuse when we bid them. I find it so here; nothing strikes me; everything I do is indifferent to me. I like the people very well, and their way of life very well; but as neither were my object, I should not much care if they were any other people, or it was any other way of life. I am out of England, and my purpose is answered.

Nothing can be more obliging than the reception I meet with everywhere. It may not be more sincere (and why should it?) than our cold and bare civility; but it is better dressed, and looks natural; one asks no more. I have begun to sup in French houses, and as Lady Hertford has left Paris to-day, shall increase my intimacies. There are swarms of English here, but most of them are going, to my great satisfaction. As the greatest part are very young, they can no more be entertaining to me than I to them, and it certainly was not my countrymen that I came to live with. Suppers please me extremely; I love to rise and breakfast late, and to trifle away the day as I like. There are sights enough to answer that end, and shops you know are an endless field for me. The city appears much worse to me than I thought I remembered it. The French music as shocking as I knew it was. The French stage is fallen off, though in the only part I have seen Le Kain I admire him extremely. He is very ugly and ill made, and yet has an heroic dignity which Garrick wants, and great fire. The Dumenil I have not seen yet, but shall in a day or two. It is a mortification that I cannot compare her with the Clairon, who has left the stage. Grandval I saw through a whole play without suspecting it was he. Alas! four-and-twenty years make strange havoc with us mortals! You cannot imagine how this struck me! The Italian comedy, now united with their *opera comique*, is their most perfect diversion; but alas! harlequin, my dear favourite harlequin, my passion, makes me more melancholy than cheerful. Instead of laughing, I sit silently reflecting how everything loses charms when one's own youth does not lend it gilding! When we are divested of that eagerness and illusion with which our youth presents objects to us, we are but the *caput mortuum* of pleasure.

Grave as these ideas are, they do not unfit me for French company. The present tone is serious enough in conscience. Unluckily, the subjects of their conversation are duller to me than my own thoughts, which may be tinged with melancholy reflections, but I doubt from my constitution will never be insipid.

The French affect philosophy, literature, and free-thinking: the first never did, and never will possess me; of the two others I have long been tired. Free-thinking is for one's self, surely not for society; besides one has settled one's way of thinking, or knows it cannot be settled, and for others I do not see why there is not as much bigotry in attempting conversions from any religion as to it. I dined to-day with a dozen *savans*, and though all the servants were waiting, the conversation was much more unrestrained, even on the Old Testament, than I would suffer at my own table in England, if a single footman was present. For literature, it is very amusing when one has nothing else to do. I think it rather pedantic in society; tiresome when displayed professedly; and, besides, in this country one is sure it is only the fashion of the day. Their taste in it is worst of all: could one believe that when they read our authors, Richardson and Mr. Hume should be their favourites? The latter is treated here with perfect veneration. His History, so falsified in many points, so partial in as many, so very unequal in its parts, is thought the standard of writing.

In their dress and equipages they are grown very simple. We English are living upon their old gods and goddesses; I roll about in a chariot decorated with cupids, and look like the grandfather of Adonis.

Of their parliaments and clergy I hear a good deal, and attend very little: I cannot take up any history in the middle, and was too sick of politics at home to enter into them here. In short, I have done with the world, and live in it rather than in a desert, like you. Few men can bear absolute retirement, and we English worst of all. We grow so humorsome, so obstinate and capricious, and so prejudiced, that it requires a fund of good-nature like yours not to grow morose. Company keeps our rind from growing too coarse and rough; and though at my return I design not to mix in public, I do not intend to be quite a recluse. My absence will put it in my power to take up or drop as much as I please. Adieu! I shall inquire about your commission of books, but having been arrived but ten days, have not yet had time. Need I say?—no I need not—that nobody can be more affectionately yours than, &c.

Letters of Horace Walpole, V2

HIS PRESENTATION AT COURT—ILLNESS OF THE DAUPHIN—DESCRIPTION OF HIS THREE SONS.

TO JOHN CHUTE, ESQ.

PARIS, *Oct.* 3, 1765.

I don't know where you are, nor when I am likely to hear of you. I write at random, and, as I talk, the first thing that comes into my pen.

I am, as you certainly conclude, much more amused than pleased. At a certain time of life, sights and new objects may entertain one, but new people cannot find any place in one's affection. New faces with some name or other belonging to them, catch my attention for a minute—I cannot say many preserve it. Five or six of the women that I have seen already are very sensible. The men are in general much inferior, and not even agreeable. They sent us their best, I believe, at first, the Duc de Nivernois. Their authors, who by the way are everywhere, are worse than their own writings, which I don't mean as a compliment to either. In general, the style of conversation is solemn, pedantic, and seldom animated, but by a dispute. I was expressing my aversion to disputes: Mr. Hume, who very gratefully admires the tone of Paris, having never known any other tone, said with great surprise, "Why, what do you like, if you hate both disputes and whisk?"

What strikes me the most upon the whole is, the total difference of manners between them and us, from the greatest object to the least. There is not the smallest similitude in the twenty-four hours. It is obvious in every trifle. Servants carry their lady's train, and put her into her coach with their hat on. They walk about the streets in the rain with umbrellas to avoid putting on their hats; driving themselves in open chaises in the country without hats, in the rain too, and yet often wear them in a chariot in Paris when it does not rain. The very footmen are powdered from the break of day, and yet wait behind their master, as I saw the Duc of Praslin's do, with a red pocket-handkerchief about their necks. Versailles, like everything else, is a mixture of parade and poverty, and in every instance exhibits something most dissonant from our manners. In the colonnades, upon the staircases, nay in the antechambers of the royal family, there are people selling all sorts of wares. While we were waiting in the Dauphin's sumptuous bedchamber, till his dressing-room door should be opened, two fellows were sweeping it, and dancing about in sabots to rub the floor.

You perceive that I have been presented. The Queen took great notice of me; none of the rest said a syllable. You are let into the King's bedchamber just as he has put on his shirt; he dresses and talks good-humouredly to a few, glares at strangers, goes to mass, to dinner, and a-hunting. The good old Queen, who is like Lady Primrose in the face, and Queen Caroline in the immensity of her cap, is at her dressing-table, attended by two or three old ladies, who are languishing to be in Abraham's bosom, as the only man's bosom to whom they can hope for admittance. Thence you go to the Dauphin, for all is done in an hour. He scarce stays a minute; indeed, poor creature, he is a ghost, and cannot possibly last three months. The Dauphiness is in her bedchamber, but dressed and standing; looks cross, is not civil, and has the true Westphalian grace and accents. The four Mesdames, who are clumsy plump old wenches, with a bad likeness to their father, stand in a bedchamber in a row, with black cloaks and knotting-bags, looking good-humoured, not knowing what to say, and wriggling as if they wanted to make water. This ceremony too is very short; then you are carried to the Dauphin's three boys, who you may be sure only bow and stare. The Duke of Berry[1] looks weak and weak-eyed: the Count de Provence is a fine boy; the Count d'Artois well enough. The whole concludes with seeing the Dauphin's little girl dine, who is as round and as fat as a pudding.

[Footnote 1: The Duc de Berri was afterwards Louis XVI.; the Comte de Provence became Louis XVIII.; and the Comte d'Artois, Charles X.]

In the Queen's antechamber we foreigners and the foreign ministers were shown the famous beast of the Gevaudan, just arrived, and covered with a cloth, which two chasseurs lifted up. It is an absolute wolf, but uncommonly large, and the expression of agony and fierceness remains strongly imprinted on its dead jaws.

I dined at the Duc of Praslin's with four-and-twenty ambassadors and envoys, who never go but on Tuesdays to Court. He does the honours sadly, and I believe nothing else well, looking important and empty. The Duc de Choiseul's face, which is quite the reverse of gravity, does not promise much more. His wife is gentle, pretty, and very agreeable. The Duchess of Praslin, jolly, red-faced, looking very vulgar, and being very attentive and civil. I saw the Duc de Richelieu in waiting, who is pale, except his nose, which is red, much wrinkled, and exactly a remnant of that age which produced General Churchill,

Wilks the player, the Duke of Argyll, &c. Adieu!

SUPPER PARTIES AT PARIS—WALPOLE WRITES A LETTER FROM LE ROI DE PRUSSE A MONSIEUR ROUSSEAU.

TO THE HON. H.S. CONWAY.

PARIS, *Jan.* 12, 1766.

I have received your letter by General Vernon, and another, to which I have writ an answer, but was disappointed of a conveyance I expected. You shall have it with additions, by the first messenger that goes; but I cannot send it by the post, as I have spoken very freely of some persons you name, in which we agree thoroughly. These few lines are only to tell you I am not idle in writing to you.

I almost repent having come hither; for I like the way of life and many of the people so well, that I doubt I shall feel more regret at leaving Paris than I expected. It would sound vain to tell you the honours and distinctions I receive, and how much I am in fashion; yet when they come from the handsomest women in France, and the most respectable in point of character, can one help being a little proud? If I was twenty years younger, I should wish they were not quite so respectable. Madame de Brionne, whom I have never seen, and who was to have met me at supper last night at the charming Madame d'Egmont's, sent me an invitation by the latter for Wednesday next. I was engaged, and hesitated. I was told, "Comment! savez-vous que c'est qu'elle ne feroit pas pour toute la France?" However, lest you should dread my returning a perfect old swain, I study my wrinkles, compare myself and my limbs to every plate of larks I see, and treat my understanding with at least as little mercy. Yet, do you know, my present fame is owing to a very trifling composition, but which has made incredible noise. I was one evening at Madame Geoffrin's joking on Rousseau's affectations and contradictions, and said some things that diverted them. When I came home, I put them into a letter, and showed it next day to Helvetius and the Duc de Nivernois; who were so pleased with it, that after telling me some faults in the language, which you may be sure there were, they encouraged me to let it be seen. As you know I willingly laugh at mountebanks, *political* or literary, let their talents be ever so great, I was not averse. The copies have spread like wild-fire; *et me voici a la mode*! I expect the end of my reign at the end of the week with great composure. Here is the letter:—

LE ROI DE PRUSSE A MONSIEUR ROUSSEAU.[1]

MON CHER JEAN JACQUES,

Vous avez renonce a Geneve votre patrie; vous vous etes fait chasser de la Suisse, pays tant vante dans vos ecrits; la France vous a decrete. Venez donz chez moi; j'admire vos talens; je m'amuse de vos reveries, qui (soit dit en passant) vous occupent trop, et trop long tems. Il faut a la fin etre sage et heureux. Vous avez fait assez parler de vous par des singularites peu convenables a un veritable grand homme. Demontrez a vos ennemis que vous pouvez avoir quelquefois le sens commun: cela les fachera, sans vous faire tort. Mes etats vous offrent une retraite paisible; je vous veux du bien, et je vous en ferai, si vous le trouvez bon. Mais si vous vous obstiniez a rejetter mons secours, attendez-vous que je ne le dirai a personne. Si vous persistez a vous creuser l'esprit pour trouver de nouveaux malheurs, choisissez les tels que vous voudrez. Je suis roi, je puis vous en procurer au gre de vos souhaits: et ce qui surement ne vous arrivera pas vis a vis de vos ennemis, je cesserai de vous persecuter quand vous cesserez de mettre votre gloire a l'etre.

Votre bon ami,

FREDERIC.

[Footnote 1: Rousseau was always ready to believe in plots to mortify and injure him; and he was so much annoyed by this composition of Walpole's, that, shortly after his arrival in England, he addressed the following letter to *The London Chronicle*:—

"WOOTTON [IN DERBYSHIRE], *March* 3, 1766

"You have failed, Sir, in the respect which every private person owes to a crowned head, in attributing publicly to the King of Prussia a letter full of extravagance and malignity, of which, for those very reasons, you ought to have known he could not be the author. You have even dared to transcribe his signature, as if you had seen him write it with his own hand. I inform you, Sir, that the letter was fabricated at Paris, and what rends my heart is that the impostor has accomplices in England. You owe to the King of Prussia, to truth, and to me to print the letter which I write to you, and which I sign, as an atonement for a fault with which you would doubtless reproach yourself severely, if you knew to what a dark transaction you have rendered yourself an accessory. I salute you, Sir, very sincerely,

"ROUSSEAU."]

The Princesse de Ligne, whose mother was an Englishwoman, made a good observation to me last night. She said, "Je suis roi, je puis vous procurer de malheurs," was plainly the stroke of an English pen. I said, then I had certainly not well imitated the character in which I wrote. You will say I am a bold man to attack both Voltaire and Rousseau. It is true; but I shoot at their heel, at their vulnerable part.

I beg your pardon for taking up your time with these trifles. The day after to-morrow we go in cavalcade with the Duchess of Richmond to her audience; I have got my cravat and shammy shoes. Adieu!

A CONSTANT ROUND OF AMUSEMENTS—A GALLERY OF FEMALE PORTRAITS—MADAME GEOFFRIN—MADAME DU DEFFAND—MADAME DE MIREPOIX—MADAME DE BOUFFLERS—MADAME DE ROCHFORT—THE MARECHALE DE LUXEMBURG—THE DUCHESSE DE CHOISEUL—AN OLD FRENCH DANDY—M. DE MAUREPAS—POPULARITY OF HIS LETTER TO ROUSSEAU.

TO MR. GRAY.

PARIS, *Jan.* 25, 1766.

I am much indebted to you for your kind letter and advice; and though it is late to thank you for it, it is at least a stronger proof that I do not forget it. However, I am a little obstinate, as you know, on the chapter of health, and have persisted through this Siberian winter in not adding a grain to my clothes, and going open-breasted without an under waistcoat. In short, though I like extremely to live, it must be in my own way, as long as I can: it is not youth I court, but liberty; and I think making oneself tender is issuing a *general warrant* against one's own person. I suppose I shall submit to confinement when I cannot help it; but I am indifferent enough to life not to care if it ends soon after my prison begins.

I have not delayed so long to answer your letter, from not thinking of it, or from want of matter, but from want of time. I am constantly occupied, engaged, amused, till I cannot bring a hundredth part of what I have to say into the compass of a letter. You will lose nothing by this: you know my volubility, when I am full of new subjects; and I have at least many hours of conversation for you at my return. One does not learn a whole nation in four or five months; but, for the time, few, I believe, have seen, studied, or got so much acquainted with the French as I have.

By what I said of their religious or rather irreligious opinions, you must not conclude their people of quality atheists—at least, not the men. Happily for them, poor souls! they are not capable of going so far into thinking. They assent to a great deal, because it is the fashion, and because they don't know how to contradict. They are ashamed to defend the Roman Catholic religion, because it is quite exploded; but I am convinced they believe it in their hearts. They hate the Parliaments and the philosophers, and are rejoiced that they may still idolise royalty. At present, too, they are a little triumphant: the Court has shown a little spirit, and the Parliaments much less: but as the Duc de Choiseul, who is very fluttering, unsettled, and inclined to the philosophers, has made a compromise with the Parliament of Bretagne, the Parliaments might venture out again, if, as I fancy will be the case, they are not glad to drop a cause, of which they began to be a little weary of the inconveniences.

The generality of the men, and more than the generality are dull and empty. They have taken up gravity, thinking it was philosophy and English, and so have acquired nothing in the room of their natural levity and cheerfulness. However, as their high opinion of their own country remains, for which they can no longer assign any reason, they are contemptuous and reserved, instead of being ridiculously, consequently pardonably, impertinent. I have wondered, knowing my own countrymen, that we had attained such a superiority. I wonder no longer, and have a little more respect for English *heads* than I had.

The women do not seem of the same country: if they are less gay than they were, they are more informed, enough to make them very conversable. I know six or seven with very superior understandings; some of them with wit, or with softness, or very good sense.

[Illustration: THOMAS GRAY, THE POET.

From a drawing in the National Portrait Gallery by James Basire, after a sketch by Gray's friend and biographer, the Rev. William Mason.]

Madame Geoffrin, of whom you have heard much, is an extraordinary woman, with more common sense than I almost ever met with. Great quickness in discovering characters, penetration in going to the bottom of them, and a pencil that never fails in a likeness—seldom a favourable one. She exacts and preserves, spite of her birth and their nonsensical prejudices about nobility, great court and attention. This she acquires by a thousand little arts and offices of friendship: and by a freedom and severity, which seem to be her sole end of drawing a concourse to her; for she insists on scolding those she inveigles to her. She has little taste and less knowledge, but protects artisans and authors, and courts a few people to have the credit of serving her dependents. She was bred under the famous Madame Tencin,[1] who advised her never to refuse any man; for, said her mistress, though nine in ten should not care a farthing for you, the tenth may live to be an useful friend. She did not adopt or reject the whole plan, but fully retained the purport of the maxim. In short, she is an epitome of empire, subsisting by rewards and punishments. Her great enemy, Madame du Deffand,[2] was for a short time mistress of the Regent, is now very old and stoneblind, but retains all her vivacity, wit, memory, judgment, passions, and agreeableness. She goes to Operas, Plays, suppers, and Versailles; gives suppers twice a week; has everything new read to her; makes new songs and epigrams, ay, admirably, and remembers every one that has been made these four-score years. She corresponds with Voltaire, dictates charming letters to him, contradicts him, is no bigot to him or anybody, and laughs both at the clergy and the philosophers. In a dispute, into which she easily falls, she is very warm, and yet scarce ever in the wrong: her judgment on every subject is as just as possible; on every point of conduct as wrong as possible: for she is all love and hatred, passionate for her friends to enthusiasm, still anxious to be loved, I don't mean by lovers, and a vehement enemy, but openly. As she can have no amusement but conversation, the least solitude and *ennui* are insupportable to her, and put her into the power of several worthless people, who eat her suppers when they can eat nobody's of higher rank; wink to one another and laugh at her; hate her because she has forty times more parts—and venture to hate her because she is not rich.[3] She has an old friend whom I must mention, a Monsieur Pondeveyle, author of the "Fatpuni," and the "Complaisant," and of those pretty novels, the "Comte de Cominge," the "Siege of Calais," and "Les Malheurs de l'Amour." Would you not expect this old man to be very agreeable? He can be so, but seldom is: yet he has another very different and very amusing talent, the art of parody, and is unique in his kind. He composes tales to the tunes of long dances: for instance, he has adapted the Regent's "Daphnis and Chloe" to one, and made it ten times more indecent; but is so old, and sings it so well, that it is permitted in all companies. He has succeeded still better in *les caracteres de la danse*, to which he has adapted words that express all the characters of love. With all this he has not the least idea of cheerfulness in conversation; seldom speaks but on grave subjects, and not often on them; is a humourist, very supercilious, and wrapt up in admiration of his own country, as the only judge of his merit. His air and look are cold and forbidding; but ask him to sing, or praise his works, his eyes and smiles open and brighten up. In short, I can show him to you: the self-applauding poet in Hogarth's Rake's Progress, the second print, is so like his very features and very wig, that you would know him by it, if you came hither—for he certainly will not go to you.

[Footnote 1: *"The famous Mme. Tencin."* "Infamous" would be more appropriate. She had been the mistress of Dubois, and was the mother of D'Alembert.]

[Footnote 2: His description of her on first making her acquaintance was not altogether complimentary. In a letter of the preceding October he calls her "an old blind debauchee of wit." In fact, she had been one of the mistresses of the Regent, Duc d'Orleans, and at first his chief inducement to court her society was to hear anecdotes of the Regent. But gradually he became so enamoured of her society that he kept up an intimacy with her till her death in 1783. There must be allowed to be much delicate perception and delineation of character in this description of the French fine ladies of the time.]

[Footnote 3: To the above portrait of Madame du Deffand it may be useful to subjoin the able development of her character which appeared in the *Quarterly Review* for May, 1811, in its critique on her Letters to Walpole:—"This lady seems to have united the lightness of the French character with the solidity of the English. She was easy and volatile, yet judicious and acute; sometimes profound and sometimes superficial. She had a wit playful, abundant, and well-toned; an admirable conception of the ridiculous, and great skill in exposing it; a turn for satire, which she indulged, not always in the best-natured manner, yet with irresistible effect; powers of expression varied, appropriate, flowing from the source, and curious without research; a refined taste for letters, and a judgment both of men and books in a high degree enlightened and accurate."]

Madame de Mirepoix's understanding is excellent of the useful kind, and can be so when she pleases of the agreeable kind. She has read, but seldom shows it, and has perfect taste. Her manner is cold, but very civil; and she conceals even the blood of Lorraine, without ever forgetting it. Nobody in France knows the world better, and nobody is personally so well with the King. She is false, artful, and insinuating beyond measure when it is her interest, but indolent and a coward. She never had any passion but gaming, and always loses. For ever paying court, the sole produce of a life of art is to get money from the King to carry on a course of paying debts or contracting new ones, which she discharges as fast as she is able. She advertised devotion to get made *dame du palais* to the Queen; and the very next day this Princess of Lorraine was seen riding backwards with Madame Pompadour in the latter's coach. When the King was stabbed, and heartily frightened, the mistress took a panic too, and consulted D'Argenson, whether she had not best make off in time. He hated her, and said, By all means. Madame de Mirepoix advised her to stay. The King recovered his spirits, D'Argenson was banished,[1] and La Marechale inherited part of the mistress's credit.—I must interrupt my history of illustrious women with an anecdote of Monsieur de Maurepas, with whom I am much acquainted, and who has one of the few heads which approach to good ones, and who luckily for us was disgraced, and the marine dropped, because it was his favourite object and province. He employed Pondeveyle to make a song on the Pompadour: it was clever and bitter, and did not spare even Majesty. This was Maurepas absurd enough to sing at supper at Versailles. Banishment ensued; and lest he should ever be restored, the mistress persuaded the King that he had poisoned her predecessor Madame de Chateauroux. Maurepas is very agreeable, and exceedingly cheerful; yet I have seen a transient silent cloud when politics are talked of.

[Footnote 1: The Comte d'Argenson was Minister at War.]

Madame de Boufflers, who was in England, is a *savante*, mistress of the Prince of Conti, and very desirous of being his wife. She is two women, the upper and the lower. I need not tell you that the lower is gallant, and still has pretensions. The upper is very sensible, too, and has a measured eloquence that is just and pleasing—but all is spoiled by an unrelaxed attention to applause. You would think she was always sitting for her picture to her biographer.

Madame de Rochfort is different from all the rest. Her understanding is just and delicate; with a finesse of wit that is the result of reflection. Her manner is soft and feminine, and though a *savante*, without any declared pretensions. She is the *decent* friend of Monsieur de Nivernois; for you must not believe a syllable of what you read in their novels. It requires the greatest curiosity, or the greatest habitude, to discover the smallest connexion between the sexes here. No familiarity, but under the veil of friendship, is permitted, and Love's dictionary is as much prohibited, as at first sight one should think his ritual was. All you hear, and that pronounced with *nonchalance*, is, that *Monsieur un tel* has had *Madame une telle*.

The Duc de Nivernois has parts, and writes at the top of the mediocre, but, as Madame Geoffrin says, is *manque par tout; guerrier manque, ambassadeur manque, homme d'affaires manque*, and *auteur manque*—no, he is not *homme de naissance manque*. He would think freely, but has some ambition of being governor to the Dauphin, and is more afraid of his wife and daughter, who are ecclesiastic fagots. The former out-chatters the Duke of Newcastle; and the latter, Madame de Gisors, exhausts Mr. Pitt's eloquence in defence of the Archbishop of Paris. Monsieur de Nivernois lives in a small circle of dependent admirers, and Madame de Rochfort is high-priestess for a small salary of credit.

The Duchess of Choiseul, the only young one of these heroines, is not very pretty, but has fine eyes, and is a little model in waxwork, which not being allowed to speak for some time as incapable, has a hesitation and modesty, the latter of which the Court has not cured, and the former of which is atoned for by the most interesting sound of voice, and forgotten in the most elegant turn and propriety of expression. Oh! it is the gentlest, amiable, civil little creature that ever came out of a fairy egg! so just in its phrases and thoughts, so attentive and good-natured! Everybody loves it but its husband, who prefers his own sister the Duchesse de Granmont, an Amazonian, fierce, haughty dame, who loves and hates arbitrarily, and is detested. Madame de Choiseul, passionately fond of her husband, was the martyr of this union, but at last submitted with a good grace; has gained a little credit with him, and is still believed to idolize him. But I doubt it—she takes too much pains to profess it.

Letters of Horace Walpole, V2

I cannot finish my list without adding a much more common character—but more complete in its kind than any of the foregoing, the Marechale de Luxembourg. She has been very handsome, very abandoned, and very mischievous. Her beauty is gone, her lovers are gone, and she thinks the devil is coming. This dejection has softened her into being rather agreeable, for she has wit and good-breeding; but you would swear, by the restlessness of her person and the horrors she cannot conceal, that she had signed the compact, and expected to be called upon in a week for the performance.

I could add many pictures, but none so remarkable. In those I send you there is not a feature bestowed gratis or exaggerated. For the beauties, of which there are a few considerable, as Mesdames de Brionne, de Monaco, et d'Egmont, they have not yet lost their characters, nor got any.

You must not attribute my intimacy with Paris to curiosity alone. An accident unlocked the doors for me. That *passe-par-tout* called the fashion has made them fly open—and what do you think was that fashion?—I myself. Yes, like Queen Eleanor in the ballad, I sunk at Charing Cross, and have risen in the Fauxbourg St. Germain. A *plaisanterie* on Rousseau, whose arrival here in his way to you brought me acquainted with many anecdotes conformable to the idea I had conceived of him, got about, was liked much more than it deserved, spread like wild-fire, and made me the subject of conversation. Rousseau's devotees were offended. Madame de Boufflers, with a tone of sentiment, and the accents of lamenting humanity, abused me heartily, and then complained to myself with the utmost softness. I acted contrition, but had liked to have spoiled all, by growing dreadfully tired of a second lecture from the Prince of Conti, who took up the ball, and made himself the hero of a history wherein he had nothing to do. I listened, did not understand half he said (nor he either), forgot the rest, said Yes when I should have said No, yawned when I should have smiled, and was very penitent when I should have rejoiced at my pardon. Madame de Boufflers was more distressed, for he owned twenty times more than I had said: she frowned, and made him signs; but she had wound up his clack, and there was no stopping it. The moment she grew angry, the lord of the house grew charmed, and it has been my fault if I am not at the head of a numerous sect; but, when I left a triumphant party in England, I did not come here to be at the head of a fashion. However, I have been sent for about like an African prince, or a learned canary-bird, and was, in particular, carried by force to the Princess of Talmond,[1] the Queen's cousin, who lives in a charitable apartment in the Luxembourg, and was sitting on a small bed hung with saints and Sobieskis, in a corner of one of those vast chambers, by two blinking tapers. I stumbled over a cat and a footstool in my journey to her presence. She could not find a syllable to say to me, and the visit ended with her begging a lap-dog. Thank the Lord! though this is the first month, it is the last week of my reign; and I shall resign my crown with great satisfaction to a *bouillie* of chestnuts, which is just invented, and whose annals will be illustrated by so many indigestions, that Paris will not want anything else these three weeks. I will enclose the fatal letter[2] after I have finished this enormous one; to which I will only add, that nothing has interrupted my Sevigne researches but the frost. The Abbe de Malesherbes has given me full power to ransack Livry. I did not tell you, that by great accident, when I thought on nothing less, I stumbled on an original picture of the Comte de Grammont. Adieu! You are generally in London in March; I shall be there by the end of it.[3]

[Footnote 1: The Princess of Talmond was born in Poland, and said to be allied to the Queen, Marie Leczinska, with whom she came to France, and there married a prince of the house of Bouillon.]

[Footnote 2: The letter from the King of Prussia to Rousseau.—WALPOLE.]

[Footnote 3: Gray, in reference to this letter, writes thus to Dr. Wharton, on the 5th of March:—"Mr. Walpole writes me now and then a long and lively letter from Paris, to which place he went the last summer, with the gout upon him; sometimes in his limbs; often in his stomach and head. He has got somehow well (not by means of the climate, one would think) goes to all public places, sees all the best company, and is very much in fashion. He says he sunk, like Queen Eleanor, at Charing Cross, and has risen again at Paris. He returns again in April; but his health is certainly in a deplorable state."—*Works by Mitford*, vol. iv. p. 79.]

SITUATION OF AFFAIRS IN ENGLAND—CARDINAL YORK—DEATH OF STANILAUS LECZINSKI, EX-KING OF POLAND.

TO SIR HORACE MANN.

PARIS, *Feb.* 29, 1766.

Letters of Horace Walpole, V2

I have received your letters very regularly, and though I have not sent you nearly so many, yet I have not been wanting to our correspondence, when I have had anything particular to say, or knew what to say. The Duke of Richmond has been gone to England this fortnight; he had a great deal of business, besides engagements here; and if he has failed writing, at least I believe he received yours. Mr. Conway, I suppose, has received them too, but not to my knowledge; for I have received but one from him this age. He has had something else to do than to think of Pretenders, and pretenders to pretensions. It has been a question (and a question scarcely decided yet) not only whether he and his friends should remain Ministers, but whether we should not draw the sword on our colonies, and provoke them and the manufacturers at home to rebellion. The goodness of Providence, or Fortune by its permission, has interposed, and I hope prevented blood; though George Grenville and the Duke of Bedford, who so mercifully checked our victories, in compassion to France, grew heroes the moment there was an opportunity of conquering our own brethren. It was actually moved by them and their banditti to send troops to America. The stout Earl of Bute, who is never afraid when not personally in danger, joined his troops to his ancient friends, late foes, and now new allies. Yet this second race of Spaniards, so fond of gold and thirsting after American blood, were routed by 274; their whole force amounting but to 134. The Earl, astonished at this defeat, had recourse to that kind of policy which Machiavel recommends in his chapter of *back-stairs*. Caesar himself disavowed his Ministers, and declared he had not been for the repeal, and that his servants had used his name without his permission. A paper was produced to his eyes, which proved this denial an equivocation. The Ministers, instead of tossing their places into the middle of the closet, as I should have done, had the courage and virtue to stand firm, and save both Europe and America from destruction.

At that instant, who do you think presented himself as Lord Bute's guardian angel? only one of his bitterest enemies: a milk-white angel [Duke of York], white even to his eyes and eyelashes, very purblind, and whose tongue runs like a fiddlestick. You have seen this divinity, and have prayed to it for a Riband. Well, this god of love became the god of politics, and contrived meetings between Bute, Grenville, and Bedford; but, what happens to highwaymen *after* a robbery, happened to them *before*; they quarrelled about the division of the plunder, before they had made the capture—and thus, when the last letters came away, the repeal was likely to pass in both houses, and tyranny once more despairs.

This is the quintessence of the present situation in England. To how many *North Britons*, No. 45, will that wretched Scot furnish matter? But let us talk of your *Cardinal Duke of York*[1]: so his folly has left his brother in a worse situation than he took him up! *York* seems a title fated to sit on silly heads—or don't let us talk of him; he is not worth it.

[Footnote 1: Cardinal York was the younger brother of Charles Edward. He lived in Italy; and, after the death of his brother, assumed the title of King of England as Henry IX. After the confiscation of the greater part of the Papal revenues by Napoleon, his chief means of livelihood was a pension of L4,000 a year allowed him by George IV. out of his private purse.]

I am so sorry for the death of Lady Hillsborough, as I suppose Mr. Skreene is glad of his consort's departure. She was a common creature, bestowed on the public by Lord Sandwich. Lady Hillsborough had sense and merit, and is a great loss to her family. By letters hither, we hear miserable accounts of poor Sir James Macdonald; pray let him know that I have written to him, and how much I am concerned for his situation.

This Court is plunged into another deep mourning for the death of old Stanislaus,[1] who fell into the fire; it caught his night-gown and burnt him terribly before he got assistance. His subjects are in despair, for he was a model of goodness and humanity; uniting or rather creating, generosity from economy. The Poles had not the sense to re-elect him, after his virtues were proved, they who had chosen him before they knew him. I am told such was the old man's affection for his country, and persuasion that he ought to do all the good he could, that he would have gone to Poland if they had offered him the crown. He has left six hundred thousand livres, and a *rente viagere* of forty thousand crowns to the Queen, saved from the sale of his Polish estates, from his pension of two millions, and from his own liberality. His buildings, his employment of the poor, his magnificence, and his economy, were constant topics of admiration. Not only the court-tables were regularly and nobly served, but he treated, and defrayed his old enemy's grand-daughter, the Princess Christina, on her journey hither to see her sister the Dauphiness. When mesdames his grand-daughters made him an unexpected visit, he was so disturbed for fear it should derange his finances, which he thought were not in advance, that he shut himself up for an hour with his treasurer, to find resources; was charmed to know he should not run in debt, and entertained them magnificently. His end was calm and gay, like his life, though he suffered terribly, and he said so extraordinary a life could not finish in a common way. To a lady who had set her ruffle on fire, and scorched her arm about the same time, he said, "Madame, nous brulons du meme feu." The poor Queen had sent him the very night-gown that occasioned his death: he wrote to her, "C'etoit pour me tenir chaud, mais il m'a tenu trop chaud."

[Footnote 1: Stanislaus Leczinski was the father of the queen of Louis XV. On the conclusion of peace between France and the Empire it was arranged that the Duke of Lorraine should exchange that duchy for Tuscany, and that Lorraine should be allotted to Stanislaus, with a reversion to his daughter and to France after his death.]

Yesterday we had the funeral oration on the Dauphin; and are soon to have one on Stanislaus. It is a noble subject; but if I had leisure, I would compose a grand funeral oration on the number of princes dead within these six months. What fine pictures, contrasts, and comparisons they would furnish! The Duke of Parma and the King of Denmark reigning virtuously with absolute power! The Emperor at the head of Europe, and encompassed with mimic Roman eagles, tied to the apron-strings, of a bigoted and jealous virago. The Dauphin cultivating virtues under the shade of so bright a crown, and shining only at the moment that he was snatched from the prospect of empire. The old Pretender wasting away in obscurity and misfortune, after surviving the Duke of Cumberland, who had given the last blow to the hopes of his family; and Stanislaus perishing by an accident,—he who had swam over the billows raised by Peter the Great and Charles XII., and reigning, while his successor and second of his name was reigning on his throne. It is not taking from the funereal part to add, that when so many good princes die, the Czarina is still living!

The public again thinks itself on the eve of a war, by the recall of Stahremberg, the Imperial Minister. It seems at least to destroy the expectation of a match between the youngest Archduchess and the Dauphin, which it was thought Stahremberg remained here to bring about. I like your Great Duke for feeling the loss of his Minister. It is seldom that a young sovereign misses a governor before he tastes the fruits of his own incapacity.

March 1_st.

We have got more letters from England, where the Ministers are still triumphant. They had a majority of 108 on the day that it was voted to bring in a bill to repeal the Stamp Act. George Grenville's ignorance and blunders were displayed to his face and to the whole world; he was hissed through the Court of Requests, where Mr. Conway was huzza'd. It went still farther for Mr. Pitt, whom the mob accompanied home with "Io Pitts!" This is new for an opposition to be so unpopular. Adieu!

SINGULAR RIOT IN MADRID—CHANGES IN THE FRENCH MINISTRY—INSURRECTIONS IN THE PROVINCES.

TO THE HON. H.S. CONWAY.

PARIS, *April* 8, 1766.

I sent you a few lines by the post yesterday with the first accounts of the insurrections at Madrid.[1] I have since seen Stahremberg, the imperial minister,[2] who has had a courier from thence; and if Lord Rochford has not sent one, you will not be sorry to know more particulars. The mob disarmed the Invalids; stopped all coaches, to prevent Squillaci's[3] flight; and meeting the Duke de Medina Celi, forced him and the Duke d'Arcos to carry their demands to the King. His most frightened Majesty granted them directly; on which his highness the people despatched a monk with their demands in writing, couched in four articles: the diminution of the gabel on bread and oil; the revocation of the ordonnance on hats and cloaks; the banishment of Squillaci; and the abolition of some other tax, I don't know what. The King signed all; yet was still forced to appear in a balcony, and promise to observe what he had granted. Squillaci was sent with an escort to Carthagena, to embark for Naples, and the first commissioner of the treasury appointed to succeed him; which does not look much like observation of the conditions. Some say Ensenada is recalled, and that Grimaldi is in no good odour with the people. If the latter and Squillaci are dismissed, we get rid of two enemies.

[Footnote 1: The Spanish Government had taken on itself to regulate dress, and to introduce French fashions into Madrid—an innovation so offensive to Spanish pride, that it gave rise to a formidable insurrection, of which the populace took advantage to demand the removal of some obnoxious taxes.]

[Footnote 2: Prince Stahremberg was the imperial ambassador at Madrid.]

[Footnote 3: Signor Squillaci, an Italian, was the Spanish Prime Minister.]

The tumult ceased on the grant of the demands; but the King retiring that night to Aranjuez, the insurrection was renewed the next morning, on pretence that this flight was a breach of the capitulation. The people seized the gates of the capital, and permitted nobody to go out. In this state were things when the courier came away. The ordonnance against going in disguise looks as if some suspicions had been conceived; and yet their confidence was so great as not to have two thousand guards in the town. The pitiful behaviour of the Court makes one think that the Italians were frightened, and that the Spanish part of the ministry were not sorry it took that turn. As I suppose there is no great city in Spain which has not at least a bigger bundle of grievances than the capital, one shall not wonder if the pusillanimous behaviour of the King encourages them to redress themselves too.

There is what is called a change of the ministry here; but it is only a crossing over and figuring in. The Duc de Praslin has wished to retire for some time; and for this last fortnight there has been much talk of his being replaced by the Duc d'Aiguillon, the Duc de Nivernois, &c.; but it is plain, though not believed till *now*, that the Duc de Choiseul is all-powerful. To purchase the stay of his cousin Praslin, on whom he can depend, and to leave no cranny open, he has ceded the marine and colonies to the Duc de Praslin, and taken the foreign and military department himself. His cousin is, besides, named *chef du conseil des finances*; a very honourable, very dignified, and very idle place, and never filled since the Duc de Bethune had it. Praslin's hopeful cub, the Viscount, whom you saw in England last year, goes to Naples; and the Marquis de Durfort to Vienna—a cold, dry, proud man, with the figure and manner of Lord Cornbury.

Great matters are expected to-day from the Parliament, which re-assembles. A *mousquetaire*, his piece loaded with a *lettre de cachet*, went about a fortnight ago to the notary who keeps the parliamentary registers, and demanded them. They were refused—but given up, on the *lettre de cachet* being produced. The Parliament intends to try the notary for breach of trust, which I suppose will make his fortune; though he has not the merit of perjury, like Carteret Webb.

There have been insurrections at Bourdeaux and Toulouse on the militia, and twenty-seven persons were killed at the latter; but both are appeased. These things are so much in vogue, that I wonder the French do not dress *a la revolte*. The Queen is in a very dangerous way. This will be my last letter; but I am not sure I shall set out before the middle of next week. Yours ever.

Letters of Horace Walpole, V2

THE BATH GUIDE—SWIFT'S CORRESPONDENCE.

TO GEORGE MONTAGU, ESQ.

STRAWBERRY HILL, *June* 20, 1766.

I don't know when I shall see you, but therefore must not I write to you? yet I have as little to say as may be. I could cry through a whole page over the bad weather. I have but a lock of hay, you know, and I cannot get it dry, unless I bring it to the fire. I would give half–a–crown for a pennyworth of sun. It is abominable to be ruined in coals in the middle of June.

What pleasure have you to come! there is a new thing published, that will make you burst your cheeks with laughing. It is called the "New Bath Guide."[1] It stole into the world, and for a fortnight no soul looked into it, concluding its name was its true name. No such thing. It is a set of letters in verse, in all kind of verses, describing the life at Bath, and incidentally everything else; but so much wit, so much humour, fun, and poetry, so much originality, never met together before. Then the man has a better ear than Dryden or Handel. *Apropos* to Dryden, he has burlesqued his St. Cecilia, that you will never read it again without laughing. There is a description of a milliner's box in all the terms of landscape, *painted lawns and chequered shades*, a Moravian ode, and a Methodist ditty, that are incomparable, and the best names that ever were composed. I can say it by heart, though a quarto, and if I had time would write it you down; for it is not yet reprinted, and not one to be had.

[Footnote 1: By Christopher Anstey. "Have you read the 'New Bath Guide'? It is the only thing in fashion, and is a new and original kind of humour. Miss Prue's conversation I doubt you will paste down, as Sir W. St. Quintyn did before he carried it to his daughter; yet I remember you all read 'Crazy Tales' without pasting" (*Gray to Wharton.—Works by Mitford*, vol. iv. p. 84).]

There are two new volumes, too, of Swift's Correspondence, that will not amuse you less in another way, though abominable, for there are letters of twenty persons now alive; fifty of Lady Betty Germain, one that does her great honour, in which she defends her friend my Lady Suffolk, with all the spirit in the world,[1] against that brute, who hated everybody that he hoped would get him a mitre, and did not. There is one to his Miss Vanhomrigh, from which I think it plain he lay with her, notwithstanding his supposed incapacity, yet not doing much honour to that capacity, for he says he can drink coffee but once a week, and I think you will see very clearly what he means by coffee. His own journal sent to Stella during the four last years of the Queen, is a fund of entertainment. You will see his insolence in full colours, and, at the same time, how daily vain he was of being noticed by the Ministers he affected to treat arrogantly. His panic at the Mohocks is comical; but what strikes one, is bringing before one's eyes the incidents of a curious period. He goes to the rehearsal of "Cato," and says the *drab* that acted Cato's daughter could not say her part. This was only Mrs. Oldfield. I was saying before George Selwyn, that this journal put me in mind of the present time, there was the same indecision, irresolution, and want of system; but I added, "There is nothing new under the sun." "No," said Selwyn, "nor under the grandson."

[Footnote 1: The letter dated Feb. 8, 1732–3.]

My Lord Chesterfield has done me much honour: he told Mrs. Anne Pitt that he would subscribe to any politics I should lay down. When she repeated this to me, I said, "Pray tell him I have laid down politics."

I am got into puns, and will tell you an excellent one of the King of France, though it does not spell any better than Selwyn's. You must have heard of Count Lauragais, and his horse-race, and his quacking his horse till he killed it.[1] At his return the King asked him what he had been doing in England? "Sire, j'ai appris a penser"—"Des chevaux?"[2] replied the King. Good night! I am tired and going to bed. Yours ever.

[Footnote 1: In a previous letter Walpole mentioned that the Count and the English Lord Forbes had had a race, which the Count lost; and that, as his horse died the following night, surgeons were employed to open the body, and they declared he had been poisoned. "The English," says Walpole, "suspect that a groom, who, I suppose, had been reading Livy or Demosthenes, poisoned it on patriotic principles to secure victory to his country. The French, on the contrary, think poison as common as oats or beans in the stables at Newmarket. In short, there is no impertinence which they have not uttered; and it has gone so far that two nights ago it was said that the King had forbidden another race which was appointed for Monday between the Prince de Nassau and a Mr. Forth, to prevent national animosities."]

[Footnote 2: Louis pretending to think he had said *pansen*.]

BATH—WESLEY.

TO JOHN CHUTE, ESQ.

BATH, *Oct.* 10, 1766.

I am impatient to hear that your charity to me has not ended in the gout to yourself—all my comfort is, if you have it, that you have good Lady Brown to nurse you.[1]

[Footnote 1: In a letter of the preceding week he mentions having gone to Bath to drink the waters there, but "is disappointed in the city. Their new buildings, that are so admired, look like a collection of little hospitals. The rest is detestable, and all crammed together, and surrounded with perpendicular hills that have no beauty. The river [the Avon] is paltry enough to be the Seine or the Tiber. Oh! how unlike my lovely Thames!"]

My health advances faster than my amusement. However, I have been to one opera, Mr. Wesley's. They have boys and girls with charming voices, that sing hymns, in parts, to Scotch ballad tunes; but indeed so long, that one would think they were already in eternity, and knew how much time they had before them. The chapel is very neat, with true Gothic windows (yet I am not converted); but I was glad to see that luxury is creeping in upon them before persecution: they have very neat mahogany stands for branches, and brackets of the same in taste. At the upper end is a broad *hautpas* of four steps, advancing in the middle: at each end of the broadest part are two of *my* eagles, with red cushions for the parson and clerk. Behind them rise three more steps, in the midst of which is a third eagle for pulpit. Scarlet armed chairs to all three. On either hand, a balcony for elect ladies. The rest of the congregation sit on forms. Behind the pit, in a dark niche, is a plain table within rails; so you see the throne is for the apostle. Wesley is a lean elderly man, fresh-coloured, his hair smoothly combed, but with a *soupcon* of curl at the ends. Wondrous clean, but as evidently an actor as Garrick. He spoke his sermon, but so fast, and with so little accent, that I am sure he has often uttered it, for it was like a lesson. There were parts and eloquence in it; but towards the end he exalted his voice, and acted very ugly enthusiasm; decried learning, and told stories, like Latimer, of the fool of his college, who said, "I *thanks* God for everything." Except a few from curiosity, and *some honourable women*, the congregation was very mean. There was a Scotch Countess of Buchan, who is carrying a pure rosy vulgar face to heaven, and who asked Miss Rich, if that was *the author of the poets*. I believe she meant me and the "Noble Authors."

The Bedfords came last night. Lord Chatham was with me yesterday two hours; looks and walks well, and is in excellent political spirits.

MINISTERIAL DIFFICULTIES—RETURN OF LORD CLIVE.

TO SIR HORACE MANN.

STRAWBERRY HILL, *July* 20, 1767.

You have heard enough, even in the late reign, of our *interministeriums*, not to be surprised that the present lasts so long. I am not writing now to tell you it is at an end; but I thought you might grow impatient.

The Parliament was scarcely separated when a negotiation was begun with the Bedfords, through Lord Gower; with a view to strengthen the remains of Administration by that faction,[1] but with no intention of including George Grenville, who is more hated at Court than he is even in other places. After some treaty, Lord Gower, much against his will, I believe, was forced to bring word, that there was no objection made by his friends to the Treasury remaining in the Duke of Grafton; that Grenville would support without a place; but Lord Temple (who the deuce thought of Lord Temple?) insisted on equal power, as he had demanded with Lord Chatham. There was no end of that treaty! Another was then begun with Lord Rockingham. He pleaded want of strength in his party, and he might have pleaded almost every other want—and asked if he might talk to the Bedfords. Yes! he might talk to whom he pleased, but the King insisted on keeping the Chancellor, "and me," said the Duke of Grafton; but added, that for himself, he was very willing to cede the Treasury to his Lordship. Away goes the Marquis to Woburn; and, to charm the King more, negotiates with both Grenvilles too. These last, who had demanded everything of the Crown, were all submission to the Marquis, and yet could not dupe him so fast as he tried to be duped. Oh! all, all were ready to stay out, or turn their friends in, or what he pleased. He took this for his own talents in negotiation, came back highly pleased, and notified his success. The Duke of Grafton wrote to him that the King meant they should come in, *to extend and strengthen his Administration.* Too elated with his imaginary power, the Marquis returned an answer, insolently civil to the Duke, and not commonly decent for the place it was to be carried to. It said, that his Lordship had laid it down for a principle of the treaty, that the present Administration was at an end. That supposed, *he* was ready to *form* a comprehensive Ministry, but first must talk to the King.

[Footnote 1: The difficulties were caused by Lord Chatham's illness. He, though Prime Minister, only held the office of Lord Privy Seal, the Duke of Grafton being First Lord of the Treasury; consequently, when Lord Chatham became incapable of transacting any business whatever, even of signing a resignation of his office, the Duke became the Prime Minister, and continued so for three years.]

Instead of such an answer as such a *remonstrance* deserved, a very prudent reply was made. The King approved the idea of a comprehensive Administration: he desired to unite the hearts of *all* his subjects: he meant to exclude men of no denomination attached to his person and government; it was such a Ministry that *he* intended to *appoint*. When his Lordship should have *formed a plan* on such views, his Majesty would be ready to receive it from him. The great statesman was wofully puzzled on receiving this message. However, he has summoned his new allies to assist in composing a scheme or list. When they bring it, how they will bring it formed, or whether they will ever bring it, the Lord knows. There the matter rests at present. If the Marquis does not alter his tone, he sinks for ever, and from being the head of a separate band, he must fall into the train of Grenville, the man whom he and his friends opposed on all the arbitrary acts of that Ministry, and whom they have irremissibly offended by repealing his darling Stamp Act. *Apropos*, America is pacified, and the two factions cannot join to fish in troubled waters, there, at least.

Lord Clive[1] is arrived, has brought a million for himself, two diamond drops worth twelve thousand pounds for the Queen, a scimitar dagger, and other matters, covered with brilliants, for the King, and worth twenty-four thousand more. These *baubles* are presents from the deposed and imprisoned Mogul, whose poverty can still afford to give such bribes. Lord Clive refused some overplus, and gave it to some widows of officers: it amounted to ninety thousand pounds. He has *reduced* the appointments of the Governor of Bengal to thirty-two thousand pounds a year; and, what is better, has left such a chain of forts and distribution of troops as will entirely secure possession of the country—till we lose it. Thus having composed the Eastern and Western worlds, we are at leisure to kick and cuff for our own little island, which is great satisfaction; and I don't doubt but my Lord Temple hopes that we shall be so far engaged before France and Spain are ripe to meddle with us, that when they do come, they will not be able to re-unite us.

[Footnote 1: It is hardly necessary to point out that this is the taker of Arcot, the victor of Plassey, and even now second to none but Warren Hastings in the splendid roll of Governors-General.]

Don't let me forget to tell you, that of all the friends you have shot flying, there is no one whose friendship for you is so little dead as Lord Hillsborough's. He spoke to me earnestly about your Riband the other day, and said he had pressed to have it given to you. Write and thank him. You have missed one by Lord Clive's returning alive, unless he should give a hamper of diamonds for the Garter.

Well! I have remembered every point but one—and see how he is forgotten! Lord Chatham! He was pressed to come forth and set the Administration on its legs again. He pleaded total incapacity; grew worse and grows better. Oh! how he ought to dread recovering!

Mr. Conway resigns the day after to-morrow. I hope in a week to tell you something more positive than the uncertainties in this letter. Good-night.

DEATH OF CHARLES TOWNSHEND AND OF THE DUKE OF YORK—WHIST THE NEW FASHION IN FRANCE.

TO SIR HORACE MANN.

PARIS, *Sept.* 27, 1767.

Since you insist on my writing from hence, I will; I intended to defer it a few days longer, as I shall set out on my return this day se'nnight.

Within the five weeks of my being here, there have happened three deaths, which certainly nobody expected six weeks ago. Yet, though the persons were all considerable, their loss will make little impression on the state of any affairs.

Monsieur de Guerchy returned from his embassy with us about a month before my arrival. He had been out of order some time, and had taken waters, yet seeing him so often I had perceived no change, till I was made to remark it, and then I did not think it considerable. On my arrival, I was shocked at the precipitate alteration. He was emaciated, yellow, and scarcely able to support himself. A fever came on in ten days, mortification ensued, and carried him off. It is said that he had concealed and tampered indiscreetly with an old complaint, acquired before his marriage. This was his radical death; I doubt, vexation and disappointment fermented the wound. Instead of the duchy he hoped, his reception was freezing. He was a frank, gallant gentleman; universally beloved with us; hated I believe by nobody, and by no means inferior in understanding to many who affected to despise his abilities.

But our comet is set too! Charles Townshend[1] is dead. All those parts and fire are extinguished; those volatile salts are evaporated; that first eloquence of the world is dumb! that duplicity is fixed, that cowardice terminated heroically. He joked on death as naturally as he used to do on the living, and not with the affectation of philosophers, who wind up their works with sayings which they hope to have remembered. With a robust person he had always a menacing constitution. He had had a fever the whole summer, recovered as it was thought, relapsed, was neglected, and it turned to an incurable putrid fever.

[Footnote 1: Mr. Townshend was Chancellor of the Exchequer; and he might have been added by Lord Macaulay to his list of men whom their eloquence had caused to be placed in offices for which they were totally unfit; for he had not only no special knowledge of finance, but he was one of the most careless and incautious of mankind, even in his oratory. In that, however, after the retirement of Lord Chatham, he seems to have had no rival in either house but Mr. Burke. It was to his heedless resumption of Grenville's plan of taxing our colonies in North America that our loss of them was owing. In his "Memoirs of the Reign of George III." Walpole gives the following description of him: "Charles Townshend, who had studied nothing with accuracy or attention, had parts that embraced all knowledge with such quickness that he seemed to create knowledge, instead of searching for it; and, ready as Burke's wit was, it appeared artificial when set by that of Townshend, which was so abundant that in him it seemed a loss of time to think. He had but to speak, and all he said was new, natural, and yet uncommon. If Burke replied extempore, his very answers that sprang from what had been said by others were so pointed and artfully arranged that they wore the appearance of study and preparation; like beautiful translations, they seemed to want the soul of the original author. Townshend's speeches, like the 'Satires' of Pope, had a thousand times more sense and meaning than the majestic blank verse of Pitt; and yet the latter, like Milton, stalked with a conscious dignity of pre-eminence, and fascinated his audience with that respect which always attends the pompous but often hollow idea of the sublime." Burke, too, in one of his speeches on American affairs, utters a still warmer panegyric on his character and abilities, while lamenting his policy and its fruits: "I speak of Charles Townshend, officially the reproducer of this fatal scheme [the taxation of the colonies], whom I cannot, even now, remember without some degree of sensibility. In truth, Sir, he was the delight and ornament of this House, and the charm of every private society which he honoured with his presence. Perhaps there never arose in this country, nor in any country, a man of a more pointed and finished wit, and (where his passions were not concerned) of a more refined, exquisite, and penetrating judgment. If he had not so great a stock, as some have had who flourished formerly, of knowledge long treasured up, he knew better by far than any man I was ever acquainted with how to bring together within a short time all that was necessary to establish, to illustrate, and to decorate that side of the question he supported. He stated his matter skillfully and powerfully. He particularly excelled in a most luminous explanation and display of his subject. His style of argument was neither trite nor vulgar, nor subtle and abstruse. He hit the House between wind and water; and, not being troubled with too anxious a zeal for any matter in question, he was never more tedious nor more earnest than the preconceived opinions and present temper of his hearers required, with whom he was always in perfect unison. He conformed exactly to the temper of the House; and he seemed to lead because he was always sure to follow it."]

The Opposition expected that the loss of this essential pin would loosen the whole frame; but it had been hard, if both his life and death were to be pernicious to the Administration. He had engaged to betray the latter to the former, as I knew early, and as Lord Mansfield has since declared. I therefore could not think the loss of him a misfortune. His seals were immediately offered to Lord North,[1] who declined them. The Opposition rejoiced; but they ought to have been better acquainted with one educated in their own school. Lord North has since accepted the seals—and the reversion of his father's pension.

[Footnote 1: Lord North succeeded Townshend as Chancellor of the Exchequer; and, when the Duke of Grafton retired, he became First Lord of the Treasury also, and continued to hold both offices till the spring of 1782.]

While that eccentric genius, Charles Townshend, whom no system could contain, is whirled out of existence, our more artificial meteor, Lord Chatham, seems to be wheeling back to the sphere of business—at least his health is declared to be re-established; but he has lost his adorers, the mob, and I doubt the wise men will not travel after his light.

You, my dear Sir, will be most concerned for the poor Duke of York,[1] who has ended his silly, good-humoured, troublesome career, in a piteous manner. He had come to the camp at Compiegne, without his brother's approbation, but had been received here not only with every proper mark of distinction, but with the utmost kindness. He had succeeded, too, was attentive, civil, obliging, lively, pleased, and very happy in his replies. Charmed with a Court so lively in comparison of the monastic scene at home, he had promised to return for Fontainebleau, and then scampered away as fast as he could ride or drive all round the South of France, intending to visit a lady at Genoa, with whom he was in love, whenever he had a minute's time. The Duc de Villars gave him a ball at his country-house, between Aix and Marseilles; the Duke of York danced at it all night as hard as if it made part of his road, and then in a violent sweat, and without changing his linen, got into his postchaise. At Marseilles the scene changed. He arrived in a fever, and found among his letters, which he had ordered to meet him there, one from the King his brother, forbidding him to go to Compiegne, by the advice of the Hereditary Prince. He was struck with this letter, which he had ignorantly disobeyed, and by the same ignorance had not answered. He proceeded, however, on his journey, but grew so ill that his gentlemen carried him to Monaco, where he arrived on the third, and languished with great suffering until the seventeenth. He behaved with the most perfect tranquillity and courage, made a short will, and the day before he died dictated to Colonel St. John, a letter to the King, in which he begged his forgiveness for every instance in which he had offended him, and entreated his favour to his servants. He would have particularly recommended St. John, but the young man said handsomely, "Sir, if the letter were written by your Royal Highness yourself, it would be most kind to me; but I cannot name myself." The Prince of Monaco, who happened to be on the spot, was unbounded in his attentions to him, both of care and honours; and visited him every hour till the Duke grew too weak to see him. Two days before he died the Duke sent for the Prince, and thanked him. The Prince burst into tears and could not speak, and retiring, begged the Duke's officers to prevent his being sent for again, for the shock was too great. They made as magnificent a coffin and pall for him as the time and place would admit, and in the evening of the 17th the body was embarked on board an English ship, which received the corpse with military honours, the cannon of the town saluting it with the same discharge as is paid to a Marshal of France. St. John and Morrison embarked with the body, and Colonel Wrottesley passed through here with the news. The poor lad was in tears the whole time he stayed....

[Footnote 1: The Duke of York was the King's younger brother.]

You tell me of the French playing at whist;[1] why, I found it established when I was last here. I told them they were very good to imitate us in anything, but that they had adopted the two dullest things we have, Whist and Richardson's Novels.

[Footnote 1: Walpole here speaks of whist as a game of but new introduction in Paris, though it had been for some time established with us. And the great authority on that scientific and beautiful game, the late Mr. James Clay, writing about twenty years ago, fixes "thirty or more years" before that date as the time when first "we began to hear of the great Paris players. There was," he says, "a wide difference between their system and our own," the special distinction being that "the English player of the old school never thought of winning the game until he saw that it was saved; the French player never thought of saving the game until he saw that he could not win it;" and "if forced to take his choice between these systems carried to their extremes." Mr. Clay "would, without hesitation, prefer the game of rash attack" (that is, the French system) "to that of over-cautious defence." And he assigns to a French player, M. Des Chapelles, "the credit of being the finest whist-player, beyond any comparison, the world has ever seen."]

So you and the Pope are going to have the Emperor! Times are a little altered; no Guelphs and Ghibellines[1] now. I do not think the Caesar of the day will hold his Holiness's stirrup[2] while he mounts his palfrey. Adieu!

[Footnote 1: "*Guelfs and Ghibellines.*" These two names were first heard in the latter part of the twelfth century, to distinguish the partisans of the Emperor and the Pope. "The Guelfs or Welfs were the ancestors of Henry the Proud, who, through his mother, represented the ancient Dukes of Saxony. The word Ghibelin is derived from Wibelung, a town in Franconia, from which the emperors of that time are said to nave sprung. The house of Swabia were considered in Germany as representing that of Franconia" (Hallam, "Middle Ages," ii. p. 101).]

[Footnote 2: "*His Holiness's stirrup.*" This refers to the humiliation imposed on the Emperor Frederic Barbarossa by Pope Alexander III., as related by Byron in his note on "Childe Harold," c. iv. st. 12.]

SOME NEW POEMS OF GRAY—WALPOLE'S "HISTORIC DOUBTS"—BOSWELL'S "CORSICA."

TO MR. GRAY.

ARLINGTON STREET, *Feb.* 18, 1768.

You have sent me a long and very obliging letter, and yet I am extremely out of humour with you. I saw *Poems* by *Mr. Gray* advertised: I called directly at Dodsley's to know if this was to be more than a new edition? He was not at home himself, but his foreman told me he thought there were some new pieces, and notes to the whole. It was very unkind, not only to go out of town without mentioning them to me, without showing them to me, but not to say a word of them in this letter. Do you think I am indifferent, or not curious about what you write? I have ceased to ask you, because you have so long refused to show me anything. You could not suppose I thought that you never write. No; but I concluded you did not intend, at least yet, to publish what you had written. As you did intend it, I might have expected a month's preference. You will do me the justice to own that I had always rather have seen your writings than have shown you mine; which you know are the most hasty trifles in the world, and which though I may be fond of the subject when fresh, I constantly forget in a very short time after they are published. This would sound like affectation to others, but will not to you. It would be affected, even to you, to say I am indifferent to fame. I certainly am not, but I am indifferent to almost anything I have done to acquire it. The greater part are mere compilations; and no wonder they are, as you say, incorrect, when they are commonly written with people in the room, as "Richard"[1] and the "Noble Authors" were. But I doubt there is a more intrinsic fault in them: which is, that I cannot correct them. If I write tolerably, it must be at once; I can neither mend nor add. The articles of Lord Capel and Lord Peterborough, in the second edition of the "Noble Authors," cost me more trouble than all the rest together: and you may perceive that the worst part of "Richard," in point of ease and style, is what relates to the papers you gave me on Jane Shore, because it was tacked on so long afterwards, and when my impetus was chilled. If some time or other you will take the trouble of pointing out the inaccuracies of it, I shall be much obliged to you: at present I shall meddle no more with it. It has taken its fate: nor did I mean to complain. I found it was condemned indeed beforehand, which was what I alluded to. Since publication (as has happened to me before) the success has gone beyond my expectation.

[Footnote 1: He is here alluding to his own very clever essay, entitled "Historic Doubts on the Life and Reign of Richard III." It failed to convince Hume; but can hardly be denied to be a singularly acute specimen of historical criticism. It does not, indeed, prove Richard to have been innocent of all the crimes imputed to him; but it proves conclusively that much of the evidence by which the various charges are supported is false. In an earlier letter he mentions having first made "a discovery, one of the most marvellous ever made. In short, it is the original Coronation Roll of Richard, by which it appears that very magnificent robes were ordered for Edward V., and that he did or was to walk at his uncle's coronation." The letter, from which this passage is an extract, was to a certain extent an answer to one from Gray, who, while praising the ingenuity of his arguments, avowed himself still unconvinced by them.]

Not only at Cambridge, but here, there have been people wise enough to think me too free with the King of Prussia! A newspaper has talked of my known inveteracy to him. Truly, I love him as well as I do most kings. The greater offence is my reflection on Lord Clarendon. It is forgotten that I had overpraised him before. Pray turn to the new State Papers, from which, *it is said*, he composed his history. You will find they are the papers from which he did *not* compose his history. And yet I admire my Lord Clarendon more than these pretended admirers do. But I do not intend to justify myself. I can as little satisfy those who complain that I do not let them know what *really did* happen. If this inquiry can ferret out any truth, I shall be glad. I have picked up a few more circumstances. I now want to know what Perkin Warbeck's Proclamation was, which Speed in his history says is preserved by Bishop Leslie. If you look in Speed perhaps you will be able to assist me.

The Duke of Richmond and Lord Lyttelton agree with you, that I have not disculpated Richard of the murder of Henry VI. I own to you, it is the crime of which in my own mind I believe him most guiltless. Had I thought he committed it, I should never have taken the trouble to apologize for the rest. I am not at all positive or obstinate on your other objections, nor know exactly what I believe on many points of this story. And I am so sincere, that, except a few notes hereafter, I shall leave the matter to be settled or discussed by others. As you have written much too little, I have written a great deal too much, and think only of finishing the two or three other things I have begun—and of those, nothing but the last volume of Painters is designed for the present public. What has one to do when turned fifty, but really think of *finishing*?

I am much obliged and flattered by Mr. Mason's approbation, and particularly by having had almost the same thought with him. I said, "People need not be angry at my excusing Richard; I have not diminished their fund of hatred, I have only transferred it from Richard to Henry." Well, but I have found you close with Mason—No doubt, cry prating I, something will come out....[1]

[Footnote 1: "*Something will come out.*" Walpole himself points out in a note that this is a quotation from Pope: "I have found him close with Swift." "Indeed?" "No doubt, (Cries prating Balbus) something will come out" (Prologue to the "Satires").]

Pray read the new Account of Corsica.[1] What relates to Paoli will amuse you much. There is a deal about the island and its divisions that one does not care a straw for. The author, Boswell, is a strange being, and, like Cambridge, has a rage of knowing anybody that ever was talked of. He forced himself upon me at Paris in spite of my teeth and my doors, and I see has given a foolish account of all he could pick up from me about King Theodore.[2] He then took an antipathy to me on Rousseau's account, abused me in the newspapers, and exhorted Rousseau to do so too: but as he came to see me no more, I forgave all the rest. I see he now is a little sick of Rousseau himself; but I hope it will not cure him of his anger to me. However, his book will I am sure entertain you.

[Footnote 1: Boswell, Dr. Johnson's celebrated biographer, had taken great interest in the affairs of Corsica, which, in this year (1768), Choiseul, the Prime Minister of France, had bought of Genoa, to which State it had long belonged. Paoli was a Corsican noble, who had roused his countrymen to throw off the domination of Genoa; and, on the arrival of French troops to take possession of their purchase, he made a vigorous resistance to the French General, the Comte de Marboeuf; but eventually he was overpowered, and forced to fly. He took refuge in England, where George III. granted him a pension, which he enjoyed till his death in 1807, when he was buried in Westminster Abbey. One of his relations was M. Charles Buonaparte, the father of Napoleon, who was only prevented from accompanying him in his abandonment of Corsica by the persuasion of his uncle, the Archdeacon of Ajaccio. Boswell, who was apt to be enthusiastic in his hero-worship and anxiety for new acquaintances (whom, it must be admitted, he commonly chose with judgement, if with little dignity), introduced him to Johnson, who also conceived a high regard for him, and on one occasion remarked that "he had the loftiest port of any man he had ever seen."]

[Footnote 2: After several outbreaks within a few years, the Corsicans in 1736 embarked in a revolt so formal and complete that they altogether threw off their allegiance to Genoa, and chose as their king Theodore Neuhof, a Westphalian baron. But Cardinal Fleury, the French Prime Minister, from a belief that Theodore was an instrument of Walpole, lent the Genoese a force of three thousand men, which at last succeeded in crushing the insurrection and expelling Theodore. (See the Editor's "France under the Bourbons," iii. 157.) Theodore is one of the six ex-kings whom, in Voltaire's "Candide," his hero met at a hotel in Venice during the carnival, when he gave a melancholy account of his reverse of fortune. "He had been called 'Your Majesty;' now he can hardly find any one to call him 'Sir.' He had coined money; now he has not a penny of his own. He had had two Secretaries of State; now he has but one valet. He had sat on a throne; but since that time he had laid on straw in a London prison." In fact, his state was so doleful, that the other ex-kings subscribed twenty sequins apiece to buy him some coats and shirts ("Candide," c. 26).]

I will add but a word or two more. I am criticised for the expression *tinker up* in the preface. Is this one of those that you object to? I own I think such a low expression, placed to ridicule an absurd instance of wise folly, very forcible. Replace it with an elevated word or phrase, and to my conception it becomes as flat as possible.

George Selwyn says I may, if I please, write Historic Doubts on the present Duke of G[loucester] too. Indeed, they would be doubts, for I know nothing certainly.

Will you be so kind as to look into Leslie "De Rebus Scotorum," and see if Perkin's Proclamation is there, and if there, how authenticated. You will find in Speed my reason for asking this. I have written in such a hurry, I believe you will scarce be able to read my letter—and as I have just been writing French, perhaps the sense may not be clearer than the writing. Adieu!

Letters of Horace Walpole, V2

WILKES IS RETURNED M.P. FOR MIDDLESEX—RIOTS IN LONDON—VIOLENCE OF THE MOB.

TO SIR HORACE MANN.

ARLINGTON STREET, *Thursday, March* 31, 1768.

I have received your letter, with the extract of that from Mr. Mackenzie. I do not think any honours will be bestowed yet. The Peerages are all postponed to an indefinite time. If you are in a violent hurry, you may petition the ghosts of your neighbours—Masaniello and the Gracchi. The spirit of one of them walks here; nay, I saw it go by my window yesterday, at noon, in a hackney chair.

Friday.

I was interrupted yesterday. The ghost is laid for a time in a red sea of port and claret. The spectre is the famous Wilkes. He appeared the moment the Parliament was dissolved. The Ministry despise him. He stood for the City of London, and was the last on the poll of seven candidates, none but the mob, and most of them without votes, favouring him. He then offered himself to the county of Middlesex. The election came on last Monday. By five in the morning a very large body of Weavers, &c., took possession of Piccadilly, and the roads and turnpikes leading to Brentford, and would suffer nobody to pass without blue cockades, and papers inscribed "*No. 45, Wilkes and Liberty*." They tore to pieces the coaches of Sir W. Beauchamp Proctor, and Mr. Cooke, the other candidates, though the latter was not there, but in bed with the gout, and it was with difficulty that Sir William and Mr. Cooke's cousin got to Brentford. There, however, lest it should be declared a void election, Wilkes had the sense to keep everything quiet. But, about five, Wilkes, being considerably ahead of the other two, his mob returned to town and behaved outrageously. They stopped every carriage, scratched and spoilt several with writing all over them "No. 45," pelted, threw dirt and stones, and forced everybody to huzza for Wilkes. I did but cross Piccadilly at eight, in my coach with a French Monsieur d'Angeul, whom I was carrying to Lady Hertford's; they stopped us, and bid us huzza. I desired him to let down the glass on his side, but, as he was not alert, they broke it to shatters. At night they insisted, in several streets, on houses being illuminated, and several Scotch refusing, had their windows broken. Another mob rose in the City, and Harley, the present Mayor, being another Sir William Walworth, and having acted formerly and now with great spirit against Wilkes, and the Mansion House not being illuminated, and he out of town, they broke every window, and tried to force their way into the House. The Trained Bands were sent for, but did not suffice. At last a party of guards, from the Tower, and some lights erected, dispersed the tumult. At one in the morning a riot began before Lord Bute's house, in Audley Street, though illuminated. They flung two large flints into Lady Bute's chamber, who was in bed, and broke every window in the house. Next morning, Wilkes and Cooke were returned members. The day was very quiet, but at night they rose again, and obliged almost every house in town to be lighted up, even the Duke of Cumberland's and Princess Amelia's. About one o'clock they marched to the Duchess of Hamilton's in Argyle Buildings (Lord Lorn being in Scotland). She was obstinate, and would not illuminate, though with child, and, as they hope, of an heir to the family, and with the Duke, her son, and the rest of her children in the house. There is a small court and parapet wall before the house: they brought iron crows, tore down the gates, pulled up the pavement, and battered the house for three hours. They could not find the key of the back door, nor send for any assistance. The night before, they had obliged the Duke and Duchess of Northumberland to give them beer, and appear at the windows, and drink "Wilkes's health." They stopped and opened the coach of Count Seilern, the Austrian ambassador, who has made a formal complaint, on which the Council met on Wednesday night, and were going to issue a Proclamation, but, hearing that all was quiet, and that only a few houses were illuminated in Leicester Fields from the terror of the inhabitants, a few constables were sent with orders to extinguish the lights, and not the smallest disorder has happened since. In short, it has ended like other election riots, and with not a quarter of the mischief that has been done in some other towns.

There are, however, difficulties to come. Wilkes has notified that he intends to surrender himself to his outlawry, the beginning of next term, which comes on the 17th of this month. There is said to be a flaw in the proceedings, in which case his election will be good, though the King's Bench may fine or imprison him on his former sentence. In my own opinion, the House of Commons is the place where he can do the least hurt, for he is a wretched speaker, and will sink to contempt, like Admiral Vernon,[1] who I remember just such an illuminated hero, with two birthdays in one year. You will say, he can write better than Vernon—true; and therefore his case is more desperate. Besides, Vernon was rich: Wilkes is undone; and, though he has had great support, his patrons will be sick of maintaining him. He must either sink to poverty and a jail, or commit new excesses, for which he will get knocked on the head. The Scotch are his implacable enemies to a man.

A Rienzi[2] cannot stop: their histories are summed up in two words—a triumph and an assassination.

[Footnote 1: In 1739 our Government had declared war against Spain. "There was at the time among the members of the Opposition in the House of Commons a naval captain named Vernon, a man of bold, blustering tongue, and presumed therefore by many to be of a corresponding readiness of action. In some of the debates he took occasion to inveigh against the timidity of our officers, who had hitherto, as he phrased it, spared Porto Bello; and he affirmed that he could take it himself with a squadron of six ships. The Ministry caught at the prospect of delivering themselves from his harangues, and gave him half as many ships again as he desired, with the temporary rank of Vice-admiral; and on July, 1739, he sailed for the American coast. When he reached it he found that the news of the rupture of the peace had not yet reached the governor of the city, and that it was in no condition to resist an attack. Many of the guns were dismounted; and for those that were serviceable there was not sufficient ammunition. A fire of musketry alone sufficed to win the fort that protected the entrance to the harbour, and an equally brief cannonade drove the garrison from the castle. The governor had no further means of defence; and thus in forty-eight hours after his arrival Vernon had accomplished his boast, and was master of the place." In a clever paper in the "Cambridge Museum Philologicum" Bishop Thirlwall compared the man and his exploit to Cleon and his achievement at Sphacteria in the Peloponnesian War. (See the Editor's "History of the British Navy," c. 9.)]

[Footnote 2: "*Rienzi.*"

> Then turn we to her latest tribune's name,
> From her ten thousand tyrants turn to thee,
> Redeemer of dark centuries of shame,
> The friend of Petrarch, hope of Italy,
> Rienzi; last of Romans.

("Childe Harold," iv. 114.)

His story is told with almost more than his usual power by Gibbon (c. 70). Born in the lowest class, "he could inherit neither dignity nor fortune; and the gift of a liberal education, which they painfully bestowed, was the cause of his glory and his untimely end." He, while still little more than a youth, had established such a reputation for eloquence, that he was one of the deputies sent by the Commons to Avignon to plead with the Pope (Clement VI.). The state of Rome, aggravated by the absence of the Pope, was miserable in the extreme. The citizens "were equally oppressed by the arrogance of the nobles and the corruption of the magistrates." Rienzi recalled to their recollection "the ancient glories of the Senate and people from whom all legal authority was derived. He raised the enthusiasm of the populace; collected a band of conspirators, at whose head, clad in complete armour, he marched to the Capitol, and assumed the government of the city, declining "the names of Senator or Consul, of King or Emperor, and preferring the ancient and modern appellation of Tribune.... Never perhaps has the energy and effect of a single mind been more remarkably felt than in the sudden, though transient, reformation of Rome by the Tribune Rienzi. A den of robbers was converted to the discipline of a camp or convent. Patient to hear, swift to redress, inexorable to punish, his tribunal was always accessible to the poor and the stranger; nor could birth, nor dignity, nor the immunities of the Church protect the offender or his accomplices." But his head was turned by his success. He even caused himself to be crowned, while "his wife, his son, and his uncle, a barber, exposed the contrast of vulgar manners and princely expense; and, without acquiring the majesty, Rienzi degenerated into the vices of a king." The people became indignant; the nobles whom he had degraded found it easy to raise the public feeling against him. Before the end of the same year (1347) he was forced to fly from Rome, and lived in exile or imprisonment at Avignon seven years; and returned to Rome in 1354, only to be murdered in an insurrection.]

I must finish, for Lord Hertford is this moment come in, and insists on my dining with the Prince of Monaco, who is come over to thank the King for the presents his Majesty sent him on his kindness and attention to the late Duke of York. You shall hear the suite of the above histories, which I sit quietly and look at, having nothing more to do with the storm, and sick of politics, but as a spectator, while they pass over the stage of the world. Adieu!

FLEETING FAME OF WITTICISMS—"THE MYSTERIOUS MOTHER."

TO GEORGE MONTAGU, ESQ.

STRAWBERRY HILL, *April* 15, 1768.

Mr. Chute tells me that you have taken a new house in Squireland, and have given yourself up for two years more to port and parsons. I am very angry, and resign you to the works of the devil or the church, I don't care which. You will get the gout, turn Methodist, and expect to ride to heaven upon your own great toe. I was happy with your telling me how well you love me, and though I don't love loving, I could have poured out all the fulness of my heart to such an old and true friend; but what am I the better for it, if I am to see you but two or three days in the year? I thought you would at last come and while away the remainder of life on the banks of the Thames in gaiety and old tales. I have quitted the stage, and the Clive[1] is preparing to leave it. We shall neither of us ever be grave: dowagers roost all around us, and you could never want cards or mirth. Will you end like a fat farmer, repeating annually the price of oats, and discussing stale newspapers? There have you got, I hear, into an old gallery, that has not been glazed since Queen Elizabeth, and under the nose of an infant Duke and Duchess, that will understand you no more than if you wore a ruff and a coif, and talk to them of a call of Serjeants the year of the Spanish Armada! Your wit and humour will be as much lost upon them, as if you talked the dialect of Chaucer; for with all the divinity of wit, it grows out of fashion like a fardingale. I am convinced that the young men at White's already laugh at George Selwyn's *bon mots* only by tradition. I avoid talking before the youth of the age as I would dancing before them; for if one's tongue don't move in the steps of the day, and thinks to please by its old graces, it is only an object of ridicule, like Mrs. Hobart in her cotillon. I tell you we should get together, and comfort ourselves with reflecting on the brave days that we have known—not that I think people were a jot more clever or wise in our youth than they are now; but as my system is always to live in a vision as much as I can, and as visions don't increase with years, there is nothing so natural as to think one remembers what one does not remember.

[Footnote 1: Mrs. Clive was a celebrated comic actress and wit, and a near neighbour of Walpole at Twickenham.]

[Illustration: STRAWBERRY HILL, FROM THE NORTH-WEST.]

I have finished my Tragedy ["The Mysterious Mother"], but as you would not bear the subject, I will say no more of it, but that Mr. Chute, who is not easily pleased, likes it, and Gray, who is still more difficult, approves it. I am not yet intoxicated enough with it to think it would do for the stage, though I wish to see it acted; but, as Mrs. Pritchard[1] leaves the stage next month, I know nobody could play the Countess; nor am I disposed to expose myself to the impertinences of that jackanapes Garrick, who lets nothing appear but his own wretched stuff, or that of creatures still duller, who suffer him to alter their pieces as he pleases. I have written an epilogue in character for the Clive, which she would speak admirably: but I am not so sure that she would like to speak it. Mr. Conway, Lady Aylesbury, Lady Lyttelton, and Miss Rich, are to come hither the day after to-morrow, and Mr. Conway and I are to read my play to them; for I have not strength enough to go through the whole alone.

[Footnote 1: Mrs. Pritchard was the most popular tragic actress of the day. Churchill gives her high praise—

In spite of outward blemishes, she shone
For humour fam'd, and humour all her own.

("Rosciad," 840.)]

My press is revived, and is printing a French play written by the old President Henault.[1] It was damned many years ago at Paris, and yet I think is better than some that have succeeded, and much better than any of our modern tragedies. I print it to please the old man, as he was exceedingly kind to me at Paris; but I doubt whether he will live till it is finished. He is to have a hundred copies, and there are to be but a hundred more, of which you shall have one.

[Footnote 1: M. Henault was President of the Parliament of Paris. His tragedy was "Cornelie." He died in 1770, at the age of eighty-six.]

Adieu! though I am very angry with you, I deserve all your friendship, by that I have for you, witness my anger and disappointment. Yours ever.

P.S.—Send me your new direction, and tell me when I must begin to use it.

CASE OF WILKES.

TO SIR HORACE MANN.

STRAWBERRY HILL, *June* 9, 1768.

To send you empty paragraphs when you expect and want news is tantalising, is it not? Pray agree with me, and then you will allow that I have acted very kindly in not writing till I had something to tell you. *Something*, of course, means Wilkes, for everything is nothing except the theme of the day. There has appeared a violent *North Briton*, addressed to, and written against Lord Mansfield, threatening a rebellion if he continued to persecute Mr. Wilkes. This paper, they say, Wilkes owned to the Chevalier de Chastelux, a French gentleman, who went to see him in the King's Bench, and who knew him at Paris. A rebellion threatened in print is not very terrible. However, it was said that the paper was outrageous enough to furnish the Law with every handle it could want. But modern mountains do not degenerate from their ancestors; their issue are still mice. You know, too, that this agrees with my system, that this is an age of abortions. Prosecutions were ordered against the publishers and vendors, and there, I suppose, it will end.

Yesterday was fixed for the appearance of Wilkes in Westminster Hall. The Judges went down by nine in the morning, but the mob had done breakfast still sooner, and was there before them; and as Judges stuffed out with dignity and lamb-skins are not absolute sprites, they had much ado to glide through the crowd. Wilkes's counsel argued against the outlawry, and then Lord Mansfield, in a speech of an hour and a half, set it aside; not on *their* reasons, but on grounds which he had discovered in it himself. I think they say it was on some flaw in the Christian name of the county, which should not have been *Middlesex to wit*,—but I protest I don't know, for I am here alone, and picked up my intelligence as I walked in our meadows by the river. You, who may be walking by the Arno, will, perhaps, think there was some timidity in this; but the depths of the Law are wonderful! So pray don't make any rash conclusions, but stay till you get better information.

Well! now he is gone to prison again,—I mean Wilkes; and on Tuesday he is to return to receive sentence on the old guilt of writing, as the Scotch would *not* call it, *the* 45,[1] though they call the rebellion so. The sentence may be imprisonment, fine, or pillory; but as I am still near the Thames, I do not think the latter will be chosen. Oh! but stay, he may plead against the indictment, and should there be an improper *Middlesex to wit* in that too, why then in that case, you know, he did *not* write *the* 45, and then he is as white as milk, and as free as air, and as good a member of Parliament as if he had never been expelled. In short, my dear Sir, I am trying to explain to you what I literally do not understand; all I do know is, that Mr. Cooke, the other member for Middlesex, is just dead, and that we are going to have another Middlesex election, which is very unpleasant to me, who hate mobs so near as Brentford. Sergeant Glynn, Wilkes's counsel, is the candidate, and I suppose the only one in the present humour of the people, who will care to have his brains dashed out, in order to sit in Parliament. In truth, this enthusiasm is confined to the very mob or little higher, and does not extend beyond the County. All other riots are ceased, except the little civil war between the sailors and coal-heavers, in which two or three lives are lost every week.

[Footnote 1: *"The 45"* here serves for the Scotch rebellion of 1745, and for No. 45 of the *North Briton*.]

What is most disagreeable, even the Emperor of Morocco has taken courage on these tumults, and has dared to mutiny for increase of wages, like our journeymen tailors. France is pert too, and gives herself airs in the Mediterranean. Our Paolists were violent for support of Corsica, but I think they are a little startled on a report that the hero Paoli is like other patriots, and is gone to Versailles, for a peerage and pension. I was told to-day that at London there are murmurs of a war. I shall be sorry if it prove so. Deaths! suspense, say victory;—how end all our victories? In debts and a wretched peace! Mad world, in the individual or the aggregate!

Well! say I to myself, and what is all this to me? Have not I done with that world? Am not I here at peace, unconnected with Courts and Ministries, and indifferent who is Minister? What is a war in Europe to me more than a war between the Turkish and Persian Emperors? True; yet self-love makes one love the nation one belongs to, and vanity makes one wish to have that nation glorious. Well! I have seen it so; I have seen its conquests spread farther than Roman eagles thought there was land. I have seen too the Pretender at Derby; and, therefore, you must know that I am content with historic seeing, and wish Fame and History would be quiet and content without entertaining me with any more sights. We were down at Derby, we were up at both Indies; I have no curiosity for any intermediate sights.

Your brother was with me just before I came out of town, and spoke of you with great kindness, and accused himself of not writing to you, but protested it was from not knowing what to say to you about the Riband. I engaged to write for him, so you must take this letter as from him too.

I hope there will be no war for some hero to take your honours out of your mouth, sword in hand. The first question I shall ask when I go to town will be, how my Lord Chatham does? I shall mind his health more than the stocks. The least symptom of a war will certainly cure him. Adieu! my dear Sir.

THE ENGLISH CLIMATE.

TO GEORGE MONTAGU, ESQ.

STRAWBERRY HILL, *June* 15, 1768.

No, I cannot be so false as to say I am glad you are pleased with your situation. You are so apt to take root, that it requires ten years to dig you out again when you once begin to settle. As you go pitching your tent up and down, I wish you were still more a Tartar, and shifted your quarters perpetually. Yes, I will come and see you; but tell me first, when do your Duke and Duchess [the Argylls] travel to the North? I know that he is a very amiable lad, and I do not know that she is not as amiable a *laddess*, but I had rather see their house comfortably when they are not there.

I perceive the deluge fell upon you before it reached us. It began here but on Monday last, and then rained near eight-and-forty hours without intermission. My poor hay has not a dry thread to its back. I have had a fire these three days. In short, every summer one lives in a state of mutiny and murmur, and I have found the reason: it is because we will affect to have a summer, and we have no title to any such thing. Our poets learnt their trade of the Romans, and so adopted the terms of their masters. They talk of shady groves, purling streams, and cooling breezes, and we get sore-throats and agues with attempting to realise these visions. Master Damon writes a song, and invites Miss Chloe to enjoy the cool of the evening, and the deuce a bit have we of any such thing as a cool evening. Zephyr is a north-east wind, that makes Damon button up to the chin, and pinches Chloe's nose till it is red and blue; and then they cry, *This is a bad summer*! as if we ever had any other. The best sun we have is made of Newcastle coal, and I am determined never to reckon upon any other. We ruin ourselves with inviting over foreign trees, and making our houses clamber up hills to look at prospects. How our ancestors would laugh at us, who knew there was no being comfortable, unless you had a high hill before your nose, and a thick warm wood at your back! Taste is too freezing a commodity for us, and, depend upon it, will go out of fashion again.

There is indeed a natural warmth in this country, which, as you say, I am very glad not to enjoy any longer; I mean the hot-house in St. Stephen's chapel. My own sagacity makes me very vain, though there was very little merit in it. I had seen so much of all parties, that I had little esteem left for any; it is most indifferent to me who is in or who is out, or which is set in the pillory, Mr. Wilkes or my Lord Mansfield. I see the country going to ruin, and no man with brains enough to save it. That is mortifying; but what signifies who has the undoing it? I seldom suffer myself to think on this subject: *my* patriotism could do no good, and my philosophy can make me be at peace.

I am sorry you are likely to lose your poor cousin Lady Hinchinbrook: I heard a very bad account of her when I was last in town. Your letter to Madame Roland shall be taken care of; but as you are so scrupulous of making me pay postage, I must remember not to overcharge you, as I can frank my idle letters no longer; therefore, good night!

P.S.—I was in town last week, and found Mr. Chute still confined. He had a return in his shoulder, but I think it more rheumatism than gout.

VOLTAIRE'S CRITICISMS ON SHAKESPEARE—PARNELL'S "HERMIT."

TO MONSIEUR DE VOLTAIRE.

STRAWBERRY HILL, *July* 27, 1768.

One can never, Sir, be sorry to have been in the wrong, when one's errors are pointed out to one in so obliging and masterly a manner. Whatever opinion I may have of Shakspeare, I should think him to blame, if he could have seen the letter you have done me the honour to write to me, and yet not conform to the rules you have there laid down. When he lived, there had not been a Voltaire both to give laws to the stage, and to show on what good sense those laws were founded. Your art, Sir, goes still farther: for you have supported your arguments, without having recourse to the best authority, your own Works. It was my interest perhaps to defend barbarism and irregularity. A great genius is in the right, on the contrary, to show that when correctness, nay, when perfection is demanded, he can still shine, and be himself, whatever fetters are imposed on him. But I will say no more on this head; for I am neither so unpolished as to tell you to your face how much I admire you, nor, though I have taken the liberty to vindicate Shakspeare against your criticisms, am I vain enough to think myself an adversary worthy of you. I am much more proud of receiving laws from you, than of contesting them. It was bold in me to dispute with you even before I had the honour of your acquaintance; it would be ungrateful now when you have not only taken notice of me, but forgiven me. The admirable letter you have been so good as to send me, is a proof that you are one of those truly great and rare men who know at once how to conquer and to pardon.

I have made all the inquiry I could into the story of M. de Jumonville; and though your and our accounts disagree, I own I do not think, Sir, that the strongest evidence is in our favour. I am told we allow he was killed by a party of our men, going to the Ohio. Your countrymen say he was going with a flag of truce. The commanding officer of our party said M. de Jumonville was going with hostile intentions; and that very hostile orders were found after his death in his pocket. Unless that officer had proved that he had previous intelligence of those orders, I doubt he will not be justified by finding them afterwards; for I am not at all disposed to believe that he had the foreknowledge of your hermit,[1] who pitched the old woman's nephew into the river, because "ce jeune homme auroit assassine sa tante dans un an."

I am grieved that such disputes should ever subsist between two nations who have everything in themselves to create happiness, and who may find enough in each other to love and admire. It is your benevolence, Sir, and your zeal for softening the manners of mankind; it is the doctrine of peace and amity which you preach, that have raised my esteem for you even more than the brightness of your genius. France may claim you in the latter light, but all nations have a right to call you their countryman *du cote du coeur*. It is on the strength of that connection that I beg you, Sir, to accept the homage of, Sir, your most obedient humble servant.[2]

[Footnote 1: The idea of Voltaire's fable in "Zadig," c. 20, is believed to have been borrowed from Parnell's "Hermit," but Mr. Wright suggests that it was more probably taken from one of the "Contes Devots, de l'Hermite qu'un ange conduisit dans le Siecle," which is published in the "Nouveau Recueil de Fabliaux et Contes."]

[Footnote 2: The letter of Voltaire to which the above is a reply, contained the following opinion of Walpole's "Historic Doubts";—"Avant le depart de ma lettre, j'ai eu le tems, Monsieur, de lire votre Richard Trois. Vous seriez un excellent attornei general; vous pesez toutes les probabilites; mais il paroit que vous avez une inclination secrete pour ce bossu. Vous voulez qu'il ait ete beau garcon, et meme galant homme. Le benedictin Calmet a fait une dissertation pour prouver que Jesus Christ avait un fort beau visage. Je veux croire avec vous, que Richard Trois n'etait ni si laid, ni si mechant, qu'on le dit; mais je n'aurais pas voulu avoir affaire a lui. Votre rose blanche et votre rose rouge avaient de terribles epines pour la nation.

"Those gracious kings are all a pack of rogues. En lisant l'histoire des York et des Lancastre, et de bien d'autres, on croit lire l'histoire des voleurs de grand chemin. Pour votre Henri Sept, il n'etait que coupeur de bourses. Be a minister or an anti-minister, a lord or a philosopher, I will be, with an equal respect, Sir, &c."]

ARRIVAL OF THE KING OF DENMARK—HIS POPULARITY WITH THE MOB.

TO THE EARL OF STRAFFORD.

STRAWBERRY HILL, *Aug.* 16, 1768.

As you have been so good, my dear lord, as twice to take notice of my letter, I am bound in conscience and gratitude to try to amuse you with anything new. A royal visitor, quite fresh, is a real curiosity—by the reception of him, I do not think many more of the breed will come hither. He came from Dover in hackney-chaises; for somehow or other the Master of the Horse happened to be in Lincolnshire; and the King's coaches having received no orders, were too good subjects to go and fetch a stranger King of their own heads. However, as his Danish Majesty travels to improve himself for the good of his people, he will go back extremely enlightened in the arts of government and morality, by having learned that crowned heads may be reduced to ride in a hired chaise.[1]

[Footnote 1: The King, travelling, as is usual with kings, *incognito*, assumed the title of the Comte de Travendahl.]

By another mistake, King George happened to go to Richmond about an hour before King Christiern arrived in London. An hour is exceedingly long; and the distance to Richmond still longer; so that with all the dispatch that could possibly be made, King George could not get back to his capital till next day at noon. Then, as the road from his closet at St. James's to the King of Denmark's apartment on t'other side of the palace is about thirty miles, which posterity, having no conception of the prodigious extent and magnificence of St. James's, will never believe, it was half an hour after three before his Danish Majesty's courier could go and return to let him know that his good brother and ally was leaving the palace in which they both were, in order to receive him at the Queen's palace, which you know is about a million of snail's paces from St. James's. Notwithstanding these difficulties and unavoidable delays, Woden, Thor, Friga, and all the gods that watch over the Kings of the North, did bring these two invincible monarchs to each other's embraces about half an hour after five that same evening. They passed an hour in projecting a family compact that will regulate the destiny of Europe to latest posterity: and then, the Fates so willing it, the British Prince departed for Richmond, and the Danish potentate repaired to the widowed mansion of his Royal Mother-in-Law, where he poured forth the fulness of his heart in praises on the lovely bride she had bestowed on him, from whom nothing but the benefit of his subjects could ever have torn him.—And here let Calumny blush, who has aspersed so chaste and faithful a monarch with low amours; pretending that he has raised to the honour of a seat in his sublime council, an artisan of Hamburgh, known only by repairing the soles of buskins, because that mechanic would, on no other terms, consent to his fair daughter's being honoured with majestic embraces. So victorious over his passions is this young Scipio from the Pole, that though on Shooter's Hill he fell into an ambush laid for him by an illustrious Countess, of blood-royal herself, his Majesty, after descending from his car, and courteously greeting her, again mounted his vehicle, without being one moment eclipsed from the eyes of the surrounding multitude.—Oh! mercy on me! I am out of breath—pray let me descend from my stilts, or I shall send you as fustian and tedious a History as that of [Lyttelton's] Henry II. Well, then, this great King is a very little one; not ugly, nor ill-made. He has the sublime strut of his grandfather, or of a cock-sparrow; and the divine white eyes of all his family by the mother's side. His curiosity seems to have consisted in the original plan of travelling, for I cannot say he takes notice of anything in particular. His manner is cold and dignified, but very civil and gracious and proper. The mob adore him and huzza him; and so they did the first instant. At present they begin to know why—for he flings money to them out of his windows; and by the end of the week I do not doubt but they will want to choose him for Middlesex. His Court is extremely well ordered; for they bow as low to him at every word as if his name was Sultan Amurat. You would take his first minister for only the first of his slaves.—I hope this example, which they have been so good as to exhibit at the opera, will contribute to civilize us. There is indeed a pert young gentleman, who a little discomposes this august ceremonial. His name is Count Holke, his age three-and-twenty; and his post answers to one that we had formerly in England, many ages ago, and which in our tongue was called the lord high favourite. Before the Danish monarchs became absolute, the most refractory of that country used to write libels, called *North Danes*, against this great officer; but that practice has long since ceased. Count Holke seems rather proud of his favour, than shy of displaying it.

I hope, my dear lord, you will be content with my Danish politics, for I trouble myself with no other. There is a long history about the Baron de Bottetourt and Sir Jeffery Amherst, who has resigned his regiment; but it is nothing to me, nor do I care a straw about it. I am deep in the anecdotes of the new Court; and if you want to know more of Count Holke or Count Molke, or the grand vizier Bernsdorff, or Mynheer Schimmelman, apply to me, and you shall be satisfied. But what do I talk of? You will see them yourself. Minerva in the shape of Count Bernsdorff, or out of all shape in the person of the Duchess of Northumberland, is to conduct Telemachus to York races; for can a monarch be perfectly accomplished in the mysteries of king-craft, as our Solomon James I. called it, unless he is initiated in the arts of jockeyship? When this northern star travels towards its own sphere, Lord Hertford will go to Ragley. I shall go with him; and, if I can avoid running foul of the magi that will be thronging from all parts to worship that star, I will endeavour to call at Wentworth Castle for a day or two, if it will not be inconvenient; I should think it would be about the second week in September, but your lordship shall hear again, unless you should forbid me, who am ever Lady Strafford's and your lordship's most faithful humble servant.

WILKES'S ELECTION—THE COMTESSE DE BARRI—THE DUC DE CHOISEUL'S INDISCRETION.

TO SIR HORACE MANN.

ARLINGTON STREET, *Jan.* 31, 1769.

Letters of Horace Walpole, V2

The affair of Wilkes is rather undecided yet, than in suspense.[1] It has been a fair trial between faction and corruption; of two such common creatures, the richest will carry it.

[Footnote 1: Wilkes had been elected a member of the Common Council.]

The Court of Aldermen set aside the election of Wilkes on some informality, but he was immediately re-chosen. This happened on Friday last, the very day of his appearance at the House of Commons. He went thither without the least disturbance or mob, having dispersed his orders accordingly, which are obeyed implicitly. He did not, however, appear at the bar till ten at night, the day being wasted in debating whether he should be suffered to enter on his case at large, or be restrained to his two chief complaints. The latter was carried by 270 to 131, a majority that he will not easily reduce. He was then called in, looked ill, but behaved decently, and demanded to take the oaths and his seat. This affair, after a short debate, was refused; and his counsel being told the restrictions imposed, the House adjourned at midnight. To-day he goes again to the House, but whatever steps he takes there, or however long debates he may occasion, you may look upon his fate as decided in that place.

We are in hourly expectation of hearing that a nymph, more common still than the two I have mentioned, has occasioned what Wilkes has failed in now, a change in an administration. I mean the Comtesse du Barri.[1] The *grands habits* are made, and nothing wanting for her presentation but—what do you think? some woman of quality to present her. In that servile Court and country, the nobility have had spirit enough to decline paying their court, though the King has stooped *a des bassesses* to obtain it. The Duc de Choiseul will be the victim; and they pretend to say that he has declared he will resign *a l'Anglaise*, rather than be *chasse* by such a creature. His indiscretion is astonishing: he has said at his own table, and she has been told so, "Madame du Barri est tres mal informee; on ne parle pas des Catins chez moi." Catin diverts herself and King Solomon the wise with tossing oranges into the air after supper, and crying, "*Saute, Choiseul! saute, Praslin!*" and then Solomon laughs heartily. Sometimes she flings powder in his sage face, and calls him *Jean Farine*! Well! we are not the foolishest nation in Europe yet! It is supposed that the Duc d'Aiguillon will be the successor.

[Footnote 1: This woman, one of the very lowest of the low, had caught the fancy of Louis XV.; and, as according to the curious etiquette of the French Court, it was indispensable that a king's mistress should be married, the Comte du Barri, a noble of old family, but ruined by gambling, was induced to marry her.]

I am going to send away this letter, because you will be impatient, and the House will not rise probably till long after the post is gone out. I did not think last May that you would hear this February that there was an end of mobs, that Wilkes was expelled, and the colonies quieted. However, pray take notice that I do not stir a foot out of the province of gazetteer into that of prophet. I protest, I know no more than a prophet what is to come. Adieu!

A GARDEN PARTY AT STRAWBERRY—A RIDOTTO AT VAUXHALL.

TO GEORGE MONTAGU, ESQ.

ARLINGTON STREET, *May* 11, 1769.

You are so wayward, that I often resolve to give you up to your humours. Then something happens with which I can divert you, and my good-nature returns. Did not you say you should return to London long before this time? At least, could you not tell me you had changed your mind? why am I to pick it out from your absence and silence, as Dr. Warburton found a future state in Moses's saying nothing of the matter! I could go on with a chapter of severe interrogatories, but I think it more cruel to treat you as a hopeless reprobate; yes, you are graceless, and as I have a respect for my own scolding, I shall not throw it away upon you.

Strawberry has been in great glory; I have given a festino there that will almost mortgage it. Last Tuesday all France dined there: Monsieur and Madame du Chatelet, the Duc de Liancourt, three more French ladies, whose names you will find in the enclosed paper, eight other Frenchmen, the Spanish and Portuguese ministers, the Holdernesses, Fitzroys, in short, we were four and twenty. They arrived at two. At the gates of the castle I received them, dressed in the cravat of Gibbons's carving, and a pair of gloves embroidered up to the elbows that had belonged to James I. The French servants stared, and firmly believed this was the dress of English country gentlemen. After taking a survey of the apartment, we went to the printing-house, where I had prepared the enclosed verses, with translations by Monsieur de Lille, one of the company. The moment they were printed off, I gave a private signal, and French horns and clarionets accompanied this compliment. We then went to see Pope's grotto and garden, and returned to a magnificent dinner in the refectory.

In the evening we walked, had tea, coffee, and lemonade in the Gallery, which was illuminated with a thousand, or thirty candles, I forget which, and played at whisk and loo till midnight. Then there was a cold supper, and at one the company returned to town, saluted by fifty nightingales, who, as tenants of the manor, came to do honour to their lord.

I cannot say last night was equally agreeable. There was what they called a *ridotto al fresco* at Vauxhall,[1] for which one paid half-a-guinea, though, except some thousand more lamps and a covered passage all round the garden, which took off from the gardenhood, there was nothing better than on a common night. Mr. Conway and I set out from his house at eight o'clock; the tide and torrent of coaches was so prodigious, that it was half-an-hour after nine before we got half way from Westminster Bridge. We then alighted; and after scrambling under bellies of horses, through wheels, and over posts and rails, we reached the gardens, where were already many thousand persons. Nothing diverted me but a man in a Turk's dress and two nymphs in masquerade without masks, who sailed amongst the company, and, which was surprising, seemed to surprise nobody. It had been given out that people were desired to come in fancied dresses without masks. We walked twice round and were rejoiced to come away, though with the same difficulties as at our entrance; for we found three strings of coaches all along the road, who did not move half a foot in half-an-hour. There is to be a rival mob in the same way at Ranelagh to-morrow; for the greater the folly and imposition the greater is the crowd. I have suspended the vestimenta[2] that were torn off my back to the god of repentance, and shall stay away. Adieu! I have not a word more to say to you. Yours ever.

P.S.—I hope you will not regret paying a shilling for this packet.

[Footnote 1: The ridotto was a Venetian entertainment—

  They went to the *Ridotto*—'tis a hall
    Where people dance, and sup, and dance again;
  Its proper name, perhaps, was a masqued ball,
    But that's of no importance to my strain;

'Tis (on a smaller scale) like our Vauxhall,
  Excepting that it can't be spoilt by rain;
The company is "mix'd"—the phrase I quote is
  As much as saying, they're below your notice.

Beppo, st. 38.]

[Footnote 2: *Vestimenta.*" Imitating Horace, who relates of himself—

  Me tabula sacer
Votiva paries indicat uvida
  Suspendisse potenti
    Vestimenta maris Deo (Od. i. 5).]

PAOLI—AMBASSADORIAL ETIQUETTE.

TO SIR HORACE MANN.

STRAWBERRY HILL, *June* 14, 1769.

I thank you for the history of the Pope and his genealogy, or, rather, for what is to be his genealogy; for I suppose all those tailors and coachmen his relations will now found noble families. They may enrich their blood with the remaining spoils of the Jesuits, unless, which would not surprise me, his new Holiness should now veer about, and endeavour to save the order; for I think the Church full as likely to fall by sacrificing its janissaries, as by any attacks that can be made upon it. *Deme unum, deme etiam unum.*

If I care little about your Roman politics, I am not so indifferent about your Corsican. Poor brave Paoli!—but he is not disgraced! We, that have sat still and seen him overwhelmed, must answer it to history. Nay, the Mediterranean will taunt us in the very next war. Choiseul triumphs over us and Madame du Barri; her star seems to have lost its influence. I do not know what another lady[1] will say to Choiseul on the late behaviour of his friend, the Ambassador, here. As the adventure will make a chapter in the new edition of Wiquefort, and, consequently, will strike *you*, I will give you the detail. At the ball on the King's birthday, Count Czernichew was sitting in the box of the Foreign

Ministers next to Count Seilern, the Imperial Ambassador. The latter, who is as fierce as the Spread Eagle itself, and as stiff as the chin of all the Ferdinands, was, according to his custom, as near to Jupiter as was possible. Monsieur du Chatelet and the Prince de Masserano came in. Chatelet sidled up to the two former, spoke to them and passed behind them, but on a sudden lifted up his leg and thrust himself in between the two Imperials. The Russian, astonished and provoked, endeavoured to push him away, and a jostle began that discomposed the faces and curls of both; and the Russian even dropped the word *impertinent*. Czernichew, however, quitted the spot of battle, and the Prince de Masserano, in support of the family-compact, hobbled into the place below Chatelet. As the two champions retired, more words at the door. However, the Russian's coach being first, he astonished everybody by proposing to set Monsieur du Chatelet down at his own house. In the coach, *it is said*, the Frenchman protested he had meant nothing personal either to Count Czernichew, or to the Russian Minister, but having received orders from his Court to take place on all occasion *next* to the Imperial Ambassador, he had but done his duty. Next morning he visited Czernichew, and they are *personally* reconciled. It was, however, feared that the dispute would be renewed, for, at the King's next levee, both were at the door, ready to push in when it should be opened; but the Russian kept behind, and at the bottom of the room without mixing with the rest of the Foreign Ministers. The King, who was much offended at what had passed, called Count Czernichew into the middle of the room, and talked to him for a very considerable time. Since then, the Lord Chamberlain has been ordered to notify to all the Foreign Ministers that the King looks on the ball at Court as a private ball, and declares, *to prevent such disagreeable altercations for the future*, that there is no precedence there. This declaration is ridiculed, because the ball at Court is almost the only ceremony that is observed there, and certainly the most formal, the princes of the blood dancing first, and everybody else being taken out according to their rank. Yet the King, being the fountain of all rank, may certainly declare what he pleases, especially in his own palace. The public papers, which seldom spare the French, are warm for the Russian. Chatelet, too, is not popular, nor well at Court. He is wrong-headed, and at Vienna was very near drawing his Court into a scrape by his haughtiness. His own friends even doubt whether this last exploit will not offend at Versailles, as the Duc de Choiseul has lately been endeavouring to soften the Czarina, wishes to send a minister thither, and has actually sent an agent. Chatelet was to have gone this week, but I believe waits to hear how his behaviour is taken. Personally, I am quite on his side, though I think him in the wrong; but he is extremely civil to me; I live much at his house, admire his wife exceedingly, and, besides, you know, have declared war with the Czarina; so what I say is quite in confidence to you, and for your information. As an Englishman, I am whatever Madam Great Britain can expect of me. As intimate with the Chatelets, and extremely attached to the Duchess of Choiseul, I detest Madame du Barri and her faction. You, who are a Foreign Minister, and can distinguish like a theologian between the *two natures* perfectly comprehend all this; and, therefore, to the charity of your casuistry I recommend myself in this jumble of contradictions, which you may be sure do not give me any sort of trouble either way. At least I have not *three* distinctions, like Chatelet when he affronted Czernichew, but neither in his private nor public capacity.

[Footnote 1: The Czarina.]

This fracas happens very luckily, as we had nothing left to talk of; for of the Pope we think no more, according to the old saying, than of the Pope of Rome. Of Wilkes there is no longer any question, and of the war under the Pole we hear nothing. Corsica, probably, will occasion murmurs, but they will be preserved in pickle till next winter. I am come hither for two months, very busy with finishing my round tower, which has stood still these five years, and with an enchanting new cottage that I have built, and other little works. In August I shall go to Paris for six weeks. In short, I am delighted with having bid adieu to Parliament and politics, and with doing nothing but what I like all the year round.

HIS RETURN TO PARIS—MADAME DEFFAND—A TRANSLATION OF "HAMLET"—MADAME DUMENIL—VOLTAIRE'S "MEROPE" AND "LES GUEBRES."

TO JOHN CHUTE, ESQ.

PARIS, *Aug.* 30, 1769.

I have been so hurried with paying and receiving visits, that I have not had a moment's worth of time to write. My passage was very tedious, and lasted near nine hours for want of wind.—But I need not talk of my journey; for Mr. Maurice, whom I met on the road, will have told you that I was safe on *terra firma*.

Judge of my surprise at hearing four days ago, that my Lord Dacre and my lady were arrived here. They are lodged within a few doors of me. He is come to consult a Doctor Pomme who has prescribed wine, and Lord Dacre already complains of the violence of his appetite. If you and I had *pommed* him to eternity, he would not have believed us. A man across the sea tells him the plainest thing in the world; that man happens to be called a doctor; and happening for novelty to talk common sense, is believed, as if he had talked nonsense! and what is more extraordinary, Lord Dacre thinks himself better, *though* he is so.

My dear old woman [Madame du Deffand] is in better health than when I left her, and her spirits so increased, that I tell her she will go mad with age. When they ask her how old she is, she answers, "J'ai soixante et mille ans." She and I went to the Boulevard last night after supper, and drove about there till two in the morning. We are going to sup in the country this evening, and are to go to-morrow night at eleven to the puppet-show. A *protege* of hers has written a piece for that theatre. I have not yet seen Madame du Barri, nor can get to see her picture at the exposition at the Louvre, the crowds are so enormous that go thither for that purpose. As royal curiosities are the least part of my *virtu*, I wait with patience. Whenever I have an opportunity I visit gardens, chiefly with a view to Rosette's having a walk. She goes nowhere else, because there is a distemper among the dogs.

There is going to be represented a translation of Hamlet; who when his hair is cut, and he is curled and powdered, I suppose will be exactly *Monsieur le Prince Oreste*. T'other night I was at "Merope." The Dumenil was as divine as Mrs. Porter[1]; they said her familiar tones were those of a *poissonniere*. In the last act, when one expected the catastrophe, Narbas, more interested than anybody to see the event, remained coolly on the stage to hear the story. The Queen's maid of honour entered without her handkerchief, and her hair most artfully undressed, and reeling as if she was maudlin, sobbed out a long narrative, that did not prove true; while Narbas, with all the good breeding in the world, was more attentive to her fright than to what had happened. So much for propriety. Now for probability. Voltaire has published a tragedy, called "Les Guebres." Two Roman colonels open the piece: they are brothers, and relate to one another, how they lately in company destroyed, by the Emperor's mandate, a city of the Guebres, in which were their own wives and children; and they recollect that they want prodigiously to know whether both their families did perish in the flames. The son of the one and the daughter of the other are taken up for heretics, and, thinking themselves brother and sister, insist upon being married, and upon being executed for their religion. The son stabs his father, who is half a Guebre, too. The high-priest rants and roars. The Emperor arrives, blames the pontiff for being a persecutor, and forgives the son for assassinating his father (who does not die) because—I don't know why, but that he may marry his cousin. The grave-diggers in Hamlet have no chance, when such a piece as the Guebres is written agreeably to all rules and unities. Adieu, my dear Sir! I hope to find you quite well at my return. Yours ever.

[Footnote 1: Mme. Dumenil, as has been mentioned in a former note, was the most popular of the French tragic actresses at this time, as Mrs. Porter was of the English actresses.]

THE FRENCH COURT—THE YOUNG PRINCES—ST. CYR—MADAME DE MAILLY.

TO GEORGE MONTAGU, ESQ.

PARIS, *Sunday night, Sept.* 17, 1769.

I am heartily tired; but, as it is too early to go to bed, I must tell you how agreeably I have passed the day. I wished for you; the same scenes strike us both, and the same kind of visions has amused us both ever since we were born.

Well then; I went this morning to Versailles with my niece Mrs. Cholmondeley, Mrs. Hart, Lady Denbigh's sister, and the Count de Grave, one of the most amiable, humane, and obliging men alive. Our first object was to see Madame du Barri. Being too early for mass, we saw the Dauphin and his brothers at dinner. The eldest is the picture of the Duke of Grafton, except that he is more fair, and will be taller. He has a sickly air, and no grace. The Count de Provence has a very pleasing countenance, with an air of more sense than the Count d'Artois, the genius of the family. They already tell as many *bon-mots* of the latter as of Henri Quatre and Louis Quatorze. He is very fat, and the most like his grandfather of all the children. You may imagine this royal mess did not occupy us long: thence to the Chapel, where a first row in the balconies was kept for us. Madame du Barri arrived over against us below, without rouge, without powder, and indeed *sans avoir fait sa toilette*; an odd appearance, as she was so conspicuous, close to the altar, and amidst both Court and people. She is pretty, when you consider her; yet so little striking, that I never should have asked who she was. There is nothing bold, assuming or affected in her manner. Her husband's sister was along with her. In the Tribune above, surrounded by prelates, was the amorous and still handsome King. One could not help smiling at the mixture of piety, pomp, and carnality. From chapel we went to the dinner of the elder Mesdames. We were almost stifled in the antechamber, where their dishes were heating over charcoal, and where we could not stir for the press. When the doors are opened, everybody rushes in, princes of the blood, *cordons bleus*, abbes, housemaids, and the Lord knows who and what. Yet, so used are their highnesses to this trade, that they eat as comfortably and heartily as you or I could do in our own parlours.

Our second act was much more agreeable. We quitted the Court and a reigning mistress, for a dead one and a Cloister. In short, I had obtained leave from the Bishop of Chartres to enter *into* St. Cyr; and, as Madame du Deffand never leaves anything undone that can give me satisfaction, she had written to the abbess to desire I might see everything that could be seen there. The Bishop's order was to admit me, *Monsieur de Grave, et les dames de ma compagnie*: I begged the abbess to give me back the order, that I might deposit it in the archives of Strawberry, and she complied instantly. Every door flew open to us: and the nuns vied in attentions to please us. The first thing I desired to see was Madame de Maintenon's apartment. It consists of two small rooms, a library, and a very small chamber, the same in which the Czar saw her, and in which she died. The bed is taken away, and the room covered now with bad pictures of the royal family, which destroys the gravity and simplicity. It is wainscotted with oak, with plain chairs of the same, covered with dark blue damask. Everywhere else the chairs are of blue cloth. The simplicity and extreme neatness of the whole house, which is vast, are very remarkable. A large apartment above (for that I have mentioned is on the ground-floor), consisting of five rooms, and destined by Louis Quatorze for Madame de Maintenon, is now the infirmary, with neat white linen beds, and decorated with every text of Scripture by which could be insinuated that the foundress was a Queen. The hour of vespers being come, we were conducted to the chapel, and, as it was *my* curiosity that had led us thither, I was placed in the Maintenon's own tribune; my company in the adjoining gallery. The pensioners, two and two, each band headed by a man, march orderly to their seats, and sing the whole service, which I confess was not a little tedious. The young ladies, to the number of two hundred and fifty, are dressed in black, with short aprons of the same, the latter and their stays bound with blue, yellow, green, or red, to distinguish the classes; the captains and lieutenants have knots of a different colour for distinction. Their hair is curled and powdered, their coiffure a sort of French round-eared caps, with white tippets, a sort of ruff and large tucker: in short, a very pretty dress. The nuns are entirely in black, with crape veils and long trains, deep white handkerchiefs, and forehead cloths, and a very long train. The chapel is plain but very pretty, and in the middle of the choir under a flat marble lies the foundress. Madame de Cambis, one of the nuns, who are about forty, is beautiful as a Madonna.[1] The abbess has no distinction but a larger and richer gold cross: her apartment consists of two very small rooms. Of Madame de Maintenon we did not see fewer than twenty pictures. The young one looking over her shoulder has a round face, without the least resemblance to those of her latter age. That in the royal mantle, of which you know I have a copy, is the most repeated; but there is another with a longer and leaner face, which has by far the most sensible look. She is in black, with a high point head and band, a long train, and is sitting in a chair of purple velvet. Before her knees stands her niece Madame de Noailles, a child; at a distance a view of Versailles or St. Cyr,[2] I could not distinguish which. We were shown some rich reliquaires and the *corpo santo* that was sent to her by the Pope. We were then carried into the public room of each class. In the first, the young ladies, who were playing at chess, were ordered to sing to us the choruses of Athaliah; in another, they danced minuets and country dances, while a nun, not quite so able as St. Cecilia, played on a violin. In the others, they acted before us the proverbs or conversations written by Madame de Maintenon for their instruction; for she was not only their foundress but their saint, and their adoration of her memory has quite eclipsed the Virgin Mary. We saw their dormitory, and saw them at supper; and at last were carried to their archives, where they produced volumes of her letters, and where one of the nuns gave me a small piece of paper with three sentences in her handwriting. I forgot to tell you, that this kind dame who took to me extremely, asked me if we had many convents and relics in England. I was much embarrassed for fear of destroying her good opinion of me, and so said we had but few now. Oh! we went too to the *apothecairie*, where they treated us with cordials, and where one of the ladies told me inoculation was a sin, as it was a voluntary detention from mass, and as voluntary a cause of eating *gras*. Our visit concluded in the garden, now grown very venerable, where the young ladies played at little games before us. After a stay of four hours we took our leave. I begged the abbess's blessing; she smiled, and said, she doubted I should not place much faith in it. She is a comely old gentlewoman, and very proud of having seen Madame de Maintenon. Well! was not I in the right to wish you with me?—could you have passed a day more agreeably.

Letters of Horace Walpole, V2

[Footnote 1: Madame du Deffand, in her letter to Walpole of the 10th of May, 1776, encloses the following portrait of Madame de Cambise, by Madame de la Valliere:—"Non, non, Madame, je ne ferai point votre portrait: vous avez une maniere d'etre si noble, si fine, si piquante, si delicate, si seduisante; votre gentilesse et vos graces changent si souvent pour n'en etre que plus aimable, que l'on ne peut saisir aucun de vos traits ni au physique ni au moral." She was niece of La Marquise de Boufflers, and, having fled to England at the breaking out of the French Revolution, resided here until her death, which took place at Richmond in January, 1809.]

[Footnote 2: St. Cyr was a school founded by Mme. de Maintenon for the education of girls of good families who were in reduced circumstances. Mme. de Maintenon was the daughter of M. D'Aubigne, a writer of fair repute both as a historian and a satirist. Her first husband had been a M. Paul Scarron, a comic poet of indifferent reputation. After his death, she was induced, after an artful show of affected reluctance, to become governess to the children of Louis XIV. and Mme. de Montespan. Louis gave her the small estate of Maintenon, and, after the death of his queen, privately married her. She became devout, and, under the tuition of the Jesuits, a violent promoter of the persecution of the Huguenots. It was probably her influence that induced Louis to issue the Edict revoking the Edict of Nantes promulgated by Henry IV. in 1598. She outlived the King, and died in 1719.]

I will conclude my letter with a most charming trait of Madame de Mailly,[1] which cannot be misplaced in such a chapter of royal concubines. Going to St. Sulpice, after she had lost the King's heart, a person present desired the crowd to make way for her. Some brutal young officers said, "Comment, pour cette catin la!" She turned to them, and with the most charming modesty said—"Messieurs, puisque vous me connoissez, priez Dieu pour moi." I am sure it will bring tears into your eyes. Was she not the Publican and Maintenon the Pharisee? Good night! I hope I am going to dream of all I have been seeing. As my impressions and my fancy, when I am pleased, are apt to be strong, my night perhaps may still be more productive of ideas than the day has been. It will be charming indeed if Madame de Cambis is the ruling tint. Adieu!

Yours ever.

[Footnote 1: Mme. de Mailly was the first of the mistresses of Louis XV. She was the elder sister of the Duchesse de Chateauroux and Mme. de Lauragais. She has the credit, such as it is, of having been really in love with the King before she became acquainted with him; but she soon retired, feeling repentance and shame at her position, and being superseded in his fancy by the more showy attractions of her younger sisters.]

A MASQUERADE—STATE OF RUSSIA.

TO SIR HORACE MANN.

ARLINGTON STREET, *Feb.* 27, 1770.

It is very lucky, seeing how much of the tiger enters into the human composition, that there should be a good dose of the monkey too. If Aesop had not lived so many centuries before the introduction of masquerades and operas, he would certainly have anticipated my observation, and worked it up into a capital fable. As we still trade upon the stock of the ancients, we seldom deal in any other manufacture; and, though nature, after new combinations, lets forth new characteristics, it is very rarely that they are added to the old fund; else how could so striking a remark have escaped being made, as mine, on the joint ingredients of tiger and monkey? In France the latter predominates, in England the former; but, like Orozmades and Arimanius,[1] they get the better by turns. The bankruptcy in France, and the rigours of the new Comptroller-General, are half forgotten, in the expectation of a new opera at the new theatre. Our civil war has been lulled asleep by a Subscription Masquerade, for which the House of Commons literally adjourned yesterday. Instead of Fairfaxes and Cromwells, we have had a crowd of Henry the Eighths, Wolseys, Vandykes, and Harlequins; and because Wilkes was not mask enough, we had a man dressed like him, with a visor, in imitation of his squint, and a Cap of Liberty on a pole. In short, sixteen or eighteen young lords have given the town a Masquerade; and politics, for the last fortnight, were forced to give way to habit-makers. The ball was last night at Soho; and, if possible, was more magnificent than the King of Denmark's. The Bishops opposed: he of London formally remonstrated to the King, who did not approve it, but could not help him. The consequence was, that four divine vessels belonging to the holy fathers, alias their wives, were at this Masquerade. Monkey again! A fair widow,[2] who once bore my whole name, and now bears half of it, was there, with one of those whom the newspapers call *great personages*—he dressed like Edward the Fourth, she like Elizabeth Woodville,[3] in grey and pearls, with a black veil. Methinks it was not very difficult to find out the meaning of those masks.

[Footnote 1: "*Orozmades and Arimanius.*" In the Persian theology Orozmades and Ahriman are the good and bad angels. In Scott's "Talisman" the disguised Saracen (Saladin) invokes Ahriman as "the dark spirit." In one of his earlier letters Walpole describes his friend Gray as Orozmades.]

[Footnote 2: "*A fair widow.*" Lady Waldegrave, a natural daughter of Walpole's uncle, married the King's favourite brother, the Duke of Gloucester, the *great personage*. The King was very indignant at the *mesalliance*; and this marriage, with that of the King's other brother, the Duke of Cumberland, to Mrs. Horton, led to the enactment of the Royal Marriage Act.]

[Footnote 3: Elizabeth Woodville was the daughter of a Sir Richard Woodville, and his wife, the Duchess of Bedford, the widow of the illustrious brother of Henry V. Her first husband had been Sir John Grey, a knight of the Lancastrian party; and, after his death, Edward IV., attracted by her remarkable beauty, married her in 1464.]

As one of my ancient passions, formerly, was Masquerades, I had a large trunk of dresses by me. I dressed out a thousand young Conways and Cholmondeleys, and went with more pleasure to see them pleased than when I formerly delighted in that diversion myself. It has cost me a great headache, and I shall probably never go to another. A symptom appeared of the change that has happened in the people.

The mob was beyond all belief: they held flambeaux to the windows of every coach, and demanded to have the masks pulled off and put on at their pleasure, but with extreme good-humour and civility. I was with my Lady Hertford and two of her daughters, in their coach: the mob took me for Lord Hertford, and huzzaed and blessed me! One fellow cried out, "Are you for Wilkes?" another said, "D—n you, you fool, what has Wilkes to do with a Masquerade?"

In good truth, that stock is fallen very low. The Court has recovered a majority of seventy-five in the House of Commons; and the party has succeeded so ill in the Lords, that my Lord Chatham has betaken himself to the gout, and appears no more. What Wilkes may do at his enlargement in April, I don't know, but his star is certainly much dimmed. The distress of France, the injustice they have been induced to commit on public credit, immense bankruptcies, and great bankers hanging and drowning themselves, are comfortable objects in our prospect; for one tiger is charmed if another tiger loses his tail.

There was a stroke of the monkey last night that will sound ill in the ears of your neighbour the Pope. The heir-apparent of the House of Norfolk, a drunken old mad fellow, was, though a Catholic, dressed like a Cardinal: I hope he was scandalised at the wives of our Bishops.

So you agree with me, and don't think that the crusado from Russia will recover the Holy Land! It is a pity; for, if the Turks kept it a little longer, I doubt it will be the Holy Land no longer. When Rome totters, poor Jerusalem! As to your Count Orloff's[1] denying the murder of the late Czar, it is no more than every felon does at the Old Bailey. If I could write like Shakspeare, I would make Peter's ghost perch on the dome of Sancta Sophia, and, when the Russian fleet comes in sight, roar, with a voice of thunder that should reach to Petersburg,

Let me sit heavy on thy soul to-morrow!

[Footnote 1: Count Orloff was one of the Czarina's earlier lovers, and was universally understood to have been the principal agent in the murder of her husband.]

We have had two or three simpletons return from Russia, charmed with the murderess, believing her innocent, *because* she spoke graciously to *them* in the drawing-room. I don't know what the present Grand Signior's name is, Osman, or Mustapha, or what, but I am extremely on his side against Catherine of Zerbst; and I never intend to ask him for a farthing, nor write panegyrics on him for pay, like Voltaire and Diderot; so you need not say a word to him of my good wishes. Benedict XIV. deserved my friendship, but being a sound Protestant, one would not, you know, make all Turk and Pagan and Infidel princes too familiar. Adieu!

[Illustration: SIR ROBERT WALPOLE

From a mezzotint by J. Simon after a picture by Sir Godfrey Kneller]

WILKES—BURKE'S PAMPHLET—PREDICTION OF AMERICAN REPUBLICS—EXTRAVAGANCE IN ENGLAND.

TO SIR HORACE MANN.

STRAWBERRY HILL, *May* 6, 1770.

I don't know whether Wilkes is subdued by his imprisonment, or waits for the rising of Parliament, to take the field; or whether his dignity of Alderman has dulled him into prudence, and the love of feasting; but hitherto he has done nothing but go to City banquets and sermons, and sit at Guildhall as a sober magistrate. With an inversion of the proverb, "Si ex quovis Mercurio fit lignum!" What do you Italians think of Harlequin Potesta?[1] In truth, his party is crumbled away strangely. Lord Chatham has talked on the Middlesex election till nobody will answer him; and Mr. Burke (Lord Rockingham's governor) has published a pamphlet[2] that has sown the utmost discord between that faction and the supporters of the Bill of Rights. Mrs. Macaulay[3] has written against it. In Parliament their numbers are shrunk to nothing, and the session is ending very triumphantly for the Court. But there is another scene opened of a very different aspect. You have seen the accounts from Boston. The tocsin seems to be sounded to America. I have many visions about that country, and fancy I see twenty empires and republics forming upon vast scales over all that continent, which is growing too mighty to be kept in subjection to half a dozen exhausted nations in Europe. As the latter sinks, and the others rise, they who live between the eras will be a sort of Noahs, witnesses to the period of the old world and origin of the new. I entertain myself with the idea of a future senate in Carolina and Virginia, where their future patriots will harangue on the austere and incorruptible virtue of the ancient English! will tell their auditors of our disinterestedness and scorn of bribes and pensions, and make us blush in our graves at their ridiculous panegyrics. Who knows but even our Indian usurpations and villanies may become topics of praise to American schoolboys? As I believe our virtues are extremely like those of our predecessors the Romans, so I am sure our luxury and extravagance are too.

[Footnote 1: Podesta was an officer in some of the smaller Italian towns, somewhat corresponding to our mayor. The name is Italianised from the Roman Potestas—

Hajus, quo trahitur, praetextam sumere mavis,
An Fidenarum, Gabiorumque esse Potestas.

(Juv., x. 100).]

[Footnote 2: The pamphlet is, "Thoughts on the Present Discontents," founding them especially on the unconstitutional influence of "the King's friends."]

[Footnote 3: Mrs. Macaulay was the wife of a London physician, and authoress of a "History of England" from the accession of James I. to that of George I., written in a spirit of the fiercest republicanism, but long since forgotten.]

What do you think of a winter Ranelagh[1] erecting in Oxford Road, at the expense of sixty thousand pounds? The new bank, including the value of the ground, and of the houses demolished to make room for it, will cost three hundred thousand; and erected, as my Lady Townley[2] says, *by sober citizens too*! I have touched before to you on the incredible profusion of our young men of fashion. I know a younger brother who literally gives a flower-woman half a guinea every morning for a bunch of roses for the nosegay in his button-hole. There has lately been an auction of stuffed birds; and, as natural history is in fashion, there are physicians and others who paid forty and fifty guineas for a single Chinese pheasant; you may buy a live one for five. After this, it is not extraordinary that pictures should be dear. We have at present three exhibitions. One West,[3] who paints history in the taste of Poussin, gets three hundred pounds for a piece not too large to hang over a chimney. He has merit, but is hard and heavy, and far unworthy of such prices. The rage to see these exhibitions is so great, that sometimes one cannot pass through the streets where they are. But it is incredible what sums are raised by mere exhibitions of anything; a new fashion, and to enter at which you pay a shilling or half-a-crown. Another rage, is for prints of English portraits: I have been collecting them above thirty years, and originally never gave for a mezzotinto above one or two shillings. The lowest are now a crown; most, from half a guinea to a guinea. Lately, I assisted a clergyman [Granger] in compiling a catalogue of them; since the publication, scarce heads in books, not worth threepence, will sell for five guineas. Then we have Etruscan vases, made of earthenware, in Staffordshire, [by Wedgwood] from two to five guineas, and *ormoulu*, never made here before, which succeeds so well, that a tea-kettle, which the inventor offered for one hundred guineas, sold by auction for one hundred and thirty. In short, we are at the height of extravagance and improvements, for we do improve rapidly in taste as well as in the former. I cannot say so much for our genius. Poetry is gone to bed, or into our prose; we are like the Romans in that too. If we have the arts of the Antonines,—we have the fustian also.

[Footnote 1: *"A winter Ranelagh."*—the Pantheon in Oxford Street.]

[Footnote 2: Lady Townley is the principal character in "The Provoked Husband."]

[Footnote 3: West, as a painter, was highly esteemed by George III., and, on the death of Sir J. Reynolds, succeeded him as President of the Royal Academy.]

Well! what becomes of your neighbours, the Pope and Turk? is one Babylon to fall, and the other to moulder away? I begin to tremble for the poor Greeks; they will be sacrificed like the Catalans, and left to be impaled for rebellion, as soon as that vainglorious woman the Czarina has glutted her lust of fame, and secured Azoph by a peace, which I hear is all she insists on keeping. What strides modern ambition takes! *We* are the successors of Aurungzebe; and a virago under the Pole sends a fleet into the Aegean Sea to rouse the ghosts of Leonidas and Epaminondas, and burn the capital of the second Roman Empire! Folks now scarce meddle with their next door neighbours; as many English go to visit St. Peter's who never thought of stepping into St. Paul's.

I shall let Lord Beauchamp know your readiness to oblige him, probably to-morrow, as I go to town. The spring is so backward here that I have little inducement to stay; not an entire leaf is out on any tree, and I have heard a syren as much as a nightingale. Lord Fitzwilliam, who, I suppose, is one of your latest acquaintance, is going to marry Lady Charlotte Ponsonby, Lord Besborough's second daughter, a pretty, sensible, and very amiable girl. I seldom tell you that sort of news, but when the parties are very fresh in your memory. Adieu!

MASQUERADES IN FASHION—A LADY'S CLUB.

TO GEORGE MONTAGU, ESQ.

STRAWBERRY HILL, *May* 6, 1770.

If you are like me, you are fretting at the weather. We have not a leaf, yet, large enough to make an apron for a Miss Eve of two years old. Flowers and fruits, if they come at all this year, must meet together as they do in a Dutch picture; our lords and ladies, however, couple as if it were the real *Gioventu dell' anno*. Lord Albemarle, you know, has disappointed all his brothers and my niece; and Lord Fitzwilliam is declared *sposo* to Lady Charlotte Ponsonby. It is a pretty match, and makes Lord Besborough as happy as possible.

Masquerades proceed in spite of Church and King. That knave the Bishop of London persuaded that good soul the Archbishop to remonstrate against them; but happily the age prefers silly follies to serious ones, and dominos, *comme de raison*, carry it against lawn sleeves.

There is a new Institution that begins to make, and if it proceeds, will make a considerable noise. It is a club of *both* sexes to be erected at Almack's, on the model of that of the men of White's. Mrs. Fitzroy, Lady Pembroke, Mrs. Meynell, Lady Molyneux, Miss Pelham, and Miss Loyd, are the foundresses. I am ashamed to say I am of so young and fashionable a society; but as they are people I live with, I choose to be idle rather than morose. I can go to a young supper, without forgetting how much sand is run out of the hour-glass. Yet I shall never pass a triste old age in turning the Psalms into Latin or English verse. My plan is to pass away calmly; cheerfully if I can; sometimes to amuse myself with the rising generation, but to take care not to fatigue them, nor weary them with old stories, which will not interest them, as their adventures do not interest me. Age would indulge prejudices if it did not sometimes polish itself against younger acquaintance; but it must be the work of folly if one hopes to contract friendships with them, or desires it, or thinks one can become the same follies, or expects that they should do more than bear one for one's good-humour. In short, they are a pleasant medicine, that one should take care not to grow fond of. Medicines hurt when habit has annihilated their force; but you see I am in no danger. I intend by degrees to decrease my opium, instead of augmenting the dose. Good night! You see I never let our long-lived friendship drop, though you give it so few opportunities of breathing.

THE PRINCESS OF WALES IS GONE TO GERMANY—TERRIBLE ACCIDENT IN PARIS.

TO SIR HORACE MANN.

ARLINGTON STREET, *June* 15, 1770.

I have no public event to tell you, though I write again sooner than I purposed. The journey of the Princess Dowager to Germany is indeed an extraordinary circumstance, but besides its being a week old, as I do not know the motives, I have nothing to say upon it. It is much canvassed and sifted, and yet perhaps she was only in search of a little repose from the torrents of abuse that have been poured upon her for some years. Yesterday they publicly sung about the streets a ballad, the burthen of which was, *the cow has left her calf*. With all this we are grown very quiet, and Lord North's behaviour is so sensible and moderate that he offends nobody.

Our family has lost a branch, but I cannot call it a misfortune. Lord Cholmondeley died last Saturday. He was seventy, and had a constitution to have carried him to a hundred, if he had not destroyed it by an intemperance, especially in drinking, that would have killed anybody else in half the time. As it was, he had outlived by fifteen years all his set, who have reeled into the ferry-boat so long before him. His grandson seems good and amiable, and though he comes into but a small fortune for an earl, five-and-twenty hundred a-year, his uncle the general may re-establish him upon a great footing—but it will not be in his life, and the general does not sail after his brother on a sea of claret.

You have heard details, to be sure, of the horrible catastrophe at the fireworks at Paris.[1] Francees, the French minister, told me the other night that the number of the killed is so great that they now try to stifle it; my letters say between five and six hundred! I think there were not fewer than ten coach-horses trodden to death. The mob had poured down from the *Etoile* by thousands and ten thousands to see the illuminations, and did not know the havoc they were occasioning. The impulse drove great numbers into the Seine, and those met with the most favourable deaths.

[Footnote 1: The Dauphin had been married to the Archduchess Marie Antoinette on May 16th, and on May 30th the city of Paris closed a succession of balls and banquets with which they had celebrated the marriage of the heir of the monarchy by a display of fireworks in the Place Louis XV., in which the ingenuity of the most fashionable pyrotechnists had been exhausted to outshine all previous displays of the sort. But towards the end of the exhibition one of the explosives set fire to a portion of the platforms on which the different figures were constructed, and in a moment the whole woodwork was in a flame. Three sides of the Place were enclosed, and the fourth was so blocked up with carriages, that the spectators, who saw themselves surrounded with flames, had no way to escape open. The carriage-horses, too, became terrified and unmanageable. In their panic-stricken flight the spectators trampled one another down; hundreds fell, and were crushed to death by their companions; hundreds were pushed into the river and drowned. The number of killed could never be precisely ascertained; but it was never estimated below six hundred, and was commonly believed to have greatly exceeded that number, as many of the victims were of the poorer class—many, too, the bread-winners of their families. The Dauphin and Dauphiness devoted the whole of their month's income to the relief of the sufferers; and Marie Antoinette herself visited many of the families whose loss seemed to have been the most severe: this personal interest in their affliction which she thus displayed making a deep impression on the citizens.]

This is a slight summer letter, but you will not be sorry it is so short, when the dearth of events is the cause. Last year I did not know but we might have a battle of Edgehill[1] by this time. At present, my Lord Chatham could as soon raise money as raise the people; and Wilkes will not much longer have more power of doing either. If you were not busy in burning Constantinople, you could not have a better opportunity for taking a trip to England. Have you never a wish this way? Think what satisfaction it would be to me?—but I never advise; nor let my own inclinations judge for my friends. I had rather suffer their absence, than have to reproach myself with having given them bad counsel. I therefore say no more on what would make me so happy. Adieu!

[Footnote 1: Edgehill was the first battle in the Great Rebellion, fought October 23, 1642.]

FALL OF THE DUC DE CHOISEUL'S MINISTRY.

TO SIR HORACE MANN.

STRAWBERRY HILL, *Saturday evening, Dec.* 29, 1770.

We are alarmed, or very glad, we don't know which. The Duke de Choiseul is fallen! but we cannot tell yet whether the mood of his successors will be peaceable or martial. The news arrived yesterday morning, and the event happened but last Monday evening. He was allowed but three hours to prepare for his journey, and ordered to retire to his seat at Chanteloup; but there are letters that say, *qu'il ira plus loin.* The Duke de Praslin is banished too—a disagreeable man; but his fate is a little hard, for he was just going to resign the Marine to Chatelet, who, by the way, is forbidden to visit Choiseul. I shall shed no tears for Chatelet, the most peevish and insolent of men, our bitter enemy, and whom M. de Choiseul may thank in some measure for his fall; for I believe while Chatelet was here, he drew the Spaniards into the attack of Falkland's Island. Choiseul's own conduct seems to have been not a little equivocal. His friends maintained that his existence as a minister depended on his preventing a war, and he certainly confuted the Comptroller-General's plan of raising supplies for it. Yet, it is now said, that on the very morning of the Duke's disgrace, the King reproached him, and said "Monsieur, je vous avois dit, que je ne voulois pas la guerre;" and the Duke d'Aiguillon's friends have officiously whispered, that if Choiseul was out it would certainly be peace; but did not Lord Chatham, immediately before he was Minister, protest not half a man should be sent to Germany, and yet, were not all our men and all our money sent thither? The Chevalier de Muy is made Secretary-at-War, and it is supposed Monsieur d'Aiguillon is, or will be, the Minister.

Thus Abishag[1] has strangled an Administration that had lasted fourteen years. I am sincerely grieved for the Duchess de Choiseul, the most perfect being I know of either sex. I cannot possibly feel for her husband: Corsica is engraved in my memory, as I believe it is on your heart. His cruelties there, I should think, would not cheer his solitude or prison. In the mean time, desolation and confusion reign all over France. They are almost bankrupts, and quite famished. The Parliament of Paris has quitted its functions, and the other tribunals threaten to follow the example. Some people say, that Maupeou,[2] the Chancellor, told the King that they were supported underhand by Choiseul, and must submit if he were removed. The suggestion is specious at least, as the object of their antipathy is the Duke d'Aiguillon. If the latter should think a war a good diversion to their enterprises, I should not be surprised if they went on, especially if a bankruptcy follows famine. The new Minister and the Chancellor are in general execration. On the latter's lately obtaining the *Cordon Bleu*,[3] this epigram appeared:—

> Ce tyran de la France, qui cherche a mettre tout en feu,
> Merite un cordon, mais ce n'est pas le cordon bleu.

[Footnote 1: Madame du Barri.—WALPOLE.]

[Footnote 2: Maupeou was the Chancellor who had just abolished the Parliaments, the restoration of which in the next reign was perhaps one of the causes which contributed to the Revolution.]

[Footnote 3: The *Cordon Bleu* was the badge of the Order of St. Louis, established by Louis XIV.; the *cordon not* blue was the hangman's rope.]

We shall see how Spain likes the fall of the author of the "Family-compact."[1] There is an Empress[2] will not be pleased with it, but it is not the Russian Empress; and much less the Turks, who are as little obliged to that bold man's intrigues as the poor Corsicans. How can one regret such a general *Boute-feu*?

[Footnote 1: Choiseul was the Minister when the "Family Compact" of 1761 was concluded between France and Spain. The Duc de Praslin, who shared his fall, had been Secretary at War, and for some little time neither his office nor that of Choiseul was filled up, but the work of their departments was performed by Secretaries of State, the Duc d'Aiguillon, in spite of the contempt in which he was deservedly held, being eventually made Secretary for Foreign Affairs through the interest of Mme. du Barri (Lacretelle, iv. 256).]

[Footnote 2: "*An Empress.*" The Empress-Queen Maria Theresa, who considered herself and her family under obligations to Choiseul for his abandonment of the long-standing policy of enmity to the house of Austria which had been the guiding principle of all French statesmen since the time of Henry IV., and for the marriage of her favourite daughter to the Dauphin.]

Perhaps our situation is not very stable neither. The world, who are ignorant of Lord Weymouth's motives, suspect a secret intelligence with Lord Chatham. Oh! let us have peace abroad before we quarrel any more at home!

Judge Bathurst is to be Lord Keeper, with many other arrangements in the law; but as you neither know the persons, nor I care about them, I shall not fill my paper with the catalogue, but reserve the rest of my letter for Tuesday, when I shall be in town. No Englishman, you know, will sacrifice his Saturday and Sunday. I have so little to do with all these matters, that I came hither this morning, and left this new chaos to arrange itself as it pleases. It certainly is an era, and may be an extensive one; not very honourable to old King Capet,[1] whatever it may be to the intrigues of his new Ministers. The Jesuits will not be without hopes. They have a friend that made mischief *ante Helenam*.

[Footnote 1: Louis XV.—WALPOLE.]

Jan. 1, 1771.

I hope the new year will end as quietly as it begins, for I have not a syllable to tell you. No letters are come from France since Friday morning, and this is Tuesday noon. As we had full time to reason—in the dark, the general persuasion is, that the French Revolution will produce peace—I mean in Europe—not amongst themselves. Probably I have been sending you little but what you will have heard long before you receive my letter; but no matter; if we did not chat about our neighbour Kings, I don't know how we should keep up our correspondence, for we are better acquainted with King Louis, King Carlos, and Empresses Katharine and Teresa, than you with the English that I live amongst, or I with your Florentines. Adieu!

PEACE WITH SPAIN—BANISHMENT OF THE FRENCH PARLIAMENT—MRS. CORNELYS'S ESTABLISHMENT—THE QUEEN OF DENMARK.

TO SIR HORACE MANN.

ARLINGTON STREET, *Feb.* 22, 1771.

Two days ago there began to be an alarm at the delay of the Spanish courier, and people were persuaded that the King of Spain had refused to ratify his ambassador's declaration; who, on the warrant of the French King, had ventured to sign it, though expecting every hour to be recalled, as he actually was two days afterwards. However, the night before last, to the great comfort of Prince Masserano and our Ministers, the ratification arrived; and, after so many delays and untoward accidents, Fortune has interposed (for there has been great luck, too, in the affair), and peace is again established. With you, I am not at all clear that Choiseul was in earnest to make it. If he was, it was entirely owing to his own ticklish situation. Other people think, that this very situation had made him desperate; and that he was on the point of striking a hardy stroke indeed; and meditated sending a strong army into Holland, to oblige the Dutch to lend twelve men-of-war to invade us. Count Welderen,[1] who is totally an anti-Gaul, assured me he did not believe this project. Still I am very glad such a *boute-feu* is removed.

[Footnote 1: The Dutch Minister in England. He married a sister of Sir John Griffin, Maid of Honour to Anne Princess of Orange.—WALPOLE.]

Letters of Horace Walpole, V2

This treaty is an epoch; and puts a total end to all our preceding histories. Long quiet is never probable, nor shall I guess who will disturb it; but, whatever happens, must be thoroughly new matter, though some of the actors perhaps may not be so. Both Lord Chatham and Wilkes are at the end of their reckoning, and the Opposition can do nothing without fresh fuel.

The scene that is closed here seems to be but opening in France. The Parliament of Paris banished; a new one arbitrarily appointed;[1] the Princes of the Blood refractory and disobedient; the other Parliament as mutinous; and distress everywhere: if the army catches the infection, what may not happen, when the King is despised, his agents detested, and no Ministry settled? Some say the mistress and her faction keep him hourly diverted or drunk; others, that he has got a new passion: how creditable at sixty! Still I think it is the crisis of their constitution. If the Monarch prevails, he becomes absolute as a Czar; if he is forced to bend, will the Parliament stop there?

[Footnote 1: "*A new one appointed.*" This is a mistake of Walpole's. A new Parliament was not, nor indeed could be, appointed; but Maupeou created six new Sovereign Courts at Arras, Blois, Chalons sur Marne, Clermont, Lyon, and Poitiers, at which "justice should be done at the sovereign's expense" (Lacretelle, iv. 264).]

In the mean time our most serious war is between two Operas. Mr. Hobart, Lord Buckingham's brother, is manager of the Haymarket. Last year he affronted Guadagni, by preferring the Zamperina, his own mistress, to the singing hero's sister. The Duchess of Northumberland, Lady Harrington, and some other great ladies, espoused the brother, and without a license erected an Opera for him at Madame Cornelys's. This is a singular dame, and you must be acquainted with her. She sung here formerly, by the name of the Pompeiati. Of late years she has been the Heidegger of the age, and presided over our diversions. Her taste and invention in pleasures and decorations are singular. She took Carlisle House in Soho Square, enlarged it, and established assemblies and balls by subscription. At first they scandalised, but soon drew in both righteous and ungodly. She went on building, and made her house a fairy palace for balls, concerts, and masquerades. Her Opera, which she called *Harmonic Meetings*, was splendid and charming. Mr. Hobart began to starve, and the managers of the theatres were alarmed. To avoid the act, she pretended to take no money, and had the assurance to advertise that the subscription was to provide coals for the poor, for she has vehemently courted the mob, and succeeded in gaining their princely favour. She then declared her Masquerades were for the benefit of commerce. I concluded she would open another sort of house next for the interests of the Foundling Hospital, and I was not quite mistaken, for they say one of her maids, gained by Mr. Hobart, affirms that she could not undergo the fatigue of managing such a house. At last Mr. Hobart informed against her, and the Bench of Justices, less soothable by music than Orpheus's beasts, have pronounced against her. Her Opera is quashed, and Guadagni, who governed so haughtily at Vienna, that, to pique some man of quality there, he named a minister to Venice, is not only fined, but was threatened to be sent to Bridewell, which chilled the blood of all the Caesars and Alexanders he had ever represented; nor could any promises of his lady-patronesses rehabilitate his courage—so for once an Act of Parliament goes for something.

You have got three new companions;[1] General Montagu, a West Indian Mr. Paine, and Mr. Lynch, your brother at Turin.

[Footnote 1: As Knights of the Bath.—WALPOLE.]

There is the devil to pay in Denmark. The Queen[1] has got the ascendant, has turned out favourites and Ministers, and literally wears the breeches, actual buckskin. There is a physician, who is said to rule both their Majesties, and I suppose is sold to France, for that is the predominant interest now at Copenhagen. The Czarina has whispered her disapprobation, and if she has a talon left, when she has done with the Ottomans, may chance to scratch the little King.

[Footnote 1: The Queen was Caroline Matilda, a sister of George III., and was accused of a criminal intimacy with Count Struenzee, the Prime Minister. Struenzee, "after a trial with only a slight semblance of the forms of justice" (to quote the words of Lord Stanhope), was convicted and executed; and the Queen was at first imprisoned in the Castle of Cronenburg, but after a time was released, and allowed to retire to Zell, Hanover, where she died in 1774.]

For eight months to come I should think we shall have little to talk of, you and I, but distant wars and distant majesties. For my part, I reckon the volume quite shut in which I took any interest. The succeeding world is young, new, and half unknown to me. Tranquillity comprehends every wish I have left, and I think I should not even ask what news there is, but for fear of seeming wedded to old stories—the rock of old men; and yet I should prefer that failing to the solicitude about a world one belongs to no more! Adieu!

QUARREL OF THE HOUSE OF COMMONS WITH THE CITY—DISSENSIONS IN THE FRENCH COURT AND ROYAL FAMILY—EXTRAVAGANCE IN ENGLAND.

TO SIR HORACE MANN.

ARLINGTON STREET, *April* 26, 1771.

You may wonder that I have been so silent, when I had announced a war between the House of Commons and the City—nay, when hostilities were actually commenced; but many a campaign languishes that has set out very flippantly. My letters depend on events, and I am like the man in the weather-house who only comes forth on a storm. The wards in the City have complimented the prisoners,[1] and some towns; but the train has not spread much. Wilkes is your only gun-powder that makes an explosion. He and his associates are more incensed at each other than against the Ministry, and have saved the latter much trouble. The Select Committees have been silent and were forgotten, but there is a talk now of their making some report before the session closes.

[Footnote 1: The prisoners were Crosby, the Lord Mayor, and Oliver, one of the aldermen, both members of Parliament. The selection of the Tower for their imprisonment was greatly remarked upon, because hitherto that had never been so used except for persons accused of high treason; while their offence was but a denial of the right of the House of Commons to arrest a liveryman within the City, and the entertaining a charge of assault against the messenger who had endeavoured to arrest him. These riots, which for the moment appeared likely to become formidable, arose out of the practice of reporting the parliamentary debates, a practice contrary to the Standing Orders of Parliament, passed as far back as the reign of Elizabeth, but the violation of which had lately begun to be attempted.]

The serious war is at last absolutely blown over. Spain has sent us word she is disarming. So are we. Who would have expected that a courtesan at Paris would have prevented a general conflagration? Madame du Barri has compensated for Madame Helen, and is *optima pacis causa*. I will not swear that the torch she snatched from the hands of Spain may not light up a civil war in France. The Princes of the Blood[1] are forbidden the Court, twelve dukes and peers, of the most complaisant, are banished, or going to be banished; and even the captains of the guard. In short, the King, his mistress, and the Chancellor, have almost left themselves alone at Versailles. But as the most serious events in France have always a ray of ridicule mixed with them, some are to be exiled *to* Paris, and some to St. Germain. How we should laugh at anybody being banished to Soho Square and Hammersmith? The Chancellor desired to see the Prince of Conti; the latter replied, "Qu'il lui donnoit rendezvous a la Greve."[2]

[Footnote 1: The "Princes of the Blood" in France were those who, though of Royal descent, were not children of a king—such, for instance, as the Dukes of Orleans and Bourbon; and they were reckoned of a rank so inferior to the princes of the Royal Family, that, as Marie Antoinette on one occasion told the Duke of Orleans, in a well-deserved reproof for his factious insolence, Princes of the Blood had never pretended to the honour of supping with the King and herself. (See the Editor's "Life of Marie Antoinette," c. 10). Their offence, in this instance, was having protested against the holding and the proceedings of a *Lit de Justice*, which had been held on April 15th, about three months after the banishment of all the members of Parliament (Lacretelle, c. 13).]

[Footnote 2: La Greve was the place of execution in Paris.

> Who has e'er been at Paris must needs know the Greve,
> The fatal retreat of th' unfortunate brave;
> Where honour and justice most oddly contribute
> To ease hero's pains by a halter and gibbet (PRIOR).]

If we laugh at the French, they stare at us. Our enormous luxury and expense astonishes them. I carried their Ambassador, and a Comte de Levi, the other morning to see the new winter Ranelagh [The Pantheon] in Oxford Road, which is almost finished. It amazed me myself. Imagine Balbec in all its glory! The pillars are of artificial *giallo antico*. The ceilings, even of the passages, are of the most beautiful stuccos in the best taste of grotesque. The ceilings of the ball-rooms and the panels painted like Raphael's *loggias* in the Vatican. A dome like the pantheon, glazed. It is to cost fifty thousand pounds. Monsieur de Guisnes said to me, "Ce n'est qu'a Londres qu'on peut faire tout cela." It is not quite a proof of the same taste, that two views of Verona, by Canaletti, have been sold by auction for five hundred and fifty guineas; and, what is worse, it is come out that they are copies by Marlow, a disciple of Scott. Both master and scholar are indeed better painters than the Venetian; but the purchasers did not mean to be so well cheated.

The papers will have told you that the wheel of fortune has again brought up Lord Holdernesse, who is made governor to the Prince of Wales. The Duchess of Queensberry, a much older veteran, is still figuring in the world, not only by giving frequent balls, but really by her beauty. Reflect, that she was a goddess in Prior's days![1] I could not help adding these lines on her—you know his end:

>   Kitty, at Heart's desire,
> Obtained the chariot for a day,
>   And set the world on fire.

This was some fifty-six years ago, or more. I gave her this stanza:

> To many a Kitty, Love his car
>   Will for a day engage,
> But Prior's Kitty, ever fair,
>   Obtained it for an age!

And she is old enough to be pleased with the compliment.

[Footnote 1: Prior died in 1721.]

My brother [Sir Edward Walpole] has lost his son; and it is no misfortune, though he was but three-and-thirty, and had very good parts; for he was sunk into such a habit of drinking and gaming, that the first ruined his constitution, and the latter would have ruined his father.

Shall I send away this short scroll, or reserve it to the end of the session? No, it is already somewhat obsolete: it shall go, and another short letter shall be the other half of it—so, good night!

GREAT DISTRESS AT THE FRENCH COURT.

TO THE HON. H.S. CONWAY.

PARIS, *July* 30, 1771.

I do not know where you are, nor where this will find you, nor when it will set out to seek you, as I am not certain by whom I shall send it. It is of little consequence, as I have nothing material to tell you, but what you probably may have heard.

The distress here is incredible, especially at Court. The King's tradesmen are ruined, his servants starving, and even angels and archangels cannot get their pensions and salaries, but sing "Woe! woe! woe!" instead of Hosannahs. Compiegne is abandoned; Villars Coterets[1] and Chantilly crowded, and Chanteloup still more in fashion, whither everybody goes that pleases; though, when they ask leave, the answer is, "Je ne le defends ni le permets." This is the first time that ever the will of a King of France was interpreted against his inclination. Yet, after annihilating his Parliament, and ruining public credit, he tamely submits to be affronted by his own servants. Madame de Beauveau, and two or three high-spirited dames, defy this Czar of Gaul. Yet they and their cabal are as inconsistent on the other hand. They make epigrams, sing vaudevilles,[2] against the mistress, hand about libels against the Chancellor [Maupeou], and have no more effect than a sky-rocket; but in three months will die to go to Court, and to be invited to sup with Madame du Barri. The only real struggle is between the Chancellor [Maupeou] and the Duc d'Aiguillon. The first is false, bold, determined, and not subject to little qualms. The other is less known, communicates himself to nobody, is suspected of deep policy and deep designs, but seems to intend to set out under a mask of very smooth varnish; for he has just obtained the payment of all his bitter enemy La Chalotais' pensions and arrears. He has the advantage, too, of being but moderately detested in comparison of his rival, and, what he values more, the interest of the mistress. The Comptroller-General[3] serves both, by acting mischief more sensibly felt; for he ruins everybody but those who purchase a respite from his mistress. He dispenses bankruptcy by retail, and will fall, because he cannot even by these means be useful enough. They are striking off nine millions from *la caisse militaire*, five from the marine, and one from the *affaires etrangeres*: yet all this will not extricate them. You never saw a great nation in so disgraceful a position. Their next prospect is not better: it rests on an *imbecille* [Louis XVI.], both in mind and body.

[Footnote 1: Villars Coterets was the country residence of the Duc d'Orleans; Chantilly that of the Prince de Conde; and Chanteloup that of the Duc de Choiseul: and the mere fact of their being in disgrace at Court was sufficient to make them popular with the people.]

[Footnote 2: The following specimen of these vaudevilles was given by Madame du Deffand to Walpole:—

"L'avez-vous vue, ma Du Barry,
  Elle a ravi mon ame;
  Pour elle j'ai perdu l'esprit,
  Des Francais j'ai le blame:
Charmants enfans de la Gourdon,
Est-elle chez vous maintenant?
  Rendez-la-moi,
  Je suis le Roi,
Soulagez mon martyre;
  Rendez-la-moi,
  Elle est a moi,
 Je suis son pauvre Sire.
L'avez-vous vue," &c.

"Je sais qu'autrefois les laquais
On fete ses jeunes attraits;
  Que les cochers,
  Les perruquiers,
L'aimaient, l'aimaient d'amour extreme,
 Mais pas autant que je l'aime.
L'avez-vous vue," &c.]

[Footnote 3: The Comptroller-General was the Abbe Terrai, notoriously as corrupt as he was incompetent. One of his measures, reducing the interest on the Debt by one-half, was tantamount to an act of bankruptcy; but the national levity comforted itself by jests, and one evening, when the pit at the theatre was crowded to suffocation, one of the sufferers carried the company with him by shouting out a suggestion to send for the Abbe Terrai to reduce them all to one-half their size.]

ENGLISH GARDENING IN FRANCE—ANGLOMANIE—HE IS WEARY OF PARIS—DEATH OF GRAY.

Letters of Horace Walpole, V2

TO JOHN CHUTE, ESQ.

Paris, *August* 5, 1771.

It is a great satisfaction to me to find by your letter of the 30th, that you have had no return of your gout. I have been assured here, that the best remedy is to cut one's nails in hot water. It is, I fear, as certain as any other remedy! It would at least be so here, if their bodies were of a piece with their understandings; or if both were as curable as they are the contrary. Your prophecy, I doubt, is not better founded than the prescription. I may be lame; but I shall never be a duck, nor deal in the garbage of the Alley.

I envy your *Strawberry tide*, and need not say how much I wish I was there to receive you. Methinks, I should be as glad of a little grass, as a seaman after a long voyage. Yet English gardening gains ground here prodigiously—not much at a time, indeed—I have literally seen one, that is exactly like a tailor's paper of patterns. There is a Monsieur Boutin, who has tacked a piece of what he calls an English garden to a set of stone terraces, with steps of turf. There are three or four very high hills, almost as high as, and exactly in the shape of, a tansy pudding. You squeeze between these and a river, that is conducted at obtuse angles in a stone channel, and supplied by a pump; and when walnuts come in I suppose it will be navigable. In a corner enclosed by a chalk wall are the samples I mentioned; there is a strip of grass, another of corn, and a third *en friche*, exactly in the order of beds in a nursery. They have translated Mr. Whately's book,[1] and the Lord knows what barbarism is going to be laid at our door. This new *Anglomanie* will literally be *mad English*.

[Footnote 1: Mr. Whately, the Secretary to the Treasury, had published an essay on Gardening.]

New *arrets*, new retrenchments, new misery, stalk forth every day. The Parliament of Besancon is dissolved; so are the *grenadiers de France*. The King's tradesmen are all bankrupt; no pensions are paid, and everybody is reforming their suppers and equipages. Despotism makes converts faster than ever Christianity did. Louis *Quinze* is the true *rex Christianissimus*, and has ten times more success than his dragooning great-grandfather. Adieu, my dear Sir! Yours most faithfully.

Friday 9th.

... It is very singular that I have not half the satisfaction in going into churches and convents that I used to have. The consciousness that the vision is dispelled, the want of fervour so obvious in the religious, the solitude that one knows proceeds from contempt, not from contemplation, make those places appear like abandoned theatres destined to destruction. The monks trot about as if they had not long to stay there; and what used to be holy gloom is now but dirt and darkness. There is no more deception than in a tragedy acted by candle-snuffers. One is sorry to think that an empire of common sense would not be very picturesque; for, as there is nothing but taste that can compensate for the imagination of madness, I doubt there will never be twenty men of taste for twenty thousand madmen. The world will no more see Athens, Rome, and the Medici again, than a succession of five good emperors, like Nerva, Trajan, Adrian, and the two Antonines.

August 13.

Mr. Edmonson has called on me; and, as he sets out to-morrow, I can safely trust my letter to him. I have, I own, been much shocked at reading Gray's[1] death in the papers. 'Tis an hour that makes one forget any subject of complaint, especially towards one with whom I lived in friendship from thirteen years old. As self lies so rooted in self, no doubt the nearness of our ages made the stroke recoil to my own breast; and having so little expected his death, it is plain how little I expect my own. Yet to you, who of all men living are the most forgiving, I need not excuse the concern I feel. I fear most men ought to apologise for their want of feeling, instead of palliating that sensation when they have it. I thought that what I had seen of the world had hardened my heart; but I find that it had formed my language, not extinguished my tenderness. In short, I am really shocked—nay, I am hurt at my own weakness, as I perceive that when I love anybody, it is for my life; and I have had too much reason not to wish that such a disposition may very seldom be put to the trial. You, at least, are the only person to whom I would venture to make such a confession.

[Footnote 1: Gray died of gout in the stomach on July 30th. He was only fifty-five.]

Adieu! my dear Sir! Let me know when I arrive, which will be about the last day of the month, when I am likely to see you. I have much to say to you. Of being here I am most heartily tired, and nothing but this dear old woman should keep me here an hour—I am weary of them to death—but that is not new! Yours ever.

SCANTINESS OF THE RELICS OF GRAY—GARRICK'S PROLOGUES, ETC.—WILKES'S SQUINT.

TO THE REV. WILLIAM COLE

ARLINGTON STREET, *Jan.* 28, 1772.

It is long indeed, dear Sir, since we corresponded. I should not have been silent if I had anything worth telling you in your way; but I grow such an antiquity myself, that I think I am less fond of what remains of our predecessors.

I thank you for Bannerman's proposal; I mean, for taking the trouble to send it, for I am not at all disposed to subscribe. I thank you more for the note on King Edward; I mean, too, for your friendship in thinking of me. Of Dean Milles I cannot trouble myself to think any more. His piece is at Strawberry: perhaps I may look at it for the sake of your note. The bad weather keeps me in town, and a good deal at home; which I find very comfortable, literally practising what so many persons pretend they intend, being quiet and enjoying my fire-side in my elderly days.

Mr. Mason has shown me the relics of poor Mr. Gray. I am sadly disappointed at finding them so very inconsiderable. He always persisted, when I inquired about his writings, that he had nothing by him. I own I doubted. I am grieved he was so very near exact—I speak of my own satisfaction; as to his genius, what he published during his life will establish his fame as long as our language lasts, and there is a man of genius left. There is a silly fellow, I don't know who, that has published a volume of Letters on the English Nation, with characters of our modern authors. He has talked such nonsense on Mr. Gray, that I have no patience with the compliments he has paid me. He must have an excellent taste! and gives me a woful opinion of my own trifles, when he likes them, and cannot see the beauties of a poet that ought to be ranked in the first line.

I am more humbled by any applause in the present age, than by hosts of such critics as Dean Milles. Is not Garrick reckoned a tolerable actor? His Cymon, his prologues and epilogues, and forty such pieces of trash, are below mediocrity, and yet delight the mob in the boxes as well as in the footman's gallery. I do not mention the things written in his praise; because he writes most of them himself. But you know any one popular merit can confer all merit. Two women talking of Wilkes, one said he squinted—t'other replied, "Squints!—well, if he does, it is not more than a man should squint." For my part, I can see how extremely well Garrick acts, without thinking him six feet high.[1]

[Footnote 1: He is quoting Churchill's "Rosciad"—

> When the pure genuine flame, by nature taught,
> Springs into sense, and every action's thought;
> Before such merit all objections fly,
> Pritchard's genteel, and Garrick six feet high—

the great actor being a short man.]

It is said Shakespeare was a bad actor; why do not his divine plays make our wise judges conclude that he was a good one? They have not a proof of the contrary, as they have in Garrick's works—but what is it to you or me what he is? We may see him act with pleasure, and nothing obliges us to read his writings.

MARRIAGE OF THE PRETENDER—THE PRINCESS LOUISE, AND HER PROTECTION OF THE CLERGY—FOX'S ELOQUENCE.

TO SIR HORACE MANN.

ARLINGTON STREET, *April* 9, 1772.

It is uncommon for *me* to send *you* news of the Pretender. He has been married in Paris by proxy, to a Princess of Stolberg. All that I can learn of her is, that she is niece to a Princess of Salm, whom I knew there, without knowing any more of her. The new Pretendress is said to be but sixteen, and a Lutheran: I doubt the latter; if the former is true, I suppose they mean to carry on the breed in the way it began, by a spurious child. A Fitz-Pretender is an excellent continuation of the patriarchal line. Mr. Chute says, when the Royal Family are prevented from marrying,[1] it is a right time for the Stuarts to marry. This event seems to explain the Pretender's disappearance last autumn; and though they sent him back from Paris, they may not dislike the propagation of thorns in our side.

Letters of Horace Walpole, V2

[Footnote 1: In a previous letter Walpole mentions the enactment of the Royal Marriage Act by a very narrow majority, after more than one violent debate. It had been insisted on by the King, who was highly indignant at his brothers, the Dukes of Gloucester and Cumberland, having married two subjects. Singularly enough they were both widows, Lady Waldegrave and Mrs. Horton. And this Act made the consent of the sovereign indispensable to the marriage of any member of the Royal Family except the descendants of princesses married to foreign princes.]

I hear the credit of the French Chancellor declines. He had strongly taken up the clergy; and Soeur Louise,[1] the King's Carmelite daughter, was the knot of the intrigue. The new Parliament has dared to remonstrate against a declaration obtained by the Chancellor for setting aside an *arret* of 1762, occasioned by the excommunication of Parma. The Spanish and Neapolitan Ministers interposed, and pronounced the declaration an infringement of the family compact: the *arret* of 1762 has been confirmed to satisfy them, and the Pope's authority, and everything that comes from Rome, except what regards *the Penitential*, (I do not know what that means,) restrained. This is supported by d'Aiguillon and all the other Ministers, who are labouring the reconciliation of the Princes of the Blood, that the Chancellor may not have the honour of reconciling them. Perhaps the Princess of Stolberg sprung out of my Sister Louise's cell. The King has demanded twelve millions of the clergy: they consent to give ten. We shall see whether Madame Louise, on her knees, or Madame du Barri will fight the better fight. I should think the King's knees were more of an age for praying, than for fighting.

[Footnote 1: The Soeur Louise was the youngest daughter of Louis XV.; and, very different from her sisters, who were ill-tempered, political intriguers. She, on the contrary, was deeply religious, and had, some years before, taken the vows of the Carmelite order; and had fixed her residence at the Convent of St. Denis, where she was more than once visited by Marie Antoinette.]

The House of Commons is embarked on the ocean of Indian affairs, and will probably make a long session. I went thither the other day to hear Charles Fox, contrary to a resolution I had made of never setting my foot there again. It is strange how disuse makes one awkward: I felt a palpitation, as if I were going to speak there myself. The object answered: Fox's abilities are amazing at so very early a period, especially under the circumstances of such a dissolute life. He was just arrived from Newmarket, had sat up drinking all night, and had not been in bed. How such talents make one laugh at Tully's rules for an orator, and his indefatigable application. His laboured orations are puerile in comparison with this boy's manly reason. We beat Rome in eloquence and extravagance; and Spain in avarice and cruelty; and, like both, we shall only serve to terrify schoolboys, and for lessons of morality! "Here stood St. Stephen's Chapel; here young Catiline spoke; here was Lord Clive's diamond-house; this is Leadenhall Street, and this broken column was part of the palace of a company of merchants[1] who were sovereigns of Bengal! They starved millions in India by monopolies and plunder, and almost raised a famine at home by the luxury occasioned by their opulence, and by that opulence raising the price of everything, till the poor could not purchase bread!" Conquest, usurpation, wealth, luxury, famine—one knows how little farther the genealogy has to go. If you like it better in Scripture phrase, here it is: Lord Chatham begot the East India Company; the East India Company begot Lord Clive; Lord Clive begot the Maccaronis, and they begot poverty; all the race are still living; just as Clodius was born before the death of Julius Caesar. There is nothing more like than two ages that are very like; which is all that Rousseau means by saying, "give him an account of any great metropolis, and he will foretell its fate." Adieu!

[Footnote 1: "*A company of merchants.*" "A mighty prince held domination over India; his name was Koompanee Jehan. Although this monarch had innumerable magnificent palaces at Delhi and Agra, at Benares, Boggleywallah, and Ahmednuggar, his common residence was in the beautiful island of Ingleez, in the midst of the capital of which, the famous city of Lundoon, Koompanee Jehan had a superb castle. It was called the Hall of Lead, and stood at the foot of the mountain of Corn, close by the verdure-covered banks of the silvery Tameez, where the cypresses wave, and zendewans, or nightingales, love to sing" (Thackeray, "Life of Sir C. Napier," iv. p. 158).]

AN ANSWER TO HIS "HISTORIC DOUBTS"—HIS EDITION OF GRAMMONT.

TO THE REV. WILLIAM COLE.

ARLINGTON STREET, *Jan.* 8, 1773.

In return to your very kind inquiries, dear Sir, I can let you know, that I am quite free from pain, and walk a little about my room, even without a stick: nay, have been four times to take the air in the Park. Indeed, after fourteen weeks this is not saying much; but it is a worse reflection, that when one is subject to the gout and far from young, one's worst account will probably be better than that after the next fit. I neither flatter myself on one hand, nor am impatient on the other—for will either do one any good? one must bear one's lot whatever it be.

I rejoice Mr. Gulston has justice,[1] though he had no bowels. How Gertrude More escaped him I do not guess. It will be wrong to rob you of her, after she has come to you through so many hazards—nor would I hear of it either, if you have a mind to keep her, or have not given up all thoughts of a collection since you have been visited by a Visigoth.

[Footnote 1: Mr. Gulston now fully remunerated Mr. Cole in a valuable present of books.—WALPOLE.]

I am much more impatient to see Mr. Gray's print, than Mr. What-d'ye-call-him's [Masters's] answer to my "Historic Doubts."[1] He may have made himself very angry; but I doubt whether he will make me at all so. I love antiquities; but I scarce ever knew an antiquary who knew how to write upon them. Their understandings seem as much in ruins as the things they describe. For the Antiquarian Society, I shall leave them in peace with Whittington and his Cat. As my contempt for them has not, however, made me disgusted with what they do not understand, antiquities, I have published two numbers of "Miscellanies," and they are very welcome to mumble them with their toothless gums. I want to send you these—not their gums, but my pieces, and a "Grammont,"[2] of which I have printed only a hundred copies, and which will be extremely scarce, as twenty-five copies are gone to France. Tell me how I shall convey them safely.

[Footnote 1: Mr. Masters's pamphlet, printed at the expense of the Antiquarian Society in the second volume of the "Archaeologia."—WALPOLE.]

[Footnote 2: He had just published a small edition of Grammont's Memoirs, "Augmentee de Notes et eclaircissemens necessaires, par M. Horace Walpole," and had dedicated it to Mme. du Deffand.]

Another thing you must tell me, if you can, is, if you know anything ancient of the Freemasons. Governor Pownall,[1] a Whittingtonian, has a mind they should have been a corporation erected by the popes. As you see what a good creature I am, and return good for evil, I am engaged to pick up what I can for him, to support this system, in which I believe no more than in the pope: and the work is to appear in a volume of the Society's pieces. I am very willing to oblige him, and turn my cheek, that they may smite that, also. Lord help them! I am sorry they are such numskulls, that they almost make me think myself something; but there are great authors enough to bring me to my senses again. Posterity, I fear, will class me with the writers of this age, or forget me with them, not rank me with any names that deserve remembrance. If I cannot survive the Milles's, the What-d'ye-call-him's [Masters's], and the compilers of catalogues of Topography, it would comfort me very little to confute them. I should be as little proud of success as if I had carried a contest for churchwarden.

[Footnote 1: Thomas Pownall, Esq., the antiquary, and a constant contributor to the "Archaeologia." Having been governor of South Carolina and other American colonies, he was always distinguished from his brother John, who was likewise an antiquary, by the title of Governor.]

Not being able to return to Strawberry Hill, where all my books and papers are, and my printer lying fallow, I want some short bills to print. Have you anything you wish printed? I can either print a few to amuse ourselves, or, if very curious, and not too dry, could make a third number of "Miscellaneous Antiquities."

I am not in any eagerness to see Mr. What-d'ye-call-him's pamphlet against me; therefore pray give yourself no trouble to get it for me. The specimens I have seen of his writing take off all edge from curiosity. A print of Mr. Gray will be a real present. Would it not be dreadful to be commended by an age that had not taste enough to admire his "Odes"? Is not it too great a compliment to me to be abused, too? I am ashamed. Indeed our antiquaries ought to like me. I am but too much on a par with them. Does not Mr. Henshaw come to London? Is he a professor, or only a lover of engraving? If the former, and he were to settle in town, I would willingly lend him heads to copy. Adieu!

POPULARITY OF LOUIS XVI—DEATH OF LORD HOLLAND—BRUCE'S "TRAVELS."

TO SIR HORACE MANN.

Letters of Horace Walpole, V2

STRAWBERRY HILL, *July* 10, 1774.

The month is come round, and I have, besides, a letter of yours to answer; and yet if I were not as regular as a husband or a merchant in paying my just dues, I think I should not perform the function, for I certainly have no natural call to it at present. Nothing in yours requires a response, and I have nothing new to tell you. Yet, if one once breaks in upon punctuality, adieu to it! I will not give out, after a perseverance of three-and-thirty years; and so far I will not resemble a husband.

The whole blood royal of France is recovered from the small-pox. Both Choiseul and Broglie are recalled, and I have some idea that even the old Parliament will be so. The King is adored, and a most beautiful compliment has been paid to him: somebody wrote under the statue of Henri Quatre, *Resurrexit*.[1]

[Footnote 1: "*Resurrexit*." A courtly picture-dealer, eager to make a market of the new sovereign's popularity, devised even a neater compliment to him, issuing a picture of the three sovereigns—Louis XII., Henri IV., and the young king—with an explanation that 4 and 12 made 16.]

Lord Holland is at last dead, and Lady Holland is at the point of death. His sons would still be in good circumstances, if they were not *his* sons; but he had so totally spoiled the two eldest, that they would think themselves bigots if they were to have common sense. The prevailing style is not to reform, though Lord Lyttelton [the bad Lord] pretends to have set the example. Gaming, for the last month, has exceeded its own outdoings, though the town is very empty. It will be quite so to-morrow, for Newmarket begins, or rather the youth adjourn thither. After that they will have two or three months of repose; but if they are not severely blooded and blistered, there will be no alteration. Their pleasures are no more entertaining to others, than delightful to themselves; one is tired of asking every day, who has won or lost? and even the portentous sums they lose, cease to make impression. One of them has committed a murder, and intends to repeat it. He betted L1,500 that a man could live twelve hours under water; hired a desperate fellow, sunk him in a ship, by way of experiment, and both ship and man have not appeared since. Another man and ship are to be tried for their lives, instead of Mr. Blake, the assassin.

Christina, Duchess of Kingston, is arrived, in a great fright, I believe, for the Duke's nephews are going to prove her first marriage, and hope to set the Will aside. It is a pity her friendship with the Pope had not begun earlier; he might have given her a dispensation. If she loses her cause, the best thing he can do will be to give her the veil.

I am sorry all Europe will not furnish me with another paragraph. Africa is, indeed, coming into fashion. There is just returned a Mr. Bruce,[1] who has lived three years in the Court of Abyssinia, and breakfasted every morning with the Maids of Honour on live oxen. Otaheite and Mr. Banks are quite forgotten; but Mr. Blake, I suppose, will order a live sheep for supper at Almack's, and ask whom he shall help to a piece of the shoulder. Oh, yes; we shall have negro butchers, and French cooks will be laid aside. My Lady Townshend [Harrison], after the Rebellion, said, everybody was so bloodthirsty, that she did not dare to dine abroad, for fear of meeting with a rebel-pie—now one shall be asked to come and eat a bit of raw mutton. In truth, I do think we are ripe for any extravagance. I am not wise enough to wish the world reasonable—I only desire to have follies that are amusing, and am sorry Cervantes laughed chivalry out of fashion. Adieu!

[Footnote 1: When Bruce's "Travels" were first published, his account of the strange incidents which had occurred to him was very generally disbelieved and ridiculed; "Baron Munchausen" was even written in derision of them; but the discoveries of subsequent travellers have confirmed his narrative in almost every respect.]

DISCONTENT IN AMERICA—MR. GRENVILLE'S ACT FOR THE TRIAL OF ELECTION PETITIONS—HIGHWAY ROBBERIES.

TO SIR HORACE MANN.

STRAWBERRY HILL, *Oct.* 6, 1774.

It would be unlike my attention and punctuality, to see so large an event as an irregular dissolution of Parliament, without taking any notice of it to you. It happened last Saturday, six months before its natural death, and without the design being known but the Tuesday before, and that by very few persons. The chief motive is supposed to be the ugly state of North America,[1] and the effects that a cross winter might have on the next elections. Whatever were the causes, the first consequences, as you may guess, were such a ferment in London as is seldom seen at this dead season of the year. Couriers, despatches, post-chaises, post-horses, hurrying every way! Sixty messengers passed through one single turnpike on Friday. The whole island is by this time in equal agitation; but less wine and money will be shed than have been at any such period for these fifty years.

[Footnote 1: "*America*"—the discontents in that country were caused by Mr. Charles Townshend's policy, who, before his death, had revived Mr. Grenville's plan of imposing taxes on the Colonies, and by the perseverance in that policy of Lord North, who succeeded him at the Exchequer, and who had also been First Lord of the Treasury since the resignation of the Duke of Grafton.]

We have a new famous Bill,[1] devised by the late Mr. Grenville, that has its first operation now; and what changes it may occasion, nobody can yet foresee. The first symptoms are not favourable to the Court; the great towns are casting off submission, and declaring for popular members. London, Westminster, Middlesex, seem to have no monarch but Wilkes, who is at the same time pushing for the Mayoralty of London, with hitherto a majority on the poll. It is strange how this man, like a phoenix, always revives from his embers! America, I doubt, is still more unpromising. There are whispers of their having assembled an armed force, and of earnest supplications arrived for succours of men and ships. A civil war is no trifle; and how we are to suppress or pursue in such a vast region, with a handful of men, I am not an Alexander to guess; and for the fleet, can we put it upon casters and wheel it from Hudson's Bay to Florida? But I am an ignorant soul, and neither pretend to knowledge nor foreknowledge. All I perceive already is, that our Parliaments are subjected to America and India, and must be influenced by their politics; yet I do not believe our senators are more universal than formerly....

[Footnote 1: Mr. Grenville's Act had been passed in 1770; but there had been no General Election since till this year. It altered the course of proceeding for the trial of election petitions, substituting for the whole House a Select Committee of fifteen members; but after a time it was found that it had not secured any greater purity of decision, but that the votes of the Committee were influenced by considerations of the interest of the dominant party as entirely as they had been in the days of Sir R. Walpole. And eventually, in the present reign, Mr. D'Israeli induced the House to surrender altogether its privilege of judging of elections, and to submit the investigation of election petitions to the only tribunal sufficiently above suspicion to command and retain the confidence of the nation, namely, the Judges of the High Court of Law. (See the Editor's "Constitutional History of England, 1760–1860," pp. 36–39.)]

In the midst of this combustion, we are in perils by land and water. It has rained for this month without intermission; there is sea between me and Richmond, and Sunday was se'nnight I was hurried down to Isleworth in the ferry–boat by the violence of the current, and had great difficulty to get to shore. Our roads are so infested by highwaymen, that it is dangerous stirring out almost by day. Lady Hertford was attacked on Hounslow Heath at three in the afternoon. Dr. Eliot was shot at three days ago, without having resisted; and the day before yesterday we were near losing our Prime Minster, Lord North; the robbers shot at the postillion, and wounded the latter. In short, all the freebooters, that are not in India, have taken to the highway. The Ladies of the Bedchamber dare not go the Queen at Kew in an evening. The lane between me and the Thames is the only safe road I know at present, for it is up to the middle of the horses in water. Next week I shall not venture to London even at noon, for the Middlesex election is to be at Brentford, where the two demagogues, Wilkes and Townshend, oppose each other; and at Richmond there is no crossing the river. How strange all this must appear to you Florentines; but you may turn to your Machiavelli and Guicciardini, and have some idea of it. I am the quietest man at present in the whole island; not but I might take some part, if I would. I was in my garden yesterday, seeing my servants lop some trees; my brewer walked in and pressed me to go to Guildhall for the nomination of members for the county. I replied, calmly, "Sir, when I would go no more to my own election, you may be very sure I will go to that of nobody else." My old tune is,

    Suave mari magno turbantibus aequora ventis, &c.

Adieu!

P.S.—ARLINGTON STREET, *7th.*

I am just come to town, and find your letter, with the notification of Lord Cowper's marriage; I recollect that I ought to be sorry for it, as you will probably lose an old friend. The approaching death of the Pope will be an event of no consequence. That old mummery is near its conclusion, at least as a political object. The history of the latter Popes will be no more read than that of the last Constantinopolitan Emperors. Wilkes is a more conspicuous personage in modern story than the Pontifex Maximus of Rome. The poll for Lord Mayor ended last night; he and his late Mayor had above 1,900 votes, and their antagonists not 1,500. It is strange that the more he is opposed, the more he succeeds!

I don't know whether Sir W. Duncan's marriage proved Platonic or not; but I cannot believe that a lady of great birth, and greater pride, quarrels with her family, to marry a Scotch physician for Platonic love, which she might enjoy without marriage. I remember an admirable *bon-mot* of George Selwyn; who said, "How often Lady Mary will repeat, with Macbeth, 'Wake, Duncan, with this knocking—would thou couldst!"

THE POPE'S DEATH—WILKES IS RETURNED FOR MIDDLESEX—A QUAKER AT VERSAILLES.

TO SIR HORACE MANN.

STRAWBERRY HILL, *Oct.* 22, 1774.

Though I have been writing two letters, of four sides each, one of which I enclose, I must answer your two last, if my fingers will move; and talk to you on the contents of the enclosed.

If the Jesuits have precipitated the Pope's death,[1] as seems more than probable, they have acted more by the spirit of their order, than by its good sense. Great crimes may raise a growing cause, but seldom retard the fall of a sinking one. This I take to be almost an infallible maxim. Great crimes, too, provoke more than they terrify; and there is no poisoning all that are provoked, and all that are terrified; who alternately provoke and terrify each other, till common danger produces common security. The Bourbon monarchs will be both angry and frightened, the Cardinals frightened. It will be the interest of both not to revive an order that bullies with arsenic in its sleeve. The poisoned host will destroy the Jesuits, as well as the Pope: and perhaps the Church of Rome will fall by a wafer, as it rose by it; for such an edifice will tumble when once the crack has begun.

[Footnote 1: Pope Benedict XIV. had died in September; but there was not any suspicion that his death had not been entirely natural.]

Our elections are almost over. Wilkes has taken possession of Middlesex without an enemy appearing against him; and, being as puissant a monarch as Henry the Eighth, and as little scrupulous, should, like him, date his acts *From our Palace of Bridewell, in the tenth year of our reign.* He has, however, met with a heroine to stem the tide of his conquests; who, though not of Arc, nor a *pucelle*, is a true *Joan* in spirit, style, and manners. This is her Grace of Northumberland [Lady Elizabeth Seymour], who has carried the mob of Westminster from him; sitting daily in the midst of Covent Garden; and will elect her son [Earl Percy] and Lord Thomas Clinton,[1] against Wilkes's two candidates, Lord Mahon[2] and Lord Mountmorris. She puts me in mind of what Charles the Second said of a foolish preacher, who was very popular in his parish: "I suppose his nonsense suits their nonsense."

[Footnote 1: Second son of Henry, Duke of Newcastle.—WALPOLE.]

[Footnote 2: Only son of Earl Stanhope.—WALPOLE.]

Let me sweeten my letter by making you smile. A Quaker has been at Versailles; and wanted to see the Comtes de Provence and D'Artois dine in public, but would not submit to pull off his hat. The Princes were told of it; and not only admitted him with his beaver on, but made him sit down and dine with them. Was it not very sensible and good-humoured? You and I know one who would not have been so gracious: I do not mean my nephew Lord Cholmondeley.[1] Adieu! I am tired to death.

[Footnote 1: He means the Duke of Gloucester.—WALPOLE.]

P.S.—I have seen the Duchess of Beaufort; who sings your praises quite in a tune I like. Her manner is much unpinioned to what it was, though her person remains as stately as ever; and powder is vastly preferable to those brown hairs, of whose preservation she was so fond. I am not so struck with the beauty of Lady Mary[1] as I was three years ago. Your nephew, Sir Horace, I see, by the papers, is come into Parliament: I am glad of it. Is not he yet arrived at Florence?

[Footnote 1: Lady Mary Somerset, youngest daughter of Charles Noel, Duke of Beaufort. She was afterwards married to the Duke of Rutland.—WALPOLE.]

BURKE'S ELECTION AT BRISTOL—RESEMBLANCE OF ONE HOUSE OF COMMONS TO ANOTHER—COMFORT OF OLD AGE.

TO THE COUNTESS OF AILESBURY.

STRAWBERRY HILL, *Nov.* 7, 1774.

I have written such tomes to Mr. Conway,[1] Madam, and so nothing new to write, that I might as well, methinks, begin and end like the lady to her husband; "Je vous ecris parceque je n'ai rien a faire: je finis parceque je n'ai rien a vous dire." Yes, I have two complaints to make, one of your ladyship, the other of myself. You tell me nothing of Lady Harriet [Stanhope]: have you no tongue, or the French no eyes? or are her eyes employed in nothing but seeing? What a vulgar employment for a fine woman's eyes after she is risen from her toilet? I declare I will ask no more questions—what is it to me, whether she is admired or not? I should know how charming she is, though all Europe were blind. I hope I am not to be told by any barbarous nation upon earth what beauty and grace are!

[Footnote 1: Mr. Conway and Lady Aylesbury were now at Paris together.—WALPOLE.]

For myself, I am guilty of the gout in my elbow; the left—witness my handwriting. Whether I caught cold by the deluge in the night, or whether the bootikins, like the water of Styx, can only preserve the parts they surround, I doubt they have saved me but three weeks, for so long my reckoning has been out. However, as I feel nothing in my feet, I flatter myself that this Pindaric transition will not be a regular ode, but a fragment, the more valuable for being imperfect.

Now for my Gazette.—Marriages—Nothing done. Intrigues—More in the political than civil way. Births—Under par since Lady Berkeley left off breeding. Gaming—Low water. Deaths—Lord Morton, Lord Wentworth, Duchess Douglas. Election stock—More buyers than sellers. Promotions—Mr. Wilkes as high as he can go.—*Apropos*, he was told the Lord Chancellor intended to signify to him, that the King did not approve the City's choice: he replied, "Then I shall signify to his lordship, that I am at least as fit to be Lord Mayor as he is to be Lord Chancellor." This being more Gospel than everything Mr. Wilkes says, the formal approbation was given.

Mr. Burke has succeeded in Bristol, and Sir James Peachey will miscarry in Sussex. But what care you, Madam, about our Parliament? You will see the *rentree* of the old one, with songs and epigrams into the bargain. We do not shift our Parliaments with so much gaiety. Money in one hand, and abuse in t'other—those are all the arts we know. *Wit and a gamut*[1] I don't believe ever signified a Parliament, whatever the glossaries may say; for they never produce pleasantry and harmony. Perhaps you may not taste this Saxon pun, but I know it will make the Antiquarian Society die with laughing.

[Footnote 1: Walpole is punning on the old Saxon name of the National Council, Witangemot.]

Expectation hangs on America. The result of the general assembly is expected in four or five days. If one may believe the papers, which one should not believe, the other side of the waterists are not *doux comme des moutons*, and yet we do intend to eat them. I was in town on Monday; the Duchess of Beaufort graced our loo, and made it as rantipole as a Quaker's meeting. *Loois Quinze*,[1] I believe, is arrived by this time, but I fear without *quinze louis*.

[Footnote 1: This was a cant name given to a lady [Lady Powis], who was very fond of loo, and who had lost much money at that game.]

Your herb-snuff and the four glasses are lying in my warehouse, but I can hear of no ship going to Paris. You are now at Fontainbleau, but not thinking of Francis I., the Queen of Sweden, and Monaldelschi. It is terrible that one cannot go to Courts that are gone! You have supped with the Chevalier de Boufflers: did he act everything in the world and sing everything in the world? Has Madame de Cambis sung to you "*Sans depit, sans legerete?*"[1] Has Lord Cholmondeley delivered my pacquet? I hear I have hopes of Madame d'Olonne. Gout or no gout, I shall be little in town till after Christmas. My elbow makes me bless myself that I am not in Paris. Old age is no such uncomfortable thing, if one gives oneself up to it with a good grace, and don't drag it about

To midnight dances and the public show.

[Footnote 1: The first words of a favourite French air.—WALPOLE.]

If one stays quietly in one's own house in the country, and cares for nothing but oneself, scolds one's servants, condemns everything that is new, and recollects how charming a thousand things were formerly that were very disagreeable, one gets over the winters very well, and the summers get over themselves.

DEATH OF LORD CLIVE—RESTORATION OF THE FRENCH PARLIAMENT—PREDICTION OF GREAT MEN TO ARISE IN AMERICA—THE KING'S SPEECH.

TO SIR HORACE MANN.

STRAWBERRY HILL, *Nov.* 24, 1774.

... A great event happened two days ago—a political and moral event; the sudden death of that second Kouli Khan, Lord Clive.[1] There was certainly illness in the case; the world thinks more than illness. His constitution was exceedingly broken and disordered, and grown subject to violent pains and convulsions. He came unexpectedly to town last Monday, and they say, ill. On Tuesday his physician gave him a dose of laudanum, which had not the desired effect. On the rest, there are two stories; one, that the physician repeated the dose; the other, that he doubled it himself, contrary to advice. In short, he has terminated at fifty a life of so much glory, reproach, art, wealth, and ostentation! He had just named ten members for the new Parliament.

[Footnote 1: Lord Clive had committed suicide in his house in Berkeley Square. As he was passing through his library his niece, who was writing a letter, asked him to mend a pen for her. He did it, and, passing on into the next room, cut his throat with the same knife he had just used. It is remarkable that, when little more than a youth, he had once tried to destroy himself. In a fit, apparently of constitutional melancholy, he had put a pistol to his head, but it did not go off. He pulled the trigger more than once; always with the same result. Anxious to see whether there was any defect in the weapon or the loading, he aimed at the door of the room, and the pistol went off, the bullet going through the door; and from that day he conceived himself reserved by Providence for great things, though in his most sanguine confidence he could never have anticipated such glory as he was destined to win.]

Next Tuesday that Parliament is to meet—and a deep game it has to play! few Parliaments a greater. The world is in amaze here that no account is arrived from America of the result of their General Congress—if any is come it is very secret; and *that* has no favourable aspect. The combination and spirit there seem to be universal, and is very alarming. I am the humble servant of events, and you know never meddle with prophecy. It would be difficult to descry good omens, be the issue what it will.

The old French Parliament is restored with great *eclat*.[1] Monsieur de Maurepas, author of the revolution, was received one night at the Opera with boundless shouts of applause. It is even said that the mob intended, when the King should go to hold the *lit de justice*,[2] to draw his coach. How singular it would be if Wilkes's case should be copied for a King of France! Do you think Rousseau was in the right, when he said that he could tell what would be the manners of any capital city from certain given lights? I don't know what he may do on Constantinople and Pekin—but Paris and London! I don't believe Voltaire likes these changes. I have seen nothing of his writing for many months; not even on the poisoning Jesuits. For our part, I repeat it, we shall contribute nothing to the *Histoire des Moeurs*, not for want of materials, but for want of writers. We have comedies without novelty, gross satires without stings, metaphysical eloquence, and antiquarians that discover nothing.

> Boeotum in crasso jurares aere natos!

[Footnote 1: In 1770 the Chancellor, Maupeou, had abolished the Parliament, as has been mentioned in a former note. Their conduct ever since the death of Richelieu had been factious and corrupt. But, though the Sovereign Courts, which Maupeou had established in their stead, had worked well, their extinction had been unpopular in Paris; and, on the accession of Louis XVI., the new Prime Minister, Maurepas, proposed their re-establishment, and the Queen, most unfortunately, was persuaded by the Duc de Choiseul to exert her influence in support of the measure. Turgot, the great Finance Minister—indeed, the greatest statesman that France ever produced—resisted it with powerful arguments, but Louis yielded to the influence of his consort. The Parliaments were re-established, and soon verified all the predictions of Turgot by conduct more factious and violent than ever. (See the Editor's "France under the Bourbons," iii. 413.)]

[Footnote 2: A *Lit de Justice* was an extraordinary meeting of the Parliament, presided over by the sovereign in person, and one in which no opposition, or even discussion, was permitted; but any edict which had been issued was at once registered.]

Don't tell me I am grown old and peevish and supercilious—name the geniuses of 1774, and I submit. The next Augustan age will dawn on the other side of the Atlantic. There will, perhaps, be a Thucydides at Boston, a Xenophon at New York, and, in time, a Virgil at Mexico, and a Newton at Peru. At last, some curious traveller from Lima will visit England and give a description of the ruins of St. Paul's, like the editions of Balbec and Palmyra; but am I not prophesying, contrary to my consummate prudence, and casting horoscopes of empires like Rousseau? Yes; well, I will go and dream of my visions.

29th.

... The Parliament opened just now—they say the speech talks of the *rebellion* of the Province of Massachusetts; but if *they–say* tells a lie, I wash my hands of it. As your gazetteer, I am obliged to send you all news, true or false. I have believed and unbelieved everything I have heard since I came to town. Lord Clive has died every death in the parish register; at present it is most fashionable to believe he cut his throat. That he is dead, is certain; so is Lord Holland—and so is not the Bishop of Worcester [Johnson]; however, to show you that I am at least as well informed as greater personages, the bishopric was on Saturday given to Lord North's brother—so for once the Irishman was in the right, and a pigeon, at least a dove, can be in two places at once.

RIOTS AT BOSTON—A LITERARY COTERIE AT BATH—EASTON.

TO THE HON. H.S. CONWAY AND LADY AYLESBURY.

ARLINGTON STREET, *Jan.* 15, 1775.

You have made me very happy by saying your journey to Naples is laid aside. Perhaps it made too great an impression on me; but you must reflect, that all my life I have satisfied myself with your being perfect, instead of trying to be so myself. I don't ask you to return, though I wish it: in truth, there is nothing to invite you. I don't want you to come and breathe fire and sword against the Bostonians,[1] like that second Duke of Alva,[2] the inflexible Lord George Germaine....

[Footnote 1: The open resistance to the new taxation of the American Colonies began at Boston, the capital of Massachusetts, where, on the arrival of the first tea-ship, a body of citizens, disguised as Red Indians, boarded the ship and threw the tea into the sea.]

[Footnote 2: The first Duke of Alva was the first Governor of the Netherlands appointed by Philip II.; and it was his bloodthirsty and intolerable cruelty that caused the revolt of the Netherlands, and cost Spain those rich provinces.]

An account is come of the Bostonians having voted an army of sixteen thousand men, who are to be called *minutemen*, as they are to be ready at a minute's warning. Two directors or commissioners, I don't know what they are called, are appointed. There has been too a kind of mutiny in the Fifth Regiment. A soldier was found drunk on his post. Gage, in his time of *danger*, thought rigour necessary, and sent the fellow to a court-martial. They ordered two hundred lashes. The General ordered them to improve their sentence. Next day it was published in the *Boston Gazette*. He called them before him, and required them on oath to abjure the communication: three officers refused. Poor Gage is to be scapegoat, not for this, but for what was a reason against employing him, incapacity. I wonder at the precedent! Howe is talked of for his successor.—Well, I have done with *you*!—Now I shall go gossip with Lady Aylesbury.

You must know, Madam, that near Bath is erected a new Parnassus, composed of three laurels, a myrtle-tree, a weeping-willow, and a view of the Avon, which has been new christened Helicon. Ten years ago there lived a Madam Riggs, an old rough humourist who passed for a wit; her daughter, who passed for nothing, married to a Captain Miller, full of good-natured officiousness. These good folks were friends of Miss Rich, who carried me to dine with them at Bath-Easton, now Pindus. They caught a little of what was then called taste, built and planted, and begot children, till the whole caravan were forced to go abroad to retrieve. Alas! Mrs. Miller is returned a beauty, a genius, a Sappho, a tenth Muse, as romantic as Mademoiselle Scuderi, and as sophisticated as Mrs. Vesey. The Captain's fingers are loaded with cameos, his tongue runs over with *virtu*, and that both may contribute to the improvement of their own country, they have introduced *bouts-rimes* as a new discovery. They hold a Parnassus fair every Thursday, give out rhymes and themes, and all the flux of quality at Bath contend for the prizes. A Roman vase dressed with pink ribbons and myrtles receives the poetry,[1] which is drawn out every festival; six judges of these Olympic games retire and select the brightest compositions, which the respective successful acknowledge, kneel to Mrs. Calliope Miller, kiss her fair hand, and are crowned by it with myrtle, with—I don't know what. You may think this is fiction, or exaggeration. Be dumb, unbelievers! The collection is printed, published.—Yes, on my faith, there are *bouts-rimes* on a buttered muffin, made by her Grace the Duchess of Northumberland; receipts to make them by Corydon the venerable, alias George Pitt; others very pretty, by Lord Palmerston; some by Lord Carlisle: many by Mrs. Miller herself, that have no fault but wanting metre; an Immorality promised to her without end or measure. In short, since folly, which never ripens to madness but in this hot climate, ran distracted, there never was anything so entertaining or so dull—for you cannot read so long as I have been telling.

[Footnote 1: Four volumes of this poetry were published under the title of "Poetical Amusements at a villa near Bath." The following lines are a fair sample of the *bouts-rimes*.

> The pen which I now take and brandish
> Has long lain useless in my standish.
> Know, every maid, from her own patten,
> To her who shines in glossy sattin,
> That could they now prepare an oglio
> From best receipt of book in folio,
> Ever so fine, for all their puffing,
> I should prefer a butter'd muffin;
> A muffin Jove himself might feast on,
> If eat with Miller at Batheaston.

The following are the concluding lines of a poem on Beauty, by Lord Palmerston:—

> In vain the stealing hand of Time
> May pluck the blossoms of their prime;
> Envy may talk of bloom decay'd,
> How lilies droop and roses fade;

But Constancy's unalter'd truth,
Regardful of the vows of youth—
Affection that recalls the past,
And bids the pleasing influence last,
Shall still preserve the lover's flame
In every scene of life the same;
And still with fond endearments blend
The wife, the mistress, and the friend!

"Lady Miller's collection of verses by fashionable people, which were put into her vase at Bath-Easton, in competition for honorary prizes, being mentioned, Dr. Johnson held them very cheap: ' *Bouts-rimes*,' said he, 'is a mere conceit, and an old conceit; I wonder how people were persuaded to write in that manner for this lady.' I named a gentleman of his acquaintance who wrote for the vase. JOHNSON—'He was a blockhead for his pains!' BOSWELL—'The Duchess of Northumberland wrote.'—'Sir, the Duchess of Northumberland may do what she pleases; nobody will say anything to a lady of her high rank: but I should be apt to throw ... verses in his face." (Boswell, vol. v. p. 227.)]

OPPOSITION OF THE FRENCH PARLIAMENTS TO TURGOT'S MEASURES.

TO DR. GEM.[1]

[Footnote 1: Dr. Gem was an English physician who had been for some time settled in Paris. He was uncle to Canning's friend and colleague, Mr. Huskisson.]

ARLINGTON STREET, *April* 4, 1776.

It is but fair, when one quits one's party, to give notice to those one abandons—at least, modern patriots, who often imbibe their principles of honour at Newmarket, use that civility. You and I, dear Sir, have often agreed in our political notions; and you, I fear, will die without changing your opinion. For my part, I must confess I am totally altered; and, instead of being a warm partisan of liberty, now admire nothing but despotism. You will naturally ask, what place I have gotten, or what bribe I have taken? Those are the criterions of political changes in England—but, as my conversion is of foreign extraction,

I shall not be the richer for it. In one word, it is the *relation du lit de justice* that has operated the miracle. When two ministers are found so humane, so virtuous, so excellent, as to study nothing but the welfare and deliverance of the people; when a king listens to such excellent men; and when a parliament, from the basest, most interested motives, interposes to intercept the blessing, must I not change my opinions, and admire arbitrary power? or can I retain my sentiments, without varying the object?

Yes, Sir, I am shocked at the conduct of the Parliament—one would think it was an English one! I am scandalised at the speeches of the *Avocat-general*,[1] who sets up the odious interests of the nobility and clergy against the cries and groans of the poor; and who employs his wicked eloquence to tempt the good young monarch, by personal views, to sacrifice the mass of his subjects to the privileges of the few—But why do I call it eloquence? The fumes of interest had so clouded his rhetoric, that he falls into a downright Iricism.—He tells the King, that the intended tax on the proprietors of land will affect the property not only of the rich, but of the poor. I should be glad to know what is the property of the poor? Have the poor landed estates? Are those who have landed estates the poor? Are the poor that will suffer by the tax, the wretched labourers who are dragged from their famishing families to work on the roads?—But *it is* wicked eloquence when it finds a reason, or gives a reason for continuing the abuse. The Advocate tells the King, those abuses *presque consacres par l'anciennete*; indeed, he says all that can be said for nobility, it is *consacree par l'anciennete*; and thus the length of the pedigree of abuses renders them respectable!

[Footnote 1: The *Avocat-General* was M. de Seguier; and, under his guidance, the Parliament had passed the monstrous resolution that "the *people* in France was liable to the tax of *la taille*, and to *corvee* at discretion" (*etait tailleable et corveable a volonte*), and that their "liability was an article of the Constitution which it was not in the power of even the King himself to change" ("France under the Bourbons," iii. 422).]

His arguments are as contemptible when he tries to dazzle the King by the great names of Henri Quatre and Sully,[1] of Louis XIV. and Colbert, two couple whom nothing but a mercenary orator would have classed together. Nor, were all four equally venerable, would it prove anything. Even good kings and good ministers, if such have been, may have erred; nay, may have done the best they could. They would not have been good, if they wished their errors should be preserved, the longer they had lasted.

[Footnote 1: Sully and Colbert were the two great Finance Ministers of Henry IV. and Louis XIV.]

In short, Sir, I think this resistance of the Parliament to the adorable reformation planned by Messrs. de Turgot and Malesherbes[1] is more phlegmatically scandalous than the wildest tyranny of despotism. I forget what the nation was that refused liberty when it was offered. This opposition to so noble a work is worse. A whole people may refuse its own happiness; but these profligate magistrates resist happiness for others, for millions, for posterity!—Nay, do they not half vindicate Maupeou, who crushed them? And you, dear Sir, will you now chide my apostasy? Have I not cleared myself to your eyes? I do not see a shadow of sound logic in all Monsieur Seguier's speeches, but in his proposing that the soldiers should work on the roads, and that passengers should contribute to their fabric; though, as France is not so luxuriously mad as England, I do not believe passengers could support the expense of their roads. That argument, therefore, is like another that the Avocat proposes to the King, and which, he modestly owns, he believes would be impracticable.

[Footnote 1: Malesherbes was the Chancellor, and in 1792 he was accepted by Louis XVI. as his counsel on his trial—a duty which he performed with an ability which drew on him the implacable resentment of Robespierre and the Jacobins, and which led to his execution in 1794.]

I beg your pardon, Sir, for giving you this long trouble; but I could not help venting myself, when shocked to find such renegade conduct in a Parliament that I was rejoiced had been restored. Poor human kind! is it always to breed serpents from its own bowels? In one country, it chooses its representatives, and they sell it and themselves; in others, it exalts despots; in another, it resists the despot when he consults the good of his people! Can we wonder mankind is wretched, when men are such beings? Parliaments run wild with loyalty, when America is to be enslaved or butchered. They rebel, when their country is to be set free! I am not surprised at the idea of the devil being always at our elbows. They who invented him, no doubt could not conceive how men could be so atrocious to one another, without the intervention of a fiend. Don't you think, if he had never been heard of before, that he would have been invented on the late partition of Poland! Adieu, dear Sir. Yours most sincerely.

HIS DECORATIONS AT "STRAWBERRY"—HIS ESTIMATE OF HIMSELF, AND HIS ADMIRATION OF CONWAY.

TO THE HON. H.S. CONWAY.

STRAWBERRY HILL, *June* 20, 1776.

I was very glad to receive your letter, not only because always most glad to hear of you, but because I wished to write to you, and had absolutely nothing to say till I had something to answer. I have lain but two nights in town since I saw you; have been, else, constantly here, very much employed, though doing, hearing, knowing exactly nothing. I have had a Gothic architect [Mr. Essex] from Cambridge to design me a gallery, which will end in a mouse, that is, in an hexagon closet of seven feet diameter. I have been making a Beauty Room, which was effected by buying two dozen of small copies of Sir Peter Lely, and hanging them up; and I have been making hay, which is not made, because I put it off for three days, as I chose it should adorn the landscape when I was to have company; and so the rain is come, and has drowned it. However, as I can even turn calculator when it is to comfort me for not minding my interest, I have discovered that it is five to one better for me that my hay should be spoiled than not; for, as the cows will eat it if it is damaged, which horses will not, and as I have five cows and but one horse, is not it plain that the worse my hay is the better? Do not you with your refining head go, and, out of excessive friendship, find out something to destroy my system. I had rather be a philosopher than a rich man; and yet have so little philosophy, that I had much rather be content than be in the right.

Mr. Beauclerk and Lady Di have been here four or five days—so I had both content and exercise for my philosophy. I wish Lady Ailesbury was as fortunate! The Pembrokes, Churchills, Le Texier, as you will have heard, and the Garricks have been with us. Perhaps, if alone, I might have come to you; but you are all too healthy and harmonious. I can neither walk nor sing; nor, indeed, am fit for anything but to amuse myself in a sedentary trifling way. What I have most certainly not been doing, is writing anything: a truth I say to you, but do not desire you to repeat. I deign to satisfy scarce anybody else. Whoever reported that I was writing anything, must have been so totally unfounded, that they either blundered by guessing without reason, or knew they lied—and that could not be with any kind intention; though saying I am going to do what I am not going to do, is wretched enough. Whatever is said of me without truth, anybody is welcome to believe that pleases.

In fact, though I have scarce a settled purpose about anything, I think I shall never write any more. I have written a great deal too much, unless I had written better, and I know I should now only write still worse. One's talent, whatever it is, does not improve at near sixty—yet, if I liked it, I dare to say a good reason would not stop my inclination;—but I am grown most indolent in that respect, and most absolutely indifferent to every purpose of vanity. Yet without vanity I am become still prouder and more contemptuous. I have a contempt for my countrymen that makes me despise their approbation. The applause of slaves and of the foolish mad is below ambition. Mine is the haughtiness of an ancient Briton, that cannot write what would please this age, and would not, if he could.

Whatever happens in America, this country is undone. I desire to be reckoned of the last age, and to be thought to have lived to be superannuated, preserving my senses only for myself and for the few I value. I cannot aspire to be traduced like Algernon Sydney, and content myself with sacrificing to him amongst my lares. Unalterable in my principles, careless about most things below essentials, indulging myself in trifles by system, annihilating myself by choice, but dreading folly at an unseemly age, I contrive to pass my time agreeably enough, yet see its termination approach without anxiety. This is a true picture of my mind; and it must be true, because drawn for you, whom I would not deceive, and could not, if I would. Your question on my being writing drew it forth, though with more seriousness than the report deserved—yet talking to one's dearest friend is neither wrong nor out of season. Nay, you are my best apology. I have always contented myself with your being perfect, or, if your modesty demands a mitigated term, I will say, unexceptionable. It is comical, to be sure, to have always been more solicitous about the virtue of one's friend than about one's own; yet, I repeat it, you are my apology—though I never was so unreasonable as to make you answerable for my faults in return; I take them wholly to myself. But enough of this. When I know my own mind, for hitherto I have settled no plan for my summer, I will come to you. Adieu!

ANGLOMANIE IN PARIS—HORSE-RACING.

TO SIR HORACE MANN.

Letters of Horace Walpole, V2

STRAWBERRY HILL, *Dec.* 1, 1776.

I don't know who the Englishwoman is of whom you give so ridiculous a description; but it will suit thousands. I distrust my age continually, and impute to it half the contempt I feel for my countrymen and women. If I think the other half well-founded, it is by considering what must be said hereafter of the present age. What is to impress a great idea of us on posterity? In truth, what do our contemporaries of all other countries think of us? They stare at and condemn our politics and follies; and if they retain any respect for us, I doubt it is for the sense we have had. I do know, indeed, one man who still worships us, but his adoration is testified so very absurdly, as not to do us much credit. It is a Monsieur de Marchais, first Valet-de-Chambre to the King of France. He has the *Anglomanie* so strong, that he has not only read more English than French books, but if any valuable work appears in his own language, he waits to peruse it till it is translated into English; and to be sure our translations of French are admirable things!

To do the rest of the French justice, I mean such as like us, they adopt only our egregious follies, and in particular the flower of them, horse-racing![1] *Le Roi Pepin*, a racer, is the horse in fashion. I suppose the next shameful practice of ours they naturalize will be the personal scurrilities in the newspapers, especially on young and handsome women, in which we certainly are originals! Voltaire, who first brought us into fashion in France, is stark mad at his own success. Out of envy to writers of his own nation, he cried up Shakspeare; and now is distracted at the just encomiums bestowed on that first genius of the world in the new translation. He sent to the French Academy an invective that bears all the marks of passionate dotage. Mrs. Montagu happened to be present when it was read. Suard, one of their writers, said to her, "Je crois, Madame, que vous etes un peu fache de ce que vous venez d'entendre." She replied, "Moi, Monsieur! point du tout! Je ne suis pas amie de Monsieur Voltaire." I shall go to town the day after to-morrow, and will add a postscript, if I hear any news.

[Footnote 1: "A rage for adopting English fashions (Anglomanie, as it was called) began to prevail; and, among the different modes in which it was exhibited, it is especially noticed that tea was introduced, and began to share with coffee the privilege of affording sober refreshment to those who aspired in their different ways to give the tone to French society. A less innocent novelty was a passion for horse-racing, in which the Comte d'Artois and the Duc de Chartres set the example of indulging, establishing a racecourse in the Bois de Boulogne. The Count had but little difficulty in persuading the Queen to attend it, and she soon showed so decided a fancy for the sport, and became so regular a visitor of it, that a small stand was built for her, which in subsequent years provoked unfavourable comments, when the Prince obtained her leave to give luncheon to some of their racing friends, who were not in every instance of a character entitled to be brought into a royal presence" (the Editor's "Life of Marie Antoinette," c. II).]

Dec. 3rd.

I am come late, have seen nobody, and must send away my letter.

OSSIAN—CHATTERTON.

TO THE REV. WILLIAM COLE.

STRAWBERRY HILL, *June* 19, 1777.

I thank you for your notices, dear Sir, and shall remember that on Prince William. I did see the *Monthly Review*, but hope one is not guilty of the death of every man who does not make one the dupe of a forgery. I believe M'Pherson's success with "Ossian"[1] was more the ruin of Chatterton[2] than I. Two years passed between my doubting the authenticity of Rowley's poems and his death. I never knew he had been in London till some time after he had undone and poisoned himself there. The poems he sent me were transcripts in his own hand, and even in that circumstance he told a lie: he said he had them from the very person at Bristol to whom he had given them. If any man was to tell you that monkish rhymes had been dug up at Herculaneum, which was destroyed several centuries before there was any such poetry, should you believe it? Just the reverse is the case of Rowley's pretended poems. They have all the elegance of Waller and Prior, and more than Lord Surrey—but I have no objection to anybody believing what he pleases. I think poor Chatterton was an astonishing genius—but I cannot think that Rowley foresaw metres that were invented long after he was dead, or that our language was more refined at Bristol in the reign of Henry V. than it was at Court under Henry VIII. One of the chaplains of the Bishop of Exeter has found a line of Rowley in "Hudibras"—the monk might foresee that too! The prematurity of Chatterton's genius is, however, full as wonderful, as that such a prodigy as Rowley should never have been heard of till the eighteenth century. The youth and industry of the former are miracles, too, yet still more credible. There is not a symptom in the poems, but the old words, that savours of Rowley's age—change the old words for modern, and the whole construction is of yesterday.

[Footnote 1: Macpherson was a Scotch literary man, who in 1760 published "Fingal" in six books, which he declared he had translated from a poem by Ossian, son of Fingal, a Gaelic prince of the third century. For a moment the work was accepted as genuine in some quarters, especially by some of the Edinburgh divines. But Dr. Johnson denounced it as an imposture from the first. He pointed out that Macpherson had never produced the manuscripts from which he professed to have translated it when challenged to do so. He maintained also that the so-called poem had no merits; that "it was a mere unconnected rhapsody, a tiresome repetition of the same images;" and his opinion soon became so generally adopted, that Macpherson wrote him a furious letter of abuse, even threatening him with personal violence; to which Johnson replied "that he would not be deterred from exposing what he thought a cheat by the menaces of a ruffian"—a reply which seems to have silenced Mr. Macpherson (Boswell's "Life of Johnson," i. 375, ii. 310).]

[Footnote 2: Chatterton's is a melancholy story. In 1768, when a boy of only sixteen, he published a volume of ballads which he described as the work of Rowley, a priest of Bristol in the fifteenth century, and which he affirmed he had found in an old chest in the crypt of the Church of St. Mary Redcliffe at Bristol, of which his father was sexton. They gave proofs of so rich and precocious a genius, that if he had published them as his own works, he would "have found himself famous" in a moment, as Byron did forty years afterwards. But people resented the attempt to impose on them, Walpole being among the first to point out the proofs of their modern composition; and consequently the admiration which his genius might have excited was turned into general condemnation of his imposture, and in despair he poisoned himself in 1770, when he was only eighteen years old.]

AFFAIRS IN AMERICA—THE CZARINA AND THE EMPEROR OF CHINA.

TO SIR HORACE MANN.

ARLINGTON STREET, *Oct.* 26, 1777.

Letters of Horace Walpole, V2

It is past my usual period of writing to you; which would not have happened but from an uncommon, and indeed, considering the moment, an extraordinary dearth of matter. I could have done nothing but describe suspense, and every newspaper told you that. Still we know nothing certain of the state of affairs in America; the very existence where, of the Howes, is a mystery. The General is said to have beaten Washington, Clinton to have repulsed three attacks, and Burgoyne[1] to be beaten. The second alone is credited. Impatience is very high, and uneasiness increases with every day. There is no sanguine face anywhere, but many alarmed ones. The pains taken, by circulating false reports, to keep up some confidence, only increase the dissatisfaction by disappointing. Some advantage gained may put off clamour for some months: but I think, the longer it is suspended, the more terrible it will be; and how the war should end but in ruin, I am not wise enough to conjecture. France suspends the blow, to make it more inevitable. She has suffered us to undo ourselves: will she allow us time to recover? We have begged her indulgence in the first: will she grant the second prayer?...

[Footnote 1: In June and July General Burgoyne, a man of some literary as well as military celebrity, achieved some trifling successes over the colonial army, alternating, however, with some defeats. He took Ticonderoga, but one of his divisions was defeated with heavy loss at Bennington—a disaster which, Lord Stanhope says, exercised a fatal influence over the rest of the campaign; and finally, a week before this letter was written, he and all his army were so hemmed in at Saratoga, that they were compelled to lay down their arms—a disgrace which was the turning-point of the war, and which is compared by Lord Stanhope to the capitulation of his own ancestor at Brihuega in the war of the Spanish Succession. The surrender of Saratoga was the event which determined the French and Spaniards to recognise the independence of the colonies, and consequently to unite with them in the war against England.]

You have heard of the inundation at Petersburg. That ill wind produced luck to somebody. As the Empress had not distressed objects enough among her own people to gratify her humanity, she turned the torrent of her bounty towards that unhappy relict the Duchess of Kingston, and ordered her Admiralty to take particular care of the marvellous yacht that bore Messalina and her fortune. Pray mind that I bestow the latter Empress's name on the Duchess, only because she married a second husband in the lifetime of the first. Amongst other benevolences, the Czarina lent her Grace a courier to despatch to England—I suppose to acquaint Lord Bristol that he is not a widower. That courier brought a letter from a friend to Dr. Hunter, with the following anecdote. Her Imperial

Majesty proposed to her brother of China to lay waste a large district that separates their two empires, lest it should, as it has been on the point of doing, produce war between them; the two empires being at the two extremities of the world, not being distance enough to keep the peace. The ill-bred Tartar sent no answer to so humane a project. On the contrary, he dispersed a letter to the Russian people, in which he tells them that a woman—he might have said the Minerva of the French *literati*—had proposed to him to extirpate all the inhabitants of a certain region belonging to him, but that he knew better what to do with his own country: however, he could but wonder that the people of all the Russias should still submit to be governed by a creature that had assassinated her husband.—Oh! if she had pulled the Ottoman by the nose in the midst of Constantinople, as she intended to do, this savage would have been more civilised. I doubt the same rude monarch is still on the throne, who would not suffer Prince Czernichew to enter his territories, when sent to notify her Majesty's *hereditary* succession to her husband; but bade him be told, he would not receive an ambassador from a murderess. Is it not shocking that the law of nations, and the law of politeness, should not yet have abrogated the laws of justice and good-sense in a nation reckoned so civilised as the Chinese? What an age do we live in, if there is still a country where the Crown does not take away all defects! Good night!

DEATH OF LORD CHATHAM—THURLOW BECOMES LORD CHANCELLOR.

TO SIR HORACE MANN.

STRAWBERRY HILL, *May* 31, 1778.

I am forced to look at the dates I keep of my letters, to see what events I have or have not told you; for at this crisis something happens every day; though nothing very striking since the death of Lord Chatham, with which I closed my last. No?—yes, but there has. All England, which had abandoned him, found out, the moment his eyes were closed, that nothing but Lord Chatham could have preserved them. How lucky for him that the experiment cannot be made! Grief is fond, and grief is generous. The Parliament will bury him; the City begs the honour of being his grave; and the important question is not yet decided, whether he is to lie at Westminster or in St. Paul's; on which it was well said, that it would be "robbing Peter to pay Paul." An annuity of four thousand pounds is settled on the title of Chatham, and twenty thousand pounds allotted to pay his debts. The Opposition and the Administration disputed zeal; and neither care a straw about him. He is already as much forgotten as John of Gaunt.

General Burgoyne has succeeded and been the topic, and for two days engrossed the attention of the House of Commons; and probably will be heard of no more. He was even forgotten for three hours while he was on the tapis, by a violent quarrel between Temple Luttrell (a brother of the Duchess of Cumberland) and Lord George Germaine; but the public has taken affection for neither them nor the General: being much more disposed at present to hate than to love—except the dead. It will be well if the ill-humour, which increases, does not break out into overt acts.

I know not what to say of war. The Toulon squadron was certainly blown back. That of Brest is supposed to be destined to invade some part of this country or Ireland; or rather, it is probable, will attempt our fleet. In my own opinion, there is no great alacrity in France—I mean, in the Court of France—for war; and, as we have had time for great preparations, their eagerness will not increase. We shall suffer as much as they can desire by the loss of America, without their risk, and in a few years shall be able to give them no umbrage; especially as our frenzy is still so strong, that, if France left us at quiet, I am persuaded we should totally exhaust ourselves in pursuing the vision of reconquest. Spain continues to disclaim hostility as you told me. If the report is true of revolts in Mexico, they would be as good as a bond under his Catholic Majesty's hand.

We shall at least not doze, as we are used to do, in summer. The Parliament is to have only short adjournments; and our senators, instead of retiring to horse-races (*their* plough), are all turned soldiers, and disciplining militia. Camps everywhere, and the ladies in the uniform of their husbands! In short, if the dose is not too strong, a little adversity would not be quite unseasonable.—A little! you will cry; why what do you call the loss of America? Oh! my dear sir, do you think a capital as enormous as London has its nerves affected by what happens beyond the Atlantic? What has become of all your reading? There is nothing so unnatural as the feelings of a million of persons who live together in one city. They have not one conception like those in villages and in the country. They presume or despond from quite different motives. They have both more sense and less, than those who are not in contact with a multitude. Wisdom forms empires, but folly dissolves them; and a great capital, which dictates to the rest of the community, is always the last to perceive the decays of the whole, because it takes its own greatness for health.

Lord Holdernesse is dead; not quite so considerable a personage as he once expected to be, though Nature never intended him for anything that he was. The Chancellor, another child of Fortune, quits the Seals; and they are, or are to be, given to the Attorney-General, Thurlow, whom nobody will reproach with want of abilities.

As the Parliament will rise on Tuesday, you will not expect my letters so frequently as of late, especially if hostilities do not commence. In fact, our newspapers tell you everything faster than I can: still I write, because you have more faith in my intelligence; yet all its merit consists in my not telling you fables. I hear no more than everybody does, but I send you only what is sterling; or, at least, give you reports for no more than they are worth. I believe Sir John Dick is much more punctual, and hears more; but, till you displace me, I shall execute my office of being your gazetteer.

EXULTATION OF FRANCE AT OUR DISASTERS IN AMERICA—FRANKLIN—NECKER—CHATTERTON.

TO THE REV. WILLIAM COLE.

STRAWBERRY HILL, *June* 3, 1778.

I will not dispute with you, dear Sir, on patriots and politics. One point is past controversy, that the Ministers have ruined this country; and if the Church of England is satisfied with being reconciled to the Church of Rome, and thinks it a compensation for the loss of America and all credit in Europe, she is as silly an old woman as any granny in an almshouse. France is very glad we have grown such fools, and soon saw that the Presbyterian Dr. Franklin[1] had more sense than our Ministers together. She has got over all her prejudices, has expelled the Jesuits, and made the Protestant Swiss, Necker,[2] her Comptroller-general. It is a little woful, that we are relapsing into the nonsense the rest of Europe is shaking off! and it is more deplorable, as we know by repeated experience, that this country has always been disgraced by Tory administrations. The rubric is the only gainer by them in a few martyrs.

[Footnote 1: Dr. Franklin, as a man of science, may almost be called the father of electrical science. He was the discoverer of the electrical character of lightning, a discovery which he followed up by the invention of iron conductors for the protection of buildings, &c., from lightning. He was also a very zealous politician, and one of the leaders of the American colonists in their resistance to the taxation imposed first by Mr. Grenville and afterwards by Mr. C. Townshend. He resided for several years in England as agent for the State of Pennsylvania, and in that character, in the year 1765, was examined before the Committee of the House of Commons on the Stamp Act of Mr. Grenville. After the civil war broke out he was elected a member of the American Congress, and was sent as an envoy to France to negotiate a treaty with that country. As early as 1758 he was elected a member of the Royal Society in England, and received the honorary degree of D.C.L. from the University of Oxford.]

[Footnote 2: Necker was originally a banker, in which business he made a large fortune; but after a time he turned his attention to politics. He began by opposing the financial and constitutional schemes of the great Turgot, and shortly after the dismissal of that Minister he himself was admitted into the Ministry as a sort of Secretary to the Treasury, his religion, as a Protestant, being a bar to his receiving the title of "Comptroller–General," though, in fact, he had the entire management of the finance of the kingdom, which, by artful misrepresentation of his measures and suppression of such important facts, that he had contracted loans to the amount of twenty millions of money, he represented as far more flourishing than in reality it was. At the end of two or three years he resigned his office in discontent at his services not receiving the rewards to which he considered himself entitled. But in 1788 he was again placed in office, on this occasion as Comptroller–General, and, practically, Prime Minister, a post for which he was utterly unfit; for he had not one qualification for a statesman, was a prey to the most overweening vanity, and his sole principles of action were a thirst for popularity and a belief in "the dominion of reason and the abstract virtues of mankind." Under the influence of these notions he frittered away the authority and dignity of the King; and, as Napoleon afterwards truly told his grandson, was, in truth, the chief cause of all the horrors of the Revolution.]

I do not know yet what is settled about the spot of Lord Chatham's interment. I am not more an enthusiast to his memory than you. I knew his faults and his defects—yet one fact cannot only not be controverted, but I doubt more remarkable every day—I mean, that under him we attained not only our highest elevation, but the most solid authority in

Europe. When the names of Marlborough and Chatham are still pronounced with awe in France, our little cavils make a puny sound. Nations that are beaten cannot be mistaken.

I have been looking out for your friend a set of my heads of Painters, and I find I want six or seven. I think I have some odd ones in town; if I have not, I will have deficiencies supplied from the plates, though I fear they will not be good, as so many have been taken off. I should be very ungrateful for all your kindnesses, if I neglected any opportunity of obliging you, dear Sir. Indeed, our old and unalterable friendship is creditable to us both, and very uncommon between two persons who differ so much in their opinions relative to Church and State. I believe the reason is, that we are both sincere, and never meant to take advantage of our principles; which I allow is too common on both sides, and I own, too, fairly more common on my side of the question than on yours. There is a reason, too, for that; the honours and emoluments are in the gift of the Crown; the nation has no separate treasury to reward its friends.

If Mr. Tyrwhitt has opened his eyes to Chatterton's forgeries,[1] there is an instance of conviction against strong prejudice! I have drawn up an account of my transaction with that marvellous young man; you shall see it one day or other, but I do not intend to print it. I have taken a thorough dislike to being an author; and if it would not look like begging you to compliment me, by contradicting me, I would tell you, what I am most seriously convinced of, that I find what small share of parts I had, grown dulled—and when I perceive it myself, I may well believe that others would not be less sharp-sighted. It is very natural; mine were spirits rather than parts; and as time has abated the one, it must surely destroy their resemblance to the other: pray don't say a syllable in reply on this head, or I shall have done exactly what I said I would not do. Besides, as you have always been too partial to me, I am on my guard, and when I will not expose myself to my enemies, I must not listen to the prejudices of my friends; and as nobody is more partial to me than you, there is nobody I must trust less in that respect. Yours most sincerely.

[Footnote 1: Mr. Tyrrhwitt, a critic of great eminence, especially as the editor of "Chaucer," had at first believed the poems published by Chatterton to be the genuine works of Rowley, but was afterwards convinced, as Dr. Johnson also was, by the inspection of the manuscripts which the poor youth called the "originals," that they were quite recent.]

ADMIRAL KEPPEL'S SUCCESS—THREATS OF INVASION—FUNERAL OF LORD CHATHAM.

TO SIR HORACE MANN.

STRAWBERRY HILL, *July 7*, 1778.

You tell me in yours of the 23rd of last month, which I received to-day, that my letters are necessary to your tranquillity. That is sufficient to make me write, though I have nothing very positive to tell you. I did not mention Admiral Keppel's skirmish with and capture of two frigates of the Brest squadron; not because I thought it trifling, but concluding that it would produce immediate declaration of war; and, for the fact itself, I knew both our papers and the French would anticipate me. Indeed, Sir John Dick has talked to me so much of his frequency and punctuality with you, that I might have concluded he would not neglect so public an event; not that I trust to anybody else for sending you intelligence.

No Declaration has followed on either side. I, who know nothing but what everybody knows, am disposed to hope that both nations are grown rational; that is, humane enough to dislike carnage. Both kings are pacific by nature, and the voice of Europe now prefers legislators to *heroes*, which is but a name for destroyers of their species.

It is true, we are threatened with invasion.[1] You ask me why I seem to apprehend less than formerly? For many reasons. In the first place, I am above thirty years older. Can one fear anything in the dregs of life as at the beginning? Experience, too, has taught me that nothing happens in proportion to our conceptions. I have learnt, too, exceedingly to undervalue human policy. Chance and folly counteract most of its wisdom. From the "Memoires de Noailles"[2] I have learnt, that, between the years 1740 and 1750, when I,—ay, and my Lord Chesterfield too,—had such gloomy thoughts, France was trembling with dread of us. These are general reasons. My particular ones are, that, if France meditated a considerable blow, she has neglected her opportunity. Last year, we had neither army nor a manned fleet at home. Now, we have a larger and better army than ever we had in the island, and a strong fleet. Within these three days, our West India and Mediterranean fleets, for which we have been in great pain, are arrived, and bring not only above two millions, but such a host of sailors as will supply the deficiencies in our unequipped men-of-war. The country is covered with camps; General Conway, who has been to one of them, speaks with astonishment of the fineness of the men, of the regiments, of their discipline and manoeuvring. In short, the French Court has taught all our young nobility to be soldiers. The Duke of Grafton, who was the most indolent of ministers, is the most indefatigable of officers. For my part, I am almost afraid that there will be a larger military spirit amongst our men of quality than is wholesome for our constitution: France will have done us hurt enough, if she has turned us into generals instead of senators.

[Footnote 1: The design of invading England, first conceived by Philip II. of Spain and the Duke of Parma, had been entertained also by Louis XIV.; and after Walpole's death ostentatious preparations for such an expedition were made in 1805 by Napoleon. But some years afterwards Napoleon told Metternich, the Austrian Prime Minister, that he had never really designed to undertake the enterprise, being convinced of the impossibility of succeeding in it, and that the sole object of his preparations and of the camp at Boulogne had been to throw Austria off her guard.]

[Footnote 2: The Duc de Noailles had been the French Commander-in-chief at the battle of Dettingen in 1743.]

I can conceive another reason why France should not choose to venture an invasion. It is certain that at least five American provinces wish for peace with us. Nor can I think that thirteen English provinces would be pleased at seeing England invaded. Any considerable blow received by us, would turn their new allies into haughty protectors. Should we accept a bad peace, America would find her treaty with them a very bad one: in short, I have treated you with speculations instead of facts. I know but one of the latter sort. The King's army has evacuated Philadelphia, from having eaten up the country, and has returned to New York. Thus it is more compact, and has less to defend.

General Howe is returned, richer in money than laurels. I do not know, indeed, that his wealth is great.

Fanaticism in a nation is no novelty; but you must know, that, though the effects were so solid, the late appearance of enthusiasm about Lord Chatham was nothing but a general affectation of enthusiasm. It was a contention of hypocrisy between the Opposition and the Court, which did not last even to his burial. Not three of the Court attended it, and not a dozen of the Minority of any note. He himself said, between his fall in the House of Lords and his death, that, when he came to himself, not one of his old acquaintance of the Court but Lord Despencer so much as asked how he did. Do you imagine people are struck with the death of a man, who were not struck with the sudden appearance of his death? We do not counterfeit so easily on a surprise, as coolly; and, when we are cool on surprise, we do not grow agitated on reflection.

The last account I heard from Germany was hostile. Four days ago both the Imperial and Prussian Ministers[1] expected news of a battle. O, ye fathers of your people, do you thus dispose of your children? How many thousand lives does a King save, who signs a peace! It was said in jest of our Charles II., that he was the real *father* of his people, so many of them did he beget himself. But tell me, ye divines, which is the most virtuous man, he who begets twenty bastards, or he who sacrifices a hundred thousand lives? What a contradiction is human nature! The Romans rewarded the man who got three children, and laid waste the world. When will the world know that peace and propagation are the two most delightful things in it? As his Majesty of France has found out the latter, I hope he will not forget the former.

[Footnote 1: Towards the close of 1777 Maximilian, the Elector of Bavaria, died, and the Emperor Joseph claimed many of his fiefs as having escheated to him. Frederic the Great, who was still jealous of Austria, endeavoured to form a league to aid the new Elector in his resistance to Joseph's demands, and even invaded Bohemia with an army of eighty thousand men; but the Austrian army was equally strong. No action of any importance took place; and in the spring of 1779 the treaty of Teschen was concluded between the Empire, Prussia, and Bavaria, by which a small portion of the district claimed by Joseph was ceded to Austria.]

SUGGESTION OF NEGOTIATIONS WITH FRANCE—PARTITION OF POLAND.

TO THE HON. H.S. CONWAY.

STRAWBERRY HILL, *July* 8, 1778.

I have had some conversation with a ministerial person, on the subject of pacification with France; and he dropped a hint, that as we should not have much of a good peace, the Opposition would make great clamour on it. I said a few words on the duty of Ministers to do what they thought right, be the consequence what it would. But as honest men do not want such lectures, and dishonest will not let them weigh, I waived that theme, to dwell on what is more likely to be persuasive, and which I am firmly persuaded is no less true than the former maxim; and that was, that the Ministers are *still* so strong, that if they could get a peace that would save the nation, though not a brilliant or glorious one, the nation in general would be pleased with it, and the clamours of the Opposition be insignificant.

I added, what I think true, too, that no time is to be lost in treating; not only for preventing a blow, but from the consequences the first misfortune would have. The nation is not yet alienated from the Court, but it is growing so; is grown so enough, for any calamity to have violent effects. Any internal disturbance would advance the hostile designs of France. An insurrection from distress would be a double invitation to invasion; and, I am sure, much more to be dreaded, even personally, by the Ministers, than the ill-humours of Opposition for even an inglorious peace. To do the Opposition justice, it is not composed of incendiaries. Parliamentary speeches raise no tumults: but tumults would be a dreadful thorough bass to speeches. The Ministers do not know the strength they have left (supposing they apply it in time), if they are afraid of making any peace. They were too sanguine in making war; I hope they will not be too timid of making peace.

What do you think of an idea of mine of offering France a neutrality? that is, to allow her to assist both us and the Americans. I know she would assist only them: but were it not better to connive at her assisting them, without attacking us, than her doing both? A treaty with her would perhaps be followed by one with America. We are sacrificing all the essentials we *can* recover, for a few words; and risking the independence of this country, for the nominal supremacy over America. France seems to leave us time for treating. She mad no scruple of begging peace of us in '63, that she might lie by and recover her advantages. Was not that a wise precedent? Does not she *now* show that it was? Is not policy the honour of nations? I mean, not morally, but has Europe left itself any other honour? And since it has really left itself no honour, and as little morality, does not the morality of a nation consist in its preserving itself in as much happiness as it can? The invasion of Portugal by Spain in the last war, and the partition of Poland,[1] have abrogated the law of nations. Kings have left no ties between one another. Their duty to their people is still allowed. He is a good King that preserves his people; and if temporising answers that end, is it not justifiable? You, who are as moral as wise, answer my questions. Grotius[2] is obsolete. Dr. Joseph and Dr. Frederic, with four hundred thousand commentators, are reading new lectures—and I should say, thank God, to one another, if the four hundred thousand commentators were not in worse danger than they. Louis XVI. is grown a casuist compared to those partitioners. Well, let us simple individuals keep our honesty, and bless our stars that we have not armies at our command, lest we should divide kingdoms that are at our *bienseance*! What a dreadful thing it is for such a wicked little imp as man to have absolute power! But I have travelled into Germany, when I meant to talk to you only of England; and it is too late to recall my text. Good night!

[Footnote 1: A partition of Poland had been proposed by the Great Elector of Brandenburgh as early as the middle of the seventeenth century, his idea being that he, the Emperor, and the King of Sweden should divide the whole country between them. At that time, however, the mutual jealousies of the three princes prevented the scheme from being carried out. But in 1770 the idea was revived by Frederic the Great, who sent his brother Henry to discuss it with the Czarina. She eagerly embraced it; and the new Emperor Joseph had so blind an admiration for Frederic, that it was not hard to induce him to become a confederate in the scheme of plunder. And the three allies had less difficulty than might have been expected in arranging the details. In extent of territory Austria was the principal gainer, her share being of sufficient importance to receive a new name as the kingdom of Galicia; the share of Prussia being West Prussia and Pomerania, with the exception of Dantzic and the fortress of Thorn; while Russia took Polish Livonia and the rich provinces to the east of the Dwina. But the spoilers were not long contented with their acquisitions. In 1791 intrigues among the Polish nobles, probably fomented by the Czarina herself, gave her a pretence for interfering in their affairs; and the result was a second partition, which gave the long-coveted port of Dantzic and a long district on the shore of the Baltic to Prussia, and such extensive provinces adjoining Russia to Catharine, that all that was left to the Polish sovereign was a small territory with a population that hardly amounted to four millions of subjects. The partition excited great indignation all over Europe, but in 1772 England was sufficiently occupied with the troubles beginning to arise in America, and France was still too completely under the profligate and imbecile rule of Louis XV. and Mme. du Barri, and too much weakened by her disasters in the Seven Years' War, for any manly counsels or indication of justice and humanity to be expected from that country.]

[Footnote 2: Grotius (a Latinised form of Groot) was an eminent statesman and jurist of Holland at the beginning of the seventeenth century. He was a voluminous author; his most celebrated works being a treatise, "De jure belli et pacis," and another on the "Truth of the Christian Religion."]

[Illustration: VIEW OF GARDEN, STRAWBERRY HILL, FROM THE GREAT BED-CHAMBER.]

UNSUCCESSFUL CRUISE OF KEPPEL—CHARACTER OF LORD CHATHAM.

TO SIR HORACE MANN.

STRAWBERRY HILL, *Oct.* 8, 1778.

As you are so earnest for news, I am concerned when I have not a paragraph to send you. It looks as if distance augmented your apprehensions; for, I assure you, at home we have lost almost all curiosity. Though the two fleets have been so long at sea, and though, before their last *sortie*, one heard nothing but *What news of the fleets?* of late there has been scarcely any inquiry; and so the French one is returned to Brest, and ours is coming home. Admiral Keppel is very unlucky in having missed them, for they had not above twenty-five ships. Letters from Paris say that their camps, too, are to break up at the end of this month: but we do not intend to be the dupes of that *finesse*, if it is one, but shall remain on our guard. One must hope that winter will produce some negotiation; and that, peace. Indeed, as war is not declared, I conclude there is always some treating on the anvil; and, should it end well, at least this age will have made a step towards humanity, in omitting the ceremonial of proclamation, which seems to make it easier to cease being at war. But I am rather making out a proxy for a letter than sending you news. But, you see, even armies of hundred thousands in Germany can execute as little as we; and you must remember what the Grand Conde, or the great Prince of Orange—I forget which—said, that unmarried girls imagine husbands are always on duty, unmilitary men that soldiers are always fighting. One of the Duke of Marlborough's Generals dining with the Lord Mayor, an Alderman who sat next to him said, "Sir, yours must be a very laborious profession."—"No," replied the General, "we fight about four hours in the morning, and two or three after dinner, and then we have all the rest of the day to ourselves."

The King has been visiting camps,—and so has Sir William Howe, who, one should think, had had enough of them; and who, one should think too, had not achieved such exploits as should make him fond of parading himself about, or expect many hosannahs. To have taken one town, and retreated from two, is not very glorious in military arithmetic; and to have marched twice to Washington, and returned without attacking him, is no addition to the sum total.

Did I tell you that Mrs. Anne Pitt is returned, and acts great grief for her brother? I suppose she was the dupe of the farce acted by the two Houses and the Court, and had not heard that none of them carried on the pantomime even to his burial. Her nephew gave a little into that mummery even to me; forgetting how much I must remember of his aversion to his uncle. Lord Chatham was a meteor, and a glorious one; people discovered that he was not a genuine luminary, and yet everybody in mimickry has been an *ignis fatuus* about him. Why not allow his magnificent enterprises and good fortune, and confess his defects; instead of being bombast in his praises, and at the same time discover that the amplification is insincere? A Minister who inspires great actions must be a great Minister; and Lord Chatham will always appear so,—by comparison with his predecessors and successors. He retrieved our affairs when ruined by a most incapable Administration; and we are fallen into a worse state since he was removed. Therefore, I doubt, posterity will allow more to his merit, than it is the present fashion to accord to it. Our historians have of late been fond of decrying Queen Elizabeth, in order if possible to raise the Stuarts: but great actions surmount foibles; and folly and guilt would always remain folly and guilt, though there had never been a great man or woman in the world. Our modern tragedies, hundreds of them do not contain a good line; nor are they a jot the better, because Shakspeare, who was superior to all mankind, wrote some whole plays that are as bad as any of our present writers.

I shall be very glad to see your nephew, and talk of you with him; which will be more satisfactory than questioning accidental travellers.

CAPTURE OF PONDICHERRY—CHANGES IN THE MINISTRY—LA FAYETTE IN AMERICA.

TO SIR HORACE MANN.

ARLINGTON STREET, *March* 22, 1779.

If your representative dignity is impaired westward, you may add to your eastern titles those of "Rose of India" and "Pearl of Pondicherry."[1] The latter gem is now set in one of the vacant sockets of the British diadem.

[Footnote 1: The authority of the great Warren Hastings, originally limited to five years, was renewed this year; and he signalised the prolongation of his authority by more vigorous attacks than ever on the French fortresses in India. He sent one body of troops against Chandemagore, their chief stronghold in Bengal; another against Pondicherry, their head-quarters in the south of Hindostan; while a third, under Colonel Goddard, defeated the two Mahratta chieftains Scindia and Holkar, and took some of their strongest fortresses.]

I have nothing to subjoin to this high-flown paragraph, that will at all keep pace with the majesty of it. I should have left to the *Gazette* to wish you joy, nor have begun a new letter without more materials, if I did not fear you would be still uneasy about your nephew. I hear he has, *since his parenthesis*, voted again with the Court; therefore he has probably not taken a new *part*, but only made a Pindaric transition on a particular question. I have seen him but twice since his arrival, and from both those visits I had no reason to expect he would act differently from what you wished. Perhaps it may never happen again. I go so little into the world, that I don't at all know what company he frequents. He talked so reasonably and tenderly with regard to you, that I shall be much deceived if he often gives you any inquietude.

The place of Secretary of State is not replenished yet. Several different successors have been talked of. At least, at present, there is a little chance of its being supplied by the Opposition. Their numbers have fallen off again, though they are more alert than they used to be. I do not love to foretell, because no Elijah left me his mantle, in which, it seems, the gift of prophecy resides; and, if I see clouds gathering, I less care to announce their contents to foreign post-offices. On the other hand, it is no secret, nor one to disguise if it were, that the French trade must suffer immensely by our captures.

Private news I know none. The Bishops are trying to put a stop to one staple commodity of that kind, Adultery. I do not suppose that they expect to lessen it; but, to be sure, it was grown to a sauciness that did call for a decenter veil. I do not think they have found out a good cure; and I am of opinion, too, that flagrancy proceeds from national depravity, which tinkering one branch will not remedy. Perhaps polished manners are a better proof of virtue in an age than of vice, though system-makers do not hold so: at least, decency has seldom been the symptom of a sinking nation.

When one talks on general themes, it is a sign of having little to say. It is not that there is a dearth of topics; but I only profess sending you information on events that really have happened, to guide you towards forming a judgment. At home, we are fed with magnificent hopes and promises that are never realized. For instance, to prove discord in America, Monsieur de la Fayette[1] was said to rail at the Congress, and their whole system and transactions. There is just published an intercourse between them that exhibits enthusiasm in him towards their cause, and the highest esteem for him on their side. For my part, I see as little chance of recovering America as of re-conquering the Holy Land. Still, I do not amuse you with visions on either side, but tell you nakedly what advantage has been gained or lost. This caution abbreviates my letters; but, in general, you can depend on what I tell you. Adieu!

[Footnote 1: Monsieur de la Fayette was a young French marquis of ancient family, but of limited fortune. He was a man of no ability, civil or military, and not even of much resolution, unless a blind fanaticism for republican principles can be called so. When the American war broke out he conceived such an admiration for Washington, that he resigned his commission in the French army to cross over to America and serve with the colonists; but it cannot be said that he was of any particular service to their cause. Afterwards, in 1789, he entered warmly into the schemes of the leaders of the Revolution, and contributed greatly to the difficulties and misfortunes of the Royal Family, especially by his conduct as Commander of the National Guard, which was a contemptible combination of treachery and imbecility.]

Tuesday 24th.

I hear this moment that an account is come this morning of D'Estaing with sixteen ships being blocked up by Byron at Martinico, and that Rowley with eight more was expected by the latter in a day or two. D'Estaing, it is supposed, will be starved to surrender, and the island too. I do not answer for this intelligence or consequences; but, if the first is believed, you may be sure the rest is.

DIVISIONS IN THE MINISTRY—CHARACTER OF THE ITALIANS AND OF THE FRENCH.

TO SIR HORACE MANN.

STRAWBERRY HILL, *July* 7, 1779.

How much larger the war will be for the addition of Spain, I do not know. Hitherto it has produced no events but the shutting of our ports against France, and the junction of nine ships from Ferrol with the French squadron. They talk of a great navy getting ready at Cadiz, and of mighty preparations in the ports of France for an embarkation. As all this must have been foreseen, I suppose we are ready to resist all attacks.

The Parliament rose last Saturday, not without an open division in the Ministry: Lord Gower, President of the Council, heading an opposition to a Bill for doubling the Militia, which had passed the Commons, and throwing it out; which Lord North as publicly resented. I make no comments on this, because I really know nothing of the motives. Thoroughly convinced that all my ideas are superannuated, and too old to learn new lessons, I only hear what passes, pretend to understand nothing, and wait patiently for events as they present themselves. I listen enough to be able to acquaint you with facts of public notoriety; but attempt to explain none of them, if they do not carry legibility in the van.

Your nephew, who lives more in the world, and is coming to you, will be far more master of the details. He called here some few days ago, as I was going out to dinner, but has kindly promised to come and dine here before he sets out. His journey is infinitely commendable, as entirely undertaken to please you. It will be very comfortable too, as surely the concourse of English must much abate, especially as France is interdicted. Travelling boys and self-sufficient governors would be an incumbrance to you, could you see more of your countrymen of more satisfactory conversation. Florence probably is improved since it had a Court of its own, and there must be men a little more enlightened than the poor Italians. Scarcely any of the latter that ever I knew but, if they had parts, were buffoons. I believe the boasted *finesse* of the ruling clergy is pretty much a traditionary notion, like their jealousy. More nations than one live on former characters after they are totally changed.

I have been often and much in France. In the provinces they may still be gay and lively; but at Paris, bating the pert *etourderie* of very young men, I protest I scarcely ever saw anything like vivacity—the Duc de Choiseul alone had more than any hundred Frenchmen I could select. Their women are the first in the world in everything but beauty; sensible, agreeable, and infinitely informed. The *philosophes*, except Buffon, are solemn, arrogant, dictatorial coxcombs—I need not say superlatively disagreeable. The rest are amazingly ignorant in general, and void of all conversation but the routine with women. My dear and very old friend [Madame du Deffand] is a relic of a better age, and at nearly eighty-four has all the impetuosity that *was* the character of the French. They have not found out, I believe, how much their nation is sunk in Europe;—probably the Goths and Vandals of the North will open their eyes before a century is past. I speak of the swarming empires that have conglomerated within our memories. *We* dispelled the vision twenty years ago: but let us be modest till we do so again....

11th.

Last night I received from town the medal you promised me on the Moorish alliance.[1] It is at least as magnificent as the occasion required, and yet not well executed. The medallist Siriez, I conclude, is grandson of my old acquaintance Louis Siriez of the Palazzo Vecchio.

[Footnote 1: A treaty had just been concluded between the Duke of Tuscany and the Emperor of Morocco.]

Yesterday's Gazette issued a proclamation on the expected invasion from Havre, where they are embarking mightily. Some think the attempt will be on Portsmouth. To sweeten this pill, Clinton has taken a fort and seventy men—not near Portsmouth, but New York; and there were reports at the latter that Charleston is likely to surrender. This would be something, if there were not a French war and a Spanish war in the way between us and

Carolina. Sir Charles Hardy is at Torbay with the whole fleet, which perhaps was not a part of the plan at Havre: we shall see, and you shall hear, if anything passes.

Friday night, July 16th.

Your nephew has sent me word that he will breakfast with me to-morrow, but shall not have time to dine. I have nothing to add to the foregoing general picture. We have been bidden even by proclamation to expect an invasion, and troops and provisions have for this week said to have been embarked. Still I do not much expect a serious descent. The French, I think, have better chances with less risk. They may ruin us in detail. The fleet is at present at home or very near, and very strong; nor do I think that the French plan is activity:—but it is idle to talk of the present moment, when it will be some time before you receive this. I am infinitely in more pain about Mr. Conway, who is in the midst of the storm in a nutshell, and I know will defend himself as if he was in the strongest fortification in Flanders—and, which is as bad, I believe the Court would sacrifice the island to sacrifice him. They played that infamous game last year on Keppel, when ten thousand times more was at stake. They look at the biggest objects through the diminishing end of every telescope; and, the higher they who look, the more malignant and mean the eye....

Adieu! my dear Sir. In what manner we are to be undone, I do not guess; but I see no way by which we can escape happily out of this crisis—I mean, preserve the country and recover the Constitution. I thought for four years that calamity would bring us to our senses: but alas! we have none left to be brought to. We shall now suffer a greal deal, submit at last to a humiliating peace, and people will be content.—So adieu, England! it will be more or less a province or kind of province to France, and its viceroy will be, in what does not concern France, its despot—and will be content too! I shall not pity the country; I shall feel only for those who grieve with me at its abject state; or for posterity, if they do not, like other degraded nations, grow callously reconciled to their ignominy.

ERUPTION OF VESUVIUS—DEATH OF LORD TEMPLE.

TO SIR HORACE MANN.

Sept. 16, 1779.

Letters of Horace Walpole, V2

I have received your letter by Colonel Floyd, and shall be surprised indeed if Caesar does not find his own purple a little rumpled, as well as his brother's mantle. But how astonished was I at finding that you did not mention the dreadful eruption of Vesuvius. Surely you had not heard of it! What are kings and their popguns to that wrath of Nature! How Sesostris, at the head of an army of nations, would have fallen prostrate to earth before a column of blazing embers eleven thousand feet high! I am impatient to hear more, as you are of the little conflict of us pigmies. Three days after my last set out, we received accounts of D'Estaing's success against Byron and Barrington, and of the capture of Grenada. I do not love to send first reports, which are rarely authentic. The subsequent narrative of the engagement is more favourable. It allows the victory to the enemy, but makes their loss of men much the more considerable. Of ships we lost but one, taken after the fight as going into port to refit. Sir Charles Hardy and D'Orvilliers have not met; the latter is at Brest, the former at Portsmouth. I never penetrated an inch into what is to be; and into some distant parts of our history, I mean the Eastern, I have never liked to look. I believe it an infamous scene; you know I have always thought it so; and the Marattas are a nation of banditti very proper to scourge the heroes of Europe, who go so far to plunder and put themselves into their way. Nature gave to mankind a beautiful world, and larger than it could occupy,—for, as to the eruption of Goths and Vandals occasioned by excess of population, I very much doubt it; and mankind prefers deforming the ready Paradise, to improving and enjoying it. Ambition and mischief, which one should not think were natural appetites, seem almost as much so as the impulse to propagation; and those pious rogues, the clergy, preach against what Nature forces us to practise (or she could not carry on her system), and not twice in a century say a syllable against the Lust of Destruction! Oh! one is lost in moralising, as one is in astronomy! In the ordinance and preservation of the great universal system one sees the Divine Artificer, but our intellects are too bounded to comprehend anything more.

Lord Temple is dead by an accident. I never had any esteem for his abilities or character. He had grown up in the bask of Lord Chatham's glory, and had the folly to mistake half the rays for his own. The world was not such a dupe; and his last years discovered a selfish restlessness, and discovered to him, too, that no mortal regarded him but himself.

The Lucans are in my neighbourhood, and talk with much affection of you. Adieu!

CHANCES OF WAR WITH HOLLAND—HIS FATHER'S POLICY—POPE—CHARACTER OF BOLINGBROKE.

TO SIR HORACE MANN.

BERKELEY SQUARE, *Jan.* 13, 1780.

In consequence of my last, it is right to make you easy, and tell you that I think we shall not have a Dutch war;[1] at least, nobody seems to expect it. What excuses we have made, I do not know; but I imagine the Hollanders are glad to gain by both sides, and glad not to be forced to quarrel with either.

[Footnote 1: Walpole was mistaken in his calculations. "Holland at this time was divided by two great parties—the party of the Staatholder, the Prince of Orange, and the party inclining to France—of which the Pensionary, Van Bethel, was among the principal members; and this party was so insulting in their tone and measures, that at the end of 1780 we were compelled to declare war against them" (Lord Stanhope, "History of England," c. 63). But the war was not signalised by any action of importance.]

What might have been expected much sooner, appears at last—a good deal of discontent; but chiefly where it was not much expected. The country gentlemen, after encouraging the Court to war with America, now, not very decently, are angry at the expense. As they have long seen the profusion, it would have been happy had they murmured sooner. Very serious associations are forming in many counties; and orders, under the title of petitions, coming to Parliament for correcting abuses. They talk of the waste of money; are silent on the thousands of lives that have been sacrificed—but when are human lives counted by any side?

The French, who may measure with us in folly, and have exceeded us in ridiculous boasts, have been extravagant in their reception of D'Estaing,[1] who has shown nothing but madness and incapacity. How the northern monarchs, who have at least exhibited talents for war and politics, must despise the last campaign of England and France!

[Footnote 1: The Comte d'Estaing was the Commander-in-chief of the French fleet in the West Indies in the years 1777-80. But, though his force was always superior to ours, he always endeavoured to avoid a battle; and succeeded in that timorous policy except on two occasions, when Lord Howe and afterwards Admiral Byron brought him to action, but only with indecisive results.]

I am once more got abroad, but more pleased to be able to do so, than charmed with anything I have to do. Having outlived the glory and felicity of my country, I carry that reflection with me wherever I go. Last night, at Strawberry Hill, I took up, to divert my thoughts, a volume of letters to Swift from Bolingbroke, Bathurst, and Gay; and what was there but lamentations on the ruin of England, in that era of its prosperity and peace, from wretches who thought their own want of power a proof that their country was undone! Oh, my father! twenty years of peace, and credit, and happiness, and liberty, were punishments to rascals who weighed everything in the scales of self? It was to the honour of Pope, that, though leagued with such a crew, and though an idolater of their archfiend Bolingbroke and in awe of the malignant Swift, he never gave in to their venomous railings; railings against a man who, in twenty years, never attempted a stretch of power, did nothing but the common business of administration, and by that temperance and steady virtue, and unalterable good-humour and superior wisdom, baffled all the efforts of faction, and annihilated the falsely boasted abilities of Bolingbroke,[1] which now appear as moderate as his character was in every light detestable. But, alas! that retrospect doubled my chagrin instead of diverting it. I soon forgot an impotent cabal of mock-patriots; but the scene they vainly sought to disturb rushed on my mind, and, like Hamlet on the sight of Yorick's skull, I recollected the prosperity of Denmark when my father ruled, and compared it with the present moment! I look about for a Sir Robert Walpole; but where is he to be found?

[Footnote: 1 It is only the excess of party spirit that could lead Walpole to call Bolingbroke's abilities moderate; and he had no attacks on his father to resent, since, though Bolingbroke was in 1724 permitted to return to England, he only received a partial pardon, and was not permitted to take his seat in Parliament. Walpole has more reason to pronounce his character detestable; for which opinion he might have quoted Dr. Johnson, who, in reference to an infidel treatise which he bequeathed to Mallet for publication, called him "a scoundrel and a coward—a scoundrel who spent his life in charging a popgun against Christianity, which he had not the courage to let off, but left it to a hungry Scotchman to pull the trigger after he was dead."]

This is not a letter, but a codicil to my last. You will soon probably have news enough—yet appearances are not always pregnancies. When there are more follies in a nation than principles and system, they counteract one another, and sometimes, as has just happened in Ireland, are composed *pulveris exigui jactu.* I sum up my wishes in that for peace: but we are not satisfied with persecuting America, though the mischief has recoiled on ourselves; nor France with wounding us, though with little other cause for exultation, and with signal mischief to her own trade, and with heavy loss of seamen; not to mention how her armies are shrunk to raise her marine, a sacrifice she will one day rue, when the *disciplined* hosts of Goths and Huns begin to cast an eye southward. But I seem to choose to read futurity, because I am not likely to see it: indeed I am most rational when I say to myself, What is all this to me? My thread is almost spun! almost all my business here is to bear pain with patience, and to be thankful for intervals of ease. Though Emperors and Kings may torment mankind, they will not disturb my bedchamber; and so I bid them and you good-night!

P.S.—I have made use of a term in this letter, which I retract, having bestowed a title on the captains and subalterns which was due only to the colonel, and not enough for his dignity. Bolingbroke was more than a rascal—he was a villain. Bathurst, I believe, was not a dishonest man, more than he was prejudiced by party against one of the honestest and best of men. Gay was a simple poor soul, intoxicated by the friendship of men of genius, and who thought *they* must be good who condescended to admire *him.* Swift was a wild beast, who baited and worried all mankind almost, because his intolerable arrogance, vanity, pride, and ambition were disappointed; he abused Lady Suffolk, who tried and wished to raise him, only because she had not power to do so: and one is sure that a man who could deify that silly woman Queen Anne, would have been more profuse of incense to Queen Caroline, who had sense, if the Court he paid to her had been crowned with success. Such were the men who wrote of virtue to one another; and even that mean, exploded miser, Lord Bath, presumed to talk of virtue too!

POLITICAL EXCITEMENT—LORD G. GORDON—EXTRAORDINARY GAMBLING AFFAIRS IN INDIA.

TO SIR HORACE MANN.

Letters of Horace Walpole, V2

STRAWBERRY HILL, *Feb.* 6, 1780.

I write only when I have facts to send. Detached scenes there have been in different provinces: they will be collected soon into a drama in St. Stephen's Chapel. One or two and twenty counties, and two or three towns, have voted petitions.[1] But in Northamptonshire Lord Spencer was disappointed, and a very moderate petition was ordered. The same happened at Carlisle. At first, the Court was struck dumb, but have begun to rally. Counter-protests have been signed in Hertford and Huntingdon shires, in Surrey and Sussex. Last Wednesday a meeting was summoned in Westminster Hall: Charles Fox harangued the people finely and warmly; and not only a petition was voted, but he was proposed for candidate for that city at the next general election, and was accepted joyfully. Wilkes was his zealous advocate: how few years since a public breakfast was given at Holland House to support Lord Luttrell against Wilkes! Charles Fox and his brother rode thence at the head of their friends to Brentford. Ovid's "Metamorphoses" contains not stranger transformations than party can work.

[Footnote 1: These petitions were chiefly for economical reform, for which Burke was preparing a Bill.]

I must introduce a new actor to you, a Lord George Gordon,—metamorphosed a little, too, for his family were Jacobites and Roman Catholics: he is the Lilburne of the Scottish Presbyterians, and an apostle against the Papists. He dresses, that is, wears long lank hair about his shoulders, like the first Methodists; though I take the modern ones to be no Anti-Catholics. This mad lord, for so all his family have been too, and are, has likewise assumed the patronage of Ireland. Last Thursday he asked an audience of the King, and, the moment he was admitted into the closet, began reading an Irish pamphlet, and continued for an hour, till it was so dark he could not see; and then left the pamphlet, exacting a promise on royal honour that his Majesty would finish it. Were I on the throne, I would make Dr. Monro a Groom of my Bedchamber: indeed it has been necessary for some time; for, of the King's lords, Lord Bolingbroke is in a mad-house, and Lord Pomfret and my nephew ought to be there. The last, being fond of onions, has lately distributed bushels of that root to his Militia; Mr. Wyndham will not be surprised.

By the tenor of the petitions you would think we were starving; yet there is a little coin stirring. Within this week there has been a cast at hazard at the Cocoa tree, the difference of which amounted to a hundred and four-score thousand pounds. Mr. O'Birne, an Irish gamester, had won one hundred thousand pounds of a young Mr. Harvey of Chigwell, just started from a midshipman[1] into an estate by his elder brother's death. O'Birne said, "You can never pay me." "I can," said the youth; "my estate will sell for the debt." "No," said O.; "I will win ten thousand—you shall throw for the odd ninety." They did, and Harvey won.

[Footnote 1: Mr. Harvey was afterwards Sir Eliab Harvey, one of Nelson's captains at Trafalgar. But unfortunately he so violently resented the appointment of Lord Cochrane, who was only a post-captain, to carry out the attack on the French fleet in Basque Roads, which he himself, who was an admiral, had also suggested, and used such violent and insubordinate language towards Lord Gambier, the Commander-in-chief (who, though a most incompetent officer, had had nothing to do with the appointment), that it was unavoidable that a court-martial should sentence him to be cashiered. He was, however, restored to his rank shortly afterwards. He was member of Parliament for Essex for many years, and died in 1830.]

However, as it is a little necessary to cast about for resources, it is just got abroad, that about a year ago we took possession of a trifling district in India called the Province of Oude,[1] which contains four millions of inhabitants, produces between three and four millions of revenue, and has an army of 30,000 men: it was scarce thought of consequence enough to deserve an article in the newspapers. If you are so *old-style* as to ask how we came to take possession, I answer, by the new law of nations; by the law by which Poland was divided. You will find it in the future editions of Grotius, tit. "Si une terre est a la bienseance d'un grand Prince." Oude appertained by that very law to the late Sujah Dowla. His successors were weak men, which *in India* is incapacity. Their Majesties the East India Company, whom God long preserve, have *succeeded*.

[Footnote 1: Warren Hastings claimed large arrears of tribute from Asaph ul Dowlah, the Nabob of Oude; but Walpole was misinformed when he understood that he had in consequence annexed the province—a measure which was never adopted till the spring of 1857, when its annexation by Lord Dalhousie was among the causes that led to the outbreak of the mutiny.]

This petty event has ascertained the existence of a certain being, who, till now, has not been much more than a matter of faith—the Grand Lama. There are some affairs of trade between the sovereigns of Oude and his Holiness the Lama. Do not imagine the East

India Company have leisure to trouble their heads about religion. Their commanding officer corresponded with the Tartar Pope, who, it seems, is a very sensible man. The Attorney-General asked this officer, who is come over, how the Lama wrote. "Oh," said he, "like any person."—"Could I see his letters?" said Mr. Wedderburne.—"Upon my word," said the officer, "when the business was settled, I threw them into the fire." However, I hear that somebody, not quite so mercantile, has published one of the Lama's letters in the "Philosophical Transactions." Well! when we break in Europe, we may pack up and remove to India, and be emperors again!

Do you believe me, my good Sir, when I tell you all these strange tales? Do you think me distracted, or that your country is so? Does not this letter seem an olio composed of ingredients picked out of the history of Charles I., of Clodius and Sesostris, and the "Arabian Nights"? Yet I could have coloured it higher without trespassing on truth; but when I, inured to the climate of my own country, can scarcely believe what I hear and see, how should you, who converse only with the ordinary race of men and women, give credit to what I have ventured to relate, merely because in forty years I have constantly endeavoured to tell you nothing but truth? Moreover, I commonly reserve passages that are not of public notoriety, not having the smallest inclination to put the credulity of foreign post-offices to the test. I would have them think that we are only mad with valour, and that Lord Chatham's cloak has been divided into shreds no bigger than a silver penny amongst our soldiers and sailors. Adieu!

RODNEY'S VICTORY—WALPOLE INCLINES TO WITHDRAW FROM AMUSEMENTS.

TO SIR HORACE MANN.

BERKELEY SQUARE, *March* 3, 1780.

As my last letter probably alarmed you, I write again to tell you that nothing decisive has happened. The troops of the Palace even rallied a little yesterday on Mr. Burke's Bill of Reformation, or Reduction, yet with evident symptoms of *caution*; for Lord North, who wished to defer the second reading, ventured to put it only to next Wednesday, instead of to-day; and would have carried a longer adjournment with still greater difficulty, for his majority was but of 35, and the minority remained 195, a very formidable number. The

Associations in the counties increase, though not rapidly: yet it will be difficult for the Court to stem such a torrent; and, I imagine, full as difficult for any man of temper to direct them wholesomely. Ireland is still more impetuous.

Fortunately, happily, the tide abroad seems turned. Sir George Rodney's victory[1] proves more considerable than it appeared at first. It secures Gibraltar, eases your Mediterranean a little, and must vex the Spaniards and their monarch, not satisfied before with his cousin of Bourbon. Admiral Parker has had great success too amongst the latter's transports. Oh! that all these elements of mischief may jumble into peace! Monsieur Necker[2] alone shines in the quarter of France; but he is carrying the war into the domains of the Church, where one cannot help wishing him success. If he can root out monks, the Pope will have less occasion to allow *gras*, because we cannot supply them with *maigre*. It is droll that the Protestant Necker, and we Protestant fishmongers, should overset the system of fasting; but ancient Alcorans could not foresee modern contingencies.

[Footnote 1: On January 8th Sir George Rodney defeated the Spanish fleet, which was on its way to join the force blockading Gibraltar, and took the commander himself, Don Juan de Langara, prisoner.]

[Footnote 2: Necker's measure, to which Walpole alludes, was the imposition of a property tax of 5 per cent. on all classes, even on the clergy.]

I have told you that politics absorb all private news. I am going to a ball this evening, which the Duke and Duchess of Bolton give to their Royal Highnesses of Gloucester, who have now a very numerous Court. It seems very improper for me to be at a ball; but you see that, on the contrary, it is propriety that carries me thither. I am heartily weary both of diversions and politics, and am more than half inclined to retire to Strawberry. I have renounced dining abroad, and hide myself as much as I can; but can one pin on one's breast a label to signify, that, though one is sensible of being Methusalem in constitution, one must sometimes be seen in a crowd for such and such reasons? I do often exaggerate my pleas of bad health; and, could I live entirely alone, would proclaim myself incurable; but, should one repent, one becomes ridiculous by returning to the world; or one must have a companion, which I never will have; or one opens a door to legatees, if one advertises ill-health. Well! I must act with as much common sense as I can; and, when one takes no part, one must temper one's conduct; and, when the world is too young for one, not shock it, nor contradict it, nor affix a peculiar character, but trust to its indifference for not drawing notice, when one does not desire to be noticed. Rabelais's "Fais ce que tu voudras" is not very difficult when one wishes to do nothing. I have always been offended at those who will belong to a world with which they have nothing to do. I have perceived that every age has not only a new language and new modes, but a new way of articulating. At first I thought myself grown deaf when with young people; but perceived that I understood my contemporaries, though they whispered. Well! I must go amongst those I do not comprehend so well, but shall leave them when they go to supper.

THE GORDON RIOTS.

TO SIR HORACE MANN.

STRAWBERRY HILL, *June* 5, 1780.

Not a syllable yet from General Clinton. There has been a battle at sea in the West Indies, which we might have gained; know we did not, but not why: and all this is forgotten already in a fresher event. I have said for some time that the field is so extensive, and the occurrences so numerous, and so much pains are taken to involve them in falsehoods and mystery, and opinions are so divided, that all evidences will be dead before a single part can be cleared up; but I have not time, nor you patience, for my reflections. I must hurry to the history of the day. The Jack of Leyden of the age, Lord George Gordon,[1] gave notice to the House of Commons last week, that he would, on Friday, bring in the petition of the Protestant Association; and he openly declared to his disciples, that he would not carry it unless *a noble army of martyrs, not fewer than forty thousand*, would accompany him. Forty thousand, led by such a lamb, were more likely to prove butchers than victims; and so, in good truth, they were very near being. Have you faith enough in me to believe that the sole precaution taken was, that the Cabinet Council on Thursday empowered the First Lord of the Treasury to give proper orders to the civil magistrates to keep the peace,—and his Lordship forgot it!

[Footnote 1: Lord George Gordon was a younger son of the Duke of Gordon; and because the Parliament had passed a Bill to relieve the Roman Catholics from some of the disabilities which seemed no longer desirable nor just to maintain, he instigated a body calling itself the Protestant Association to present a monster petition to the House of Commons, and headed a procession of at least fifty thousand to march with it to the House. The processionists behaved with great violence on their march, insulting those members of both Houses whom they thought unfavourable to their views; and, when the House adjourned without taking their petition into consideration, they began to commit the most violent outrages. They burnt Newgate; they burnt the house of the great Chief Justice, Lord Mansfield; and for two days seemed masters of London, till the King himself summoned a Privy Council, and issued orders for the troops to put down the rioters. Many of the rioters were brought to trial and executed. Lord George, being prosecuted for high treason, to which his offence did not amount, instead of for sedition, was acquitted, to the great indignation of the French historian, Lacretelle, that "Cet extravagant scelerat ne paya point de sa tete un tel crime."]

Early on Friday morning the conservators of the Church of England assembled in *St. George's* Fields to encounter the dragon, the old serpent, and marched in lines of six and six—about thirteen thousand only, as they were computed—with a petition as long as the procession, which the apostle himself presented; but, though he had given out most Christian injunctions for peaceable behaviour, he did everything in his power to promote a massacre. He demanded immediate repeal of toleration, told Lord North he could have him torn to pieces, and, running every minute to the door or windows, bawled to the populace that Lord North would give them no redress, and that now this member, now that, was speaking against them.

In the mean time, the Peers, going to their own Chamber, and as yet not concerned in the petition, were assaulted; many of their glasses were broken, and many of their persons torn out of the carriages. Lord Boston was thrown down and almost trampled to death; and the two Secretaries of State, the Master of the Ordnance, and Lord Willoughby were stripped of their bags or wigs, and the three first came into the House with their hair all dishevelled. The chariots of Sir George Savile and Charles Turner, two leading advocates for the late toleration, though in Opposition, were demolished; and the Duke of Richmond and Burke were denounced to the mob as proper objects for sacrifice. Lord Mahon laboured to pacify the tempest, and towards eight and nine, prevailed on so many to disperse, that the Lords rose and departed in quiet; but every avenue to the other House was besieged and blockaded, and for four hours they kept their doors locked, though some of the warmest members proposed to sally out, sword in hand, and cut their way. Lord North and that House behaved with great firmness, and would not submit to give any other satisfaction to the rioters, than to consent to take the Popish laws into consideration on the following Tuesday; and, calling the Justices of the Peace, empowered them to call out the whole force of the country to quell the riot.

The magistrates soon brought the Horse and Foot Guards, and the pious ragamuffins soon fled; so little enthusiasm fortunately had inspired them; at least all their religion consisted in outrage and plunder; for the Duke of Northumberland, General Grant, Mr. Mackinsy, and others, had their pockets picked of their watches and snuff-boxes. Happily, not a single life was lost.

This tumult, which was over between nine and ten at night, had scarce ceased before it broke out in two other quarters. Old Haslang's[1] Chapel was broken open and plundered; and, as he is a Prince of Smugglers as well as Bavarian Minister, great quantities of run tea and contraband goods were found in his house. This one cannot lament; and still less, as the old wretch has for these forty years usurped a hired house, and, though the proprietor for many years has offered to remit his arrears of rent, he will neither quit the house nor pay for it.

[Footnote 1: Count Haslang was the Bavarian Minister.]

Monsieur Cordon, the Sardinian Minister, suffered still more. The mob forced his chapel, stole two silver lamps, demolished everything else, threw the benches into the street, set them on fire, carried the brands into the chapel, and set fire to that; and, when the engines came, would not suffer them to play till the Guards arrived, and saved the house and probably all that part of the town. Poor Madame Cordon was confined by illness. My cousin, Thomas Walpole, who lives in Lincoln's Inn Fields, went to her rescue, and dragged her, for she could scarce stand with terror and weakness, to his own house.

I doubt this narrative will not re-approach you and Mr. Wyndham. I have received yours of the 20th of last month.

You will be indignant that such a mad dog as Lord George should not be knocked on the head. Colonel Murray did tell him in the House, that, if any lives were lost, his Lordship should join the number. Nor yet is he so lunatic as to deserve pity. Besides being very debauched, he has more knavery than mission. What will be decided on him, I do not know; every man that heard him can convict him of the worst kind of sedition: but it is dangerous to constitute a rascal a martyr. I trust we have not much holy fury left; I am persuaded that there was far more dissoluteness than enthusiasm in the mob: yet the episode is very disagreeable. I came from town yesterday to avoid the birthday [June 4]. We have a report here that the Papists last night burnt a Presbyterian meeting–house, but I credit nothing now on the first report. It was said to be intended on Saturday, and the Guards patrolled the streets at night; but it is very likely that Saint George Gordon spread the insinuation himself.

My letter cannot set out before to-morrow; therefore I will postpone the conclusion. In the mean time I must scold you very seriously for the cameo you have sent me by Mr. Morrice. This house is full of your presents and of my blushes. I love any one of them as an earnest of your friendship; but I hate so many. You force upon me an air most contrary to my disposition. I cannot thank you for your kindness; I entreated you to send me nothing more. You leave me no alternative but to seem interested or ungrateful. I can only check your generosity by being brutal. If I had a grain of power, I would affront you and call your presents bribes. I never gave you anything but a coffee-pot. If I could buy a diamond as big as the Caligula, and a less would not be so valuable, I would send it you. In one word, I will not accept the cameo, unless you give me a promise under your hand that it shall be the last present you send me. I cannot stir about this house without your gifts staring me in the face. Do you think I have no conscience? I am sorry Mr. Morrice is no better, and wonder at his return. What can invite him to this country? Home never was so homely.

6th.

It is not true that a meeting-house has been burnt. I believe a Popish chapel in the city has been attacked: and they talk here of some disturbance yesterday, which is probable; for, when grace, robbery, and mischief make an alliance, they do not like to give over:—but ten miles from the spot are a thousand from truth. My letter must go to town before night, or would be too late for the post. If you do not hear from me again immediately, you will be sure that this *bourrasque* has subsided.

Thursday 8th.

I am exceedingly vexed. I sent this letter to Berkeley Square on Tuesday, but by the present confusions my servant did not receive it in time. I came myself yesterday, and found a horrible scene. Lord Mansfield's house was just burnt down, and at night there were shocking disorders. London and Southwark were on fire in six places; but the regular troops quelled the sedition by daybreak, and everything now is quiet. A camp of ten thousand men is formed in Hyde Park, and regiments of horse and foot arrive every hour.

Friday morn, 9th.

All has been quiet to-night. I am going to Strawberry for a little rest. Your nephew told me last night that he sends you constant journals just now.

HOGARTH—COLONEL CHARTERIS—ARCHBISHOP BLACKBURNE—JERVAS—RICHARDSON'S POETRY.

TO SIR DAVID DALRYMPLE.

Dec. 11, 1780.

I should have been shamefully ungrateful, Sir, if I could ever forget all the favours I have received from you, and had omitted any mark of respect to you that it was in my power to show. Indeed, what you are so good as to thank me for was a poor trifle, but it was all I had or shall have of the kind. It was imperfect too, as some painters of name have died since it was printed, which was nine years ago. They will be added with your kind notices, should I live, which is not probable, to see a new edition wanted. Sixty-three years, and a great deal of illness, are too speaking mementos not to be attended to; and when the public has been more indulgent than one had any right to expect, it is not decent to load it with one's dotage!

I believe, Sir, that I may have been over-candid to Hogarth, and that his spirit and youth and talent may have hurried him into more real caricatures than I specified; yet he certainly restrained his bent that way pretty early. Charteris,[1] I have seen; but though some years older than you, Sir, I cannot say I have at all a perfect idea of him; nor did I ever hear the curious anecdote you tell me of the banker and my father. I was much better acquainted with Archbishop Blackburne. He lived within two doors of my father in Downing Street, and took much notice of me when I was near man.... He was a little hurt at not being raised to Canterbury on Wake's death [1737], and said to my father, "You did not think on me; but it is true, I am too old, I am too old." Perhaps, Sir, these are gossiping stories, but at least they hurt nobody now.

[Footnote 1: Colonel Charteris, satirised by Hogarth's introduction of his portrait in the "Harlot's Progress," was at his death still more bitterly branded by Swift's friend, Dr. Arbuthnot, in the epitaph he proposed for him: "Here continueth to rot the body of Francis Charteris, who, in the course of his long life, displayed every vice except prodigality and hypocrisy. His insatiable avarice saved him from the first: his matchless impudence from the second." And he concludes it with the explanation that his life was not useless, since "it was intended to show by his example of how small estimation inordinate wealth is in the sight of Almighty God, since He bestowed it on the most unworthy of mortals."]

I can say little, Sir, for my stupidity or forgetfulness about Hogarth's poetry, which I still am not sure I ever heard, though I knew him so well; but it is an additional argument for my distrusting myself, if my memory fails, which is very possible. A whole volume of Richardson's[1] poetry has been published since my volume was printed, not much to the honour of his muse, but exceedingly so to that of his piety and amiable heart. You will be pleased, too, Sir, with a story Lord Chesterfield told me (too late too) of Jervas,[2] who piqued himself on the reverse, on total infidelity. One day that he had talked very indecently in that strain, Dr. Arbuthnot,[3] who was as devout as Richardson, said to him, "Come, Jervas, this is all an air and affectation; nobody is a sounder believer than you."—"I!" said Jervas, "I believe nothing."—"Yes, but you do," replied the Doctor; "nay, you not only believe, but practise: you are so scrupulous an observer of the commandments, that you never make the likeness of anything that is in heaven above, or on the earth beneath, or," &c.

[Footnote 1: Richardson was a London bookseller, the author of the three longest novels in the English language—"Pamela," "Clarissa Harbour," and "Sir Charles Grandison." They were extravagantly praised in their day. But it was to ridicule "Pamela" that Fielding wrote "Joseph Andrews."]

[Footnote 2: Jervas was a fashionable portrait-painter in the first half of the century. Lady Mary Montague, in one of her letters, speaks of him in terms of the highest praise.]

[Footnote 3: Dr. Arbuthnot was the author of the celebrated satire on the Partition Treaties, entitled "The History of John Bull," to which Englishmen have ever since owed their popular nickname. It is to him also that Pope dedicated the Prologue to his "Satires and Epistles."]

I fear, Sir, this letter is too long for thanks, and that I have been proving what I have said, of my growing superannuated; but, having made my will in my last volume, you may look on this as a codicil.

P.S.—I had sealed my letter, Sir, but break it open, lest you should think soon, that I do not know what I say, or break my resolution lightly. I shall be able to send you in about two months a very curious work that I am going to print, and is actually in the press; but there is not a syllable of my writing in it. It is a discovery just made of two very ancient manuscripts, copies of which were found in two or three libraries in Germany, and of which there are more complete manuscripts at Cambridge. They are of the eleventh century at lowest, and prove that painting in oil was then known, above three hundred years before the pretended invention of Van Eyck. The manuscripts themselves will be printed, with a full introductory Dissertation by the discoverer, Mr. Raspe, a very learned German, formerly librarian to the Landgrave of Hesse, and who writes English surprisingly well. The manuscripts are in the most barbarous monkish Latin, and are much such works as our booksellers publish of receipts for mixing colours, varnishes, &c. One of the authors, who calls himself Theophilus, was a monk; the other, Heraclius, is totally unknown; but the proofs are unquestionable. As my press is out of order, and that besides it would take up too much time to print them there, they will be printed here at my expense, and if there is any surplus, it will be for Raspe's benefit.

THE PRINCE OF WALES—HURRICANE AT BARBADOES—A "VOICE FROM ST. HELENA."

TO SIR HORACE MANN.

BERKELEY SQUARE, *Dec.* 31, 1780.

I have received, and thank you much for the curious history of the Count and Countess of Albany; what a wretched conclusion of a wretched family! Surely no royal race was ever so drawn to the dregs! The other Countess [Orford] you mention seems to approach still nearer to dissolution. Her death a year or two ago might have prevented the sale of the pictures,—not that I know it would. Who can say what madness in the hands of villany would or would not have done? Now, I think, her dying would only put more into the reach of rascals. But I am indifferent what they do; nor, but thus occasionally, shall I throw away a thought on that chapter.

All chance of accommodation with Holland is vanished. Count Welderen and his wife departed this morning. All they who are to gain by privateers and captures are delighted with a new field of plunder. Piracy is more practicable than victory. Not being an admirer of wars, I shall reserve my *feux de joie* for peace.

My letters, I think, are rather eras than journals. Three days ago commenced another date—the establishment of a family for the Prince of Wales. I do not know all the names, and fewer of the faces that compose it; nor intend. I, who kissed the hand of George I., have no colt's tooth for the Court of George IV. Nothing is so ridiculous as an antique face in a juvenile drawing-room. I believe that they who have spirits enough to be absurd in their decrepitude, are happy, for they certainly are not sensible of their folly; but I, who have never forgotten what I thought in my youth of such superannuated idiots, dread nothing more than misplacing myself in my old age. In truth, I feel no such appetite; and, excepting the young of my own family, about whom I am interested, I have mighty small satisfaction in the company of *posterity*; for so the present generation seem to me. I would contribute anything to their pleasure, but what cannot contribute to it—my own presence. Alas! how many of this age are swept away before me: six thousand have been mowed down at once by the late hurricane at Barbadoes alone! How Europe is paying the debts it owes to America! Were I a poet, I would paint hosts of Mexicans and Peruvians crowding the shores of Styx, and insulting the multitudes of the usurpers of their continent that have been sending themselves thither for these five or six years. The poor Africans, too, have no call to be merciful to European ghosts. Those miserable slaves have just now seen whole crews of men-of-war swallowed by the late hurricane.

We do not yet know the extent of our loss. You would think it very slight, if you saw how little impression it makes on a luxurious capital. An overgrown metropolis has less sensibility than marble; nor can it be conceived by those not conversant in one. I remember hearing what diverted me then; a young gentlewoman, a native of our rock, St. Helena, and who had never stirred beyond it, being struck with the emotion occasioned there by the arrival of one or two of our China ships, said to the captain, "There must be a great solitude in London as often as the China ships come away!" Her imagination could not have compassed the idea, if she had been told that six years of war, the absence of an army of fifty or sixty thousand men of all our squadrons, and a new debt of many, many millions, would not make an alteration in the receipts at the door of a single theatre in London. I do not boast of, or applaud, this profligate apathy. When pleasure is our business, our business is never pleasure; and, if four wars cannot awaken us, we shall die in a dream!

NAVAL MOVEMENTS—SIEGE OF GIBRALTAR—FEMALE FASHIONS.

TO SIR HORACE MANN.

BERKELEY SQUARE, *Sept.* 7, 1781.

The combined fleets, to the amount of forty-seven or forty-nine sail, brought news of their own arrival at the mouth of the Channel a day or two before your letter, of August the 18th, brought an account of that probability, and of the detachment for Minorca. Admiral Darby, on a false alarm, or perhaps, a true one, had returned to Torbay a week ago, where he is waiting for reinforcements. This is the fourth or fifth day since the appearance of the enemy off Scilly. It is thought, I find here (whither I came to-day), that the great object is our Jamaica fleet; but that a detachment is gone to Ireland to do what mischief they can on the coast before our ally, the Equinox, will beseech them to retire. Much less force than this Armada would have done more harm two years ago, when they left a card at Plymouth, than this can do; as Plymouth is now very strong, and that there are great disciplined armies now in both islands. Of Gibraltar we have no apprehensions.[1] I know less of Minorca.

[Footnote 1: The Spaniards and French had been blockading Gibraltar for more than two years, and continued the siege till the autumn of 1782, when the blockading fleet was totally destroyed by the Governor, General Eliot, who was created Lord Heathfield for the achievement.]

Lord George Gordon is standing candidate for the City of London on an accidental vacancy; but his premature alarm last year has had a sinister effect. In short, those riots have made mankind sick of them, and give him no chance of success.

What can I say more? Nothing at present; but I will the moment any event presents itself. My hope is that, after a fermentation, there will be a settlement, and that peace will arise out of it.

The decree[1] you sent me against high heads diverted me. It is as necessary here, but would not have such expeditious effect. The Queen has never admitted feathers at Court; but, though the nation has grown excellent courtiers, Fashion remained in opposition, and not a plume less was worn anywhere else. Some centuries ago, the Clergy preached against monstrous head-dresses; but Religion had no more power than our Queen. It is better to leave the Mode to its own vagaries; if she is not contradicted, she seldom remains long in the same mood. She is very despotic; but, though her reign is endless, her laws are repealed as fast as made.

[Footnote 1: *"The decree."* The Grand Duke of Tuscany had just issued an order prohibiting high head-dresses.]

Mrs. Damer,[1] General Conway's daughter, is going abroad to confirm a very delicate constitution—I believe, at Naples. I will say very few words on her, after telling you that, besides being his daughter, I love her as my own child. It is not from wanting matter, but from having too much. She has one of the most solid understandings I ever knew, astonishingly improved, but with so much reserve and modesty, that I have often told Mr. Conway he does not know the extent of her capacity and the solidity of her reason. We have by accident discovered, that she writes Latin like Pliny, and is learning Greek. In Italy she will be a prodigy. She models like Bernini, has excelled the moderns in the similitudes of her busts, and has lately begun one in marble. You must keep all knowledge of these talents and acquisitions to yourself; she would never forgive my mentioning, at least her mental qualities. You may just hint that I talked of her statuary, as you may assist her if she has a mind to borrow anything to copy from the Great Duke's collection. Lady William Campbell, her uncle's widow, accompanies, who is a very reasonable woman too, and equally shy. If they return through Florence, pray give them a parcel of my letters. I had been told your nephew would make you a visit this autumn, but I have heard nothing from him. If you should see him, pray give him the parcel, for he will return sooner than they.

[Footnote 1: Mrs. Damer had devoted herself to sculpture with an ability which has given her a high place among artists. The bust of Nelson in the armoury at Windsor is her work.]

I have a gouty pain in my hand, that would prevent my saying more, had I more to say.

CAPITULATION OF LORD CORNWALLIS—PITT AND FOX.

TO SIR HORACE MANN.

Nov. 29, 1781.

Your nephew is arrived, as he has told you himself; the sight of him, for he called on me the next morning, was more than ordinarily welcome, though your letter of the 10th, which I received the night before, had dispelled many of my fears. I will now unfold them to you. A packet-boat from Ostend was lost last week, and your nephew was named for one of the passengers. As Mrs. Noel had expected him for a fortnight, I own my apprehensions were strengthened; but I will say no more on a dissipated panic. However, this incident and his half-wreck at Lerici will, I hope, prevent him from the future from staying with you so late in the year; and I see by your letter that you agree with me, of which I should be sure though you had not said so.

I mentioned on Tuesday the captivity of Lord Cornwallis and his army, the Columbus who was to bestow America on us again. A second army[1] taken in a drag-net is an uncommon event, and happened but once to the Romans, who sought adventures everywhere. We have not lowered our tone on this new disgrace, though I think we shall talk no more of insisting on *implicit submission*, which would rather be a gasconade than firmness. In fact, there is one very unlucky circumstance already come out, which must drive every American, to a man, from ever calling himself our friend. By the tenth article of the capitulation, Lord Cornwallis demanded that the loyal Americans in his army should not be punished. This was flatly refused, and he has left them to be hanged. I doubt no vote of Parliament will be able to blanch such a—such a—I don't know what the word is for it; he must get his uncle the Archbishop to christen it; there is no name for it in any Pagan vocabulary. I suppose it will have a patent for being called Necessity. Well! there ends another volume of the American war. It looks a little as if the history of it would be all we should have for it, except forty millions[2] of debt, and three other wars that have grown out of it, and that do not seem so near to a conclusion. They say that Monsieur de Maurepas, who is dying, being told that the Duc de Lauzun had brought the news of Lord Cornwallis's surrender, said, from Racine's "Mithridate" I think:—

Mes derniers regards out vu fuir les Romains.

How Lord Chatham will frown when they meet! for, since I began my letter, the papers say that Maurepas is dead. The Duc de Nivernois, it is said, is likely to succeed him as Minister; which is probable, as they were brothers-in-law and friends, and the one would naturally recommend the other. Perhaps, not for long, as the Queen's influence gains ground.

[Footnote 1: The capitulation of Burgoyne at Saratoga has been mentioned in a previous letter; and in October, 1781, Lord Cornwallis, whose army was reduced to seven thousand men, was induced to surrender to Washington, who, with eighteen thousand, had blockaded him at a village called Yorktown; and it was the news of this disaster which at last compelled the King to consent to relinquish the war.]

[Footnote 2: "*Forty millions.*" Burke, in one of his speeches, asserted the expense to have been L70,000,000, "besides one hundred thousand men."]

The warmth in the House of Commons is prodigiously rekindled; but Lord Cornwallis's fate has cost the Administration no ground *there*. The names of most *eclat* in the Opposition are two names to which those walls have been much accustomed at the same period—CHARLES FOX and WILLIAM PITT, second son of Lord Chatham.[1] Eloquence is the only one of our brilliant qualities that does not seem to have degenerated rapidly—but I shall leave debates to your nephew, now an ear-witness: I could only re-echo newspapers. Is it not another odd coincidence of events, that while the father Laurens is prisoner to Lord Cornwallis as Constable of the Tower, the son Laurens signed the capitulation by which Lord Cornwallis became prisoner? It is said too, I don't know if truly, that this capitulation and that of Saratoga were signed on the same anniversary. These are certainly the speculations of an idle man, and the more trifling when one considers the moment. But alas! what would *my* most grave speculations avail? From the hour that fatal egg, the Stamp Act, was laid, I disliked it and all the vipers hatched from it. I now hear many curse it, who fed the vermin with poisonous weeds. Yet the guilty and the innocent rue it equally hitherto! I would not answer for what is to come! Seven years of miscarriages may sour the sweetest tempers, and the most sweetened. Oh! where is the Dove with the olive-branch? Long ago I told you that you and I might not live to see an end of the American war. It is very near its end indeed now—its consequences are far from a conclusion. In some respects, they are commencing a new date, which will reach far beyond *us*. I desire not to pry into that book of futurity. Could I finish my course in peace—but one must take the chequered scenes of life as they come. What signifies whether the elements are serene or turbulent, when a private old man slips away? What has he and the world's concerns to do with one another? He may sigh for his country, and babble about it; but he might as well sit quiet and read or tell old stories; the past is as important to him as the future.

[Footnote 1: Charles Fox and William Pitt were the second sons of the first Lord Holland and the first Lord Chatham, Fox being by some years the older. They were both men of great eloquence; but in this (as in every other point) Pitt was the superior, even by the confession of Lord Macaulay. As Prime Minister from 1783 to 1801, and afterwards in 1804-5, Pitt proved himself the greatest statesman, the man more in advance of his age than any of his predecessors or successors; while Fox's career was for the most part one of an opposition so rancorous, and so destitute of all patriotism, that he even exulted over the disasters of Burgoyne and Cornwallis, and afterwards over the defeat of the Austrians at Marengo in 1800, avowedly because the Austrians were our allies, and it was a heavy blow to Pitt and his policy.]

Dec. 3.

I had not sealed my letter, as it cannot set out till to-morrow; and since I wrote it I have received yours, of the 20th of November, by your courier.

I congratulate you on the success of your attempts, and admire the heroic refusal of the General.[1] I shall certainly obey you, and not mention it. Indeed, it would not easily be believed here, where as many pence are irresistible....

[Footnote 1: General the Hon. James Murray was governor of Minorca, which was besieged by the Spaniards, and was offered a vast bribe by the Duc de Crillon, the commander of the besiegers, to give up Port St. Philip.]

Don't trouble yourself about the third set of "Galuzzi." They are to be had here now, and those for whom I intended them can buy them. I have not made so much progress as I intended, and have not yet quite finished the second volume. I detest Cosmo the Great. I am sorry, either that he was so able a man, or so successful a man. When tyrants are great men they should miscarry; if they are fools, they will miscarry of course. Pray, is there any picture of Camilla Martelli, Cosmo's last wife? I had never heard of her. The dolt, his son, I find used her ill, and then did the same thing. Our friend, Bianca Capello, it seems, was a worthless creature. I don't expect much entertainment but from the Life of Ferdinand the Great. It is true I have dipped into the others, particularly into the story of Cosmo the Third's wife, of whom I had read much in French Memoires; and into that of John Gaston, which was so fresh when I was at Florence; but as the author, in spite of the Great Duke's injunctions, has tried to palliate some of the worst imputations on Cosmo and his son Ferdinand, so he has been mighty modest about the Caprean amours of John Gaston and his eldest brother. Adieu! I have been writing a volume here myself. Pray remember to answer me about Camilla Martelli.

P.S.—Is there any china left in the Great Duke's collection, made by Duke Francis the First himself? Perhaps it was lately sold with what was called the refuse of the wardrobe, whence I hear some charming things were purchased, particularly the Medallions of the Medici, by Benvenuto Cellini. That sale and the "History" are enough to make the old Electress[1] shudder in her coffin.

[Footnote 1: The Electress Palatine Dowager was sister of John Gaston, the last Grand Duke of the House of Medici; after her husband's death she returned to Florence and died there.]

THE LANGUAGE PROPER FOR INSCRIPTIONS IN ENGLAND—FALL OF LORD NORTH'S MINISTRY—BRYANT.

TO THE REV. WILLIAM COLE.

April 13, 1782.

Your partiality to me, my good Sir, is much overseen, if you think me fit to correct your Latin. Alas! I have not skimmed ten pages of Latin these dozen years. I have dealt in nothing but English, French, and a little Italian; and do not think, if my life depended on it, I could write four lines of pure Latin. I have had occasion once or twice to speak that language, and soon found that all my verbs were Italian with Roman terminations. I would not on any account draw you into a scrape, by depending on my skill in what I have half forgotten. But you are in the metropolis of Latium. If you distrust your own knowledge, which I do not, especially from the specimen you have sent me, surely you must have good critics at your elbow to consult.

In truth, I do not love Roman inscriptions in lieu of our own language,[1] though, if anywhere, proper in an University; neither can I approve writing what the Romans themselves would not understand. What does it avail to give a Latin tail to a Guildhall? Though the words are used by moderns, would *major* convey to Cicero the idea of a *mayor*? *Architectus*, I believe, is the right word; but I doubt whether *veteris jam perantiquae* is classic for a dilapidated building—but do not depend on me; consult some better judges.

[Footnote 1: Walpole certainly here shows himself superior in judgement to Johnson, who, when Burke, Reynolds, and others, in a "round-robin," requested that the epitaph on Goldsmith, which was entrusted to him to draw up, should be in English instead of Latin, refused, with the absurd expression that "he would never be guilty of defacing Westminster Abbey with an English inscription."]

Though I am glad of the late *revolution*,[1] a word for which I have great reverence, I shall certainly not dispute with you thereon. I abhor exultation. If the change produces peace, I shall make a bonfire in my heart. Personal interest I have none; you and I shall certainly never profit by the politics to which we are attached. The "Archaeologic Epistle" I admire exceedingly, though I am sorry it attacks Mr. Bryant,[2] whom I love and respect. The Dean is so absurd an oaf, that he deserves to be ridiculed. Is anything more hyperbolic than his preferences of Rowley to Homer, Shakspeare, and Milton? Whether Rowley or Chatterton was the author, are the poems in any degree comparable to those authors? is not a ridiculous author an object of ridicule? I do not even guess at your meaning in your conclusive paragraph on that subject: Dictionary-writer I suppose alludes to Johnson; but surely you do not equal the compiler of a dictionary to a genuine poet? Is a brickmaker on a level with Mr. Essex? Nor can I hold that exquisite wit and satire are Billingsgate; if they were, Milles and Johnson would be able to write an answer to the "Epistle." I do as little guess whom you mean that got a pension by Toryism: if Johnson too, he got a pension for having abused pensioners, and yet took one himself, which was contemptible enough. Still less know I who preferred opposition to principles, which is not a very common case; whoever it was, as Pope says,

The way he took was strangely round about.

[Footnote 1: In March Lord North resigned, and been replaced by Lord Rockingham, who had been Prime Minister before in 1765.]

[Footnote 2: Bryant, the celebrated or notorious critic, who published a treatise in which he denied the existence of Troy, and even called in question that of Homer—a work which, whether Walpole agreed with him on this point or not, afterwards drew down on him the indignant denunciations of Byron. It was well for him that he wrote before the discoveries of Dr. Schliemann.]

HIGHWAYMEN AND FOOTPADS.

TO SIR HORACE MANN.

STRAWBERRY HILL, *Sept.* 8, 1782.

... I am perfectly ignorant of the state of the war abroad; they say we are in no pain for Gibraltar: but I know that we are in a state of war at home that is shocking. I mean, from the enormous profusion of housebreakers, highwaymen, and footpads; and, what is worse, from the savage barbarities of the two latter, who commit the most wanton cruelties. This evil is another fruit of the American war. Having no vent for the convicts that used to be transported to our late colonies, a plan was adopted for confining them on board of lighters for the term of their sentences. In those colleges, undergraduates in villainy commence Masters of Arts, and at the expiration of their studies issue as mischievous as if they had taken their degrees in law, physic, or divinity, at one of our regular universities; but, having no profession, nor testimonial to their characters, they can get no employment, and therefore live upon the public. In short, the grievance is so crying, that one dare not stir out after dinner but well-armed. If one goes abroad to dinner, you would think one was going to the relief of Gibraltar. You may judge how depraved we are, when the war has not consumed half the reprobates, nor press-gangs thinned their numbers! But no wonder—how should the morals of the people be purified, when such frantic dissipation reigns above them? Contagion does not mount, but descend. A new theatre is going to be erected merely for people of fashion, that they may not be confined to vulgar hours—that is, to day or night. Fashion is always silly, for, before it can spread far, it must be calculated for silly people; as examples of sense, wit, or ingenuity could be imitated only by a few. All the discoveries that I can perceive to have been made by the present age, is to prefer riding about the streets rather than on the roads or on the turf, and being too late for everything. Thus, though we have more public diversions than would suffice for two capitals, nobody goes to them till they are over. This is literally true. Ranelagh, that is, the music there, finishes at half an hour after ten at night; but the most fashionable set out for it, though above a mile out of town, at eleven or later. Well! but is not this censure being old and cross? were not the charming people of my youth guilty of equivalent absurdities? Oh yes; but the sensible folks of my youth had not lost America, nor dipped us in wars with half Europe, that cost us fifteen millions a year. I believe the Jews went to Ranelagh at midnight, though Titus was at Knightsbridge. But Titus demolished their Ranelagh as well as Jerusalem. Adieu!

FOX'S INDIA BILL—BALLOONS.

TO SIR HORACE MANN.

BERKELEY SQUARE, *Dec.* 2, 1783.

... Your nephew is in town, but confined by the gout. I called on him, but did not see him; yet you may be very easy, for he expects to be abroad in a day or two. I can make you as easy about another point, too; but, if you have not learnt it from him, do not take notice to him that you know it. Mrs. Noel has informed me that his daughter's treaty of marriage is broken off, and in a fortunate way. The peer, father of the lover, obliged *him* to declare off; and Mrs. Noel says that your niece is in good spirits. All this is just what one should have wished. Your nephew has sent me a good and most curious print from you of the old Pretender's marriage: I never saw one before. It is a great present to my collection of English portraits. The Farnesian books I have not yet received, and have forgotten the name of the gentleman to whom you entrusted them, and must search among your letters for it; or, tell it me again.

The politicians of London, who at present are not the most numerous corporation, are warm on a Bill for a new regulation of the East Indies, brought in by Mr. Fox.[1] Some even of his associates apprehended his being defeated, or meant to defeat him; but his marvellous abilities have hitherto triumphed conspicuously, and on two divisions in the House of Commons he had majorities of 109 and 114. On *that* field he will certainly be victorious: the forces will be more nearly balanced when the Lords fight the battle; but, though the Opposition will have more generals and more able, he is confident that his troops will overmatch theirs; and, in Parliamentary engagements, a superiority of numbers is not vanquished by the talents of the commanders, as often happens in more martial encounters. His competitor, Mr. Pitt, appears by no means an adequate rival. Just like their fathers, Mr. Pitt has brilliant language, Mr. Fox solid sense; and such luminous powers of displaying it clearly, that mere eloquence is but a Bristol stone, when set by the diamond Reason.

[Footnote 1: In the session of 1783 Fox, as the leader of the Coalition Ministry in the House of Commons, brought in a Bill for the reform of the government of India on the expiration of the existing Charter of the Company. It was denounced by Pitt as having for its principal object the perpetuation of the administration by the enormous patronage it would place at the disposal of the Treasury; and, through the interposition of the King, whose conduct on this occasion must be confessed to have been wholly unconstitutional, it was defeated in the House of Lords. The King on this dismissed the Ministry, and Pitt became Prime Minister.]

Do not wonder that we do not entirely attend to things of earth: Fashion has ascended to a higher element. All our views are directed to the air. *Balloons* occupy senators, philosophers, ladies, everybody. France gave us the *ton*; and, as yet, we have not come up to our model. Their monarch is so struck with the heroism of two of his subjects who adventured their persons in two of these new *floating batteries*, that he has ordered statues of them, and contributed a vast sum towards their marble immortality. All this may be very important: to me it looks somewhat foolish. Very early in my life I remember this town at gaze on a man who *flew down* a rope from the top of St. Martin's steeple; now, late in my day, people are staring at a voyage to the moon. The former Icarus broke his neck at a subsequent flight: when a similar accident happens to modern knights–errant, adieu to air–balloons.

Apropos, I doubt these new kites have put young Astley's nose out of joint, who went to Paris lately under their Queen's protection,[1] and expected to be Prime Minister, though he only ventured his neck by dancing a minuet on three horses at full gallop, and really in that attitude has as much grace as the Apollo Belvedere. When the arts are brought to such perfection in Europe, who would go, like Sir Joseph Banks, in search of islands in the Atlantic, where the natives in six thousand years have not improved the science of carving fishing-hooks out of bones or flints! Well! I hope these new mechanic meteors will prove only playthings for the learned and the idle, and not be converted into new engines of destruction to the human race, as is so often the case of refinements or discoveries in science. *The wicked wit of man always studies to apply the result of talents to enslaving, destroying, or cheating his fellow-creatures.* Could we reach the moon, we should think of reducing it to a province of some European kingdom.

[Footnote 1: In the spring Montgolfier had made the first ascent in a balloon, which as a novelty created great excitement in Paris. The Queen gave permission for the balloon to be called by her name; and the next year, during a visit of Gustavus, King of Sweden, to Versailles, it went up from the grounds of the Trianon, and made a successful voyage to Chantilly (the Editor's "Life of Marie Antoinette," c. 19).]

5th.

P.S.—The Opposition in the House of Commons were so humbled by their two defeats, that, though Mr. Pitt had declared he would contest every clause (of the India Bill) in the committee, (where in truth, if the Bill is so bad as he says, he ought at least to have tried to amend it,) that he slunk from the contest, and all the blanks were filled up without obstruction, the opponents promising only to resist it in its last stage on Monday next; but really, having no hopes but in the House of Lords, where, however, I do not believe they expect to succeed. Mr. Pitt's reputation is much sunk; nor, though he is a much more correct logician than his father, has he the same firmness and perseverance. It is no wonder that he was dazzled by his own premature fame; yet his late checks may be of use to him, and teach him to appreciate his strength better, or to wait till it is confirmed. Had he listed under Mr. Fox, who loved and courted him, he would not only have discovered modesty, but have been more likely to succeed him, than by commencing his competitor. But what have I to do to look into futurity?[1]

[Footnote 1: Evidently not much: as few prophecies have been more strikingly and speedily falsified.]

BALLOONS.

TO THE HON. H.S. CONWAY.

STRAWBERRY HILL, *Oct.* 15, 1784.

As I have heard nothing from you, I flatter myself Lady Aylesbury mends, or I think you would have brought her again to the physicians: you will, I conclude, next week, as towards the end of it the ten days they named will be expired. I must be in town myself about Thursday on some little business of my own.

As I was writing this, my servants called me away to see a balloon; I suppose Blanchard's, that was to be let off from Chelsea this morning. I saw it from the common field before the window of my round tower. It appeared about a third of the size of the moon, or less, when setting, something above the tops of the trees on the level horizon. It was then descending; and, after rising and declining a little, it sunk slowly behind the trees, I should think about or beyond Sunbury, at five minutes after one. But you know I am a very inexact guesser at measures and distances, and may be mistaken in many miles; and you know how little I have attended to these *airgonauts*: only t'other night I diverted myself with a sort of meditation on future *airgonation*, supposing that it will not only be perfected, but will depose navigation. I did not finish it, because I am not skilled, like the gentleman that used to write political ship-news, in that style which I wanted to perfect my essay: but in the prelude I observed how ignorant the ancients were in supposing Icarus melted the wax of his wings by too near access to the sun, whereas he would have been frozen to death before he made the first post on that road. Next, I discovered an alliance between Bishop Wilkins's[1] art of flying and his plan of universal language; the latter of which he no doubt calculated to prevent the want of an interpreter when he should arrive at the moon.

[Footnote 1: Dr. Wilkins, Bishop of Chester in the reign of Charles II., was chiefly instrumental in the foundation of the Royal Society. Among his works was a treatise to prove that "It is probable there may be another habitable world in the moon, with a discourse concerning the possibility of a passage thither." Burnet ("Hist. of his Own Times," Anno 1661) says of him, "He was a great observer and promoter of experimental philosophy, which was then a new thing. He was naturally ambitious, but was the wisest clergyman I ever knew." He married Cromwell's sister, and his daughter was the wife of Archbishop Tillotson.]

But I chiefly amused myself with ideas of the change that would be made in the world by the substitution of balloons to ships. I supposed our seaports to become *deserted villages*; and Salisbury Plain, Newmarket Heath, (another canvass for alteration of ideas,) and all downs (but *the* Downs) arising into dockyards for aerial vessels. Such a field would be ample in furnishing new speculations. But to come to my ship-news:—

"The good balloon Daedalus, Captain Wing-ate, will fly in a few days for China; he will stop at the top of the Monument to take in passengers.

"Arrived on Brand-sands, the Vulture, Captain Nabob; the Tortoise snow, from Lapland; the Pet-en-l'air, from Versailles; the Dreadnought, from Mount Etna, Sir W. Hamilton, commander; the Tympany, Montgolfier; and the Mine-A-in-a-bandbox, from the Cape of Good Hope. Foundered in a hurricane, the Bird of Paradise, from Mount Ararat. The Bubble, Sheldon, took fire, and was burnt to her gallery; and the Phoenix is to be cut down to a second-rate."

In those days Old Sarum will again be a town and have houses in it. There will be fights in the air with wind-guns and bows and arrows; and there will be prodigious increase of land for tillage, especially in France, by breaking up all public roads as useless. But enough of my fooleries; for which I am sorry you must pay double postage.

HIS LETTERS ON LITERATURE—DISADVANTAGE OF MODERN WRITERS—COMPARISON OF LADY MARY WORTLEY WITH MADAME DE SEVIGNE.

TO JOHN PINKERTON, ESQ.

June 22, 1785.

Letters of Horace Walpole, V2

Since I received your book,[1] Sir, I scarce ceased from reading till I had finished it; so admirable I found it, and so full of good sense, brightly delivered. Nay, I am pleased with myself, too, for having formed the same opinions with you on several points, in which we do not agree with the generality of men. On some topics, I confess frankly, I do not concur with you: considering how many you have touched, it would be wonderful if we agreed on all, or I should not be sincere if I said I did. There are others on which I have formed no opinion; for I should give myself an impertinent air, with no truth, if I pretended to have any knowledge of many subjects, of which, young as you are, you seem to have made yourself master. Indeed, I have gone deeply into nothing, and therefore shall not discuss those heads on which we differ most; as probably I should not defend my own opinions well. There is but one part of your work to which I will venture any objection, though you have considered it much, and I little, very little indeed, with regard to your proposal, which to me is but two days old: I mean your plan for the improvement of our language, which I allow has some defects, and which wants correction in several particulars. The specific amendment which you propose, and to which I object, is the addition of *a's* and *o's* to our terminations. To change *s* for *a* in the plural number of our substantives and adjectives, would be so violent an alteration, that I believe neither the power of Power nor the power of Genius would be able to effect it. In most cases I am convinced that very strong innovations are more likely to make impression than small and almost imperceptible differences, as in religion, medicine, politics, &c.; but I do not think that language can be treated in the same manner, especially in a refined age.

[Footnote 1: Mr. Pinkerton was a Scotch lawyer, who published a volume entitled "Letters on Literature" under the name of Heron; which, however, he afterwards suppressed, as full of ill-considered ideas, which was not strange, as he was only twenty-five.]

When a nation first emerges from barbarism, two or three masterly writers may operate wonders; and the fewer the number of writers, as the number is small at such a period, the more absolute is their authority. But when a country has been polishing itself for two or three centuries, and when, consequently, authors are innumerable, the most super-eminent genius (or whoever is esteemed so, though without foundation) possesses very limited empire, and is far from meeting implicit obedience. Every petty writer will contest very novel institutions: every inch of change in any language will be disputed; and the language will remain as it was, longer than the tribunal which should dictate very heterogeneous alterations. With regard to adding *a* or *o* to final consonants, consider, Sir, should the usage be adopted, what havoc it would make! All our poetry would be defective in metre, or would become at once as obsolete as Chaucer; and could we promise ourselves, that, though we should acquire better harmony and more rhymes, we should have a new crop of poets, to replace Milton, Dryden, Gray, and, I am sorry you will not allow me to add, Pope! You might enjoin our prose to be reformed, as you have done by the "Spectator" in your thirty-fourth Letter; but try Dryden's "Ode" by your new institution.

I beg your pardon for these trivial observations: I assure you I could write a letter ten times as long, if I were to specify all I like in your work. I more than like most of it; and I am charmed with your glorious love of liberty, and your other humane and noble sentiments. Your book I shall with great pleasure send to Mr. Colman[1]: may I tell him, without naming you, that it is written by the author of the comedy I offered to him? He must be struck with your very handsome and generous conduct in printing your encomiums on him, after his rejecting your piece. It is as great as uncommon, and gives me as good an opinion of your heart, Sir, as your book does of your great sense. Both assure me that you will not take ill the liberty I have used in expressing my doubts on your plan for amending our language, or for any I may use in dissenting from a few other sentiments in your work; as I shall in what I think your too low opinion of some of the French writers, of your preferring Lady Mary Wortley to Madame de Sevigne, and of your esteeming Mr. Hume a man of deeper and more solid understanding than Mr. Gray. In the two last articles it is impossible to think more differently than we do.[2] In Lady Mary's "Letters," which I never could read but once, I discovered no merit of any sort; yet I have seen others by her (unpublished) that have a good deal of wit; and for Mr. Hume, give me leave to say that I think your opinion, "that he might have ruled a state," ought to be qualified a little; as in the very next page you say, his "History" is "a mere apology for prerogative," and a very weak one. If he could have ruled a state, one must presume, at best, that he would have been an able tyrant; and yet I should suspect that a man, who, sitting coolly in his chamber, could forge but a weak apology for the prerogative, would not have exercised it very wisely. I knew personally and well both Mr. Hume and Mr. Gray, and thought there was no degree of comparison between their understandings; and, in fact, Mr. Hume's writings were so superior to his conversation, that I frequently said he understood nothing till he had written upon it. What you say, Sir, of the discord in his "History" from his love of prerogative and hatred of churchmen, flatters me much; as I have taken notice of that very unnatural discord in a piece I printed some years ago, but did not publish, and which I will show to you when I have the pleasure of seeing you here; a satisfaction I shall be glad to taste, whenever you will let me know you are at leisure after the beginning of next week. I have the honour to be, Sir, &c.

[Footnote 1: Mr. Colman was manager of the Haymarket Theatre.]

[Footnote 2: It is difficult to judge what were the published letters of Lady Mary which Walpole could have seen. If Mr. Pinkerton preferred them to those of Mme. de Sevigne, he could certainly have adduced plausible reasons for his preference. There is far greater variety in them, as was natural from the different lives led by the two fair writers. Mme. de Sevigne's was almost confined to Paris and the Court; Lady Mary was a great traveller. Her husband was English ambassador at Constantinople and other places, and her letters give descriptions of that city, of Vienna, the Hague, Venice, Rome, Naples, &c., &c. It may be fitly pointed out here that in a letter to Lord Strafford Walpole expresses an opinion that letter-writing is a branch of literature in which women are likely to excel men; "for our sex is too jealous of the reputation of good sense to hazard a thousand trifles and negligences which give grace, ease, and familiarity to correspondence."]

CRITICISM ON VARIOUS AUTHORS: GREEK, LATIN, FRENCH, AND ENGLISH—HUMOUR OF ADDISON, AND OF FIELDING—WALLER—MILTON—BOILEAU'S "LUTRIN"—"THE RAPE OF THE LOCK"—MADAME DE SEVIGNE.

TO JOHN PINKERTON, ESQ.

June 26, 1785.

I have sent your book to Mr. Colman, Sir, and must desire you in return to offer my grateful thanks to Mr. Knight, who has done me an honour, to which I do not know how I am entitled, by the present of his poetry, which is very classic, and beautiful, and tender, and of chaste simplicity.

Letters of Horace Walpole, V2

To *your* book, Sir, I am much obliged on many accounts; particularly for having recalled my mind to subjects of delight, to which it was grown dulled by age and indolence. In consequence of your reclaiming it, I asked myself whence you feel so much disregard for certain authors whose fame is established: you have assigned good reasons for withholding your approbation from some, on the plea of their being imitators: it was natural, then, to ask myself again, whence they had obtained so much celebrity. I think I have discovered a cause, which I do not remember to have seen noted; and *that* cause I suspect to have been, that certain of those authors possessed grace:—do not take me for a disciple of Lord Chesterfield, nor imagine that I mean to erect grace into a capital ingredient of writing, but I do believe that it is a perfume that will serve from putrefaction, and is distinct even from style, which regards expression. *Grace*, I think, belongs to *manner*. It is from the charm of grace that I believe some authors, not in your favour, obtained part of their renown; Virgil, in particular: and yet I am far from disagreeing with you on his subject in general. There is such a dearth of invention in the Aeneid (and when he did invent, it was often so foolishly), so little good sense, so little variety, and so little power over the passions, that I have frequently said, from contempt for his matter, and from the charm of his harmony, that I believe I should like his poem better, if I was to hear it repeated, and did not understand Latin. On the other hand, he has more than harmony: whatever he utters is said gracefully, and he ennobles his images, especially in the Georgics; or, at least, it is more sensible there, from the humility of the subject. A Roman farmer might not understand his diction in agriculture; but he made a Roman courtier understand farming, the farming of that age, and could captivate a lord of Augustus's bedchamber, and tempt him to listen to themes of rusticity. On the contrary, Statius and Claudian, though talking of war, would make a soldier despise them as bullies. That graceful manner of thinking in Virgil seems to me to be more than style, if I do not refine too much: and I admire, I confess, Mr. Addison's phrase, that Virgil "tossed about his dung with an air of majesty." A style may be excellent without grace: for instance, Dr. Swift's. Eloquence may bestow an immortal style, and one of more dignity; yet eloquence may want that ease, that genteel air that flows from or constitutes grace. Addison himself was master of that grace, even in his pieces of humour, and which do not owe their merit to style; and from that combined secret he excels all men that ever lived; but Shakspeare, in humour,[1] by never dropping into an approach towards burlesque and buffoonery, when even his humour descended to characters that in other hands would have been vulgarly low. Is not it clear that Will Wimble was a gentleman, though he always lived at a distance from good company? Fielding had as much humour, perhaps, as Addison; but, having no idea of grace, is perpetually disgusting. His innkeepers and parsons are the grossest of their profession; and his gentlemen are awkward when they should be at their ease.

[Footnote 1: "*Addison's humour.*" Undoubtedly there is much gentlemanlike humour in Addison's Sir Roger de Coverley; but to say that he "excels all men that ever lived" in that quality is an exaggeration hardly to be understood in a man who had seen the "Rivals" and the "Critic." In the present day no one, it may be supposed, would echo it, after Scott with the Baron, the Antiquary, Dalgetty, &c., and Thackeray with Mrs. O'Dowd, Major Pendennis, and Colonel Newcome. The epithet "*Vafer*" applied to Horace by Persius is not inapplicable to Addison. There is a slyness about some of his sketches which breathes something of the Horatian facetiousness. It is remarkable that in all this long and varied criticism Walpole scarcely mentions *wit*, which he seems to allow to no one but Horace and Boileau. His comparative denial of it to Aristophanes and Lucian creates a supposition that his Greek was inferior to his Latin scholarship. It is not always easy to distinguish humour from wit; of the two, the former seems the higher quality. Wit is verbal, conversant with language, combining keenness and terseness of expression with a keen perception of resemblances or differences; humour has, comparatively speaking, little to do with language, and is of different kinds, varying with the class of composition in which it is found. In one of his "Imaginary Conversations" Savage Landor remarks that "It is no uncommon thing to hear, 'Such an one has humour rather than wit.' Here the expression can only mean *pleasantry*, for whoever has humour has wit, although it does not follow that whoever has wit has humour.... The French have little humour, because they have little *character*; they excel all nations in wit, because of their levity and sharpness."]

The Grecians had grace in everything; in poetry, in oratory, in statuary, in architecture, and probably, in music and painting. The Romans, it is true, were their imitators; but, having grace too, imparted it to their copies, which gave them a merit that almost raises them to the rank of originals. Horace's "Odes" acquired their fame, no doubt, from the graces of his manner and purity of his style—the chief praise of Tibullus and Propertius, who certainly cannot boast of more meaning than Horace's "Odes."

Waller, whom you proscribe, Sir, owed his reputation to the graces of his manner, though he frequently stumbled, and even fell flat; but a few of his smaller pieces are as graceful as possible: one might say that he excelled in painting ladies in enamel, but could not succeed in portraits in oil, large as life. Milton had such superior merit, that I will only say, that if his angels, his Satan, and his Adam have as much dignity as the Apollo Belvedere, his Eve has all the delicacy and graces of the Venus of Medicis; as his description of Eden has the colouring of Albano. Milton's tenderness imprints ideas as graceful as Guido's Madonnas: and the "Allegro," "Penseroso," and "Comus" might be denominated from the three Graces; as the Italians gave similar titles to two or three of Petrarch's best sonnets.

Cowley, I think, would have had grace (for his mind was graceful) if he had had any ear, or if his task had not been vitiated by the pursuit of wit; which, when it does not offer itself naturally, degenerates into tinsel or pertness. Pertness is the mistaken affection of grace, as pedantry produces erroneous dignity; the familiarity of the one, and the clumsiness of the other, distort or prevent grace. Nature, that furnishes samples of all qualities, and on the scale of gradation exhibits all possible shades, affords us types that are more apposite than words. The eagle is sublime, the lion majestic, the swan graceful, the monkey pert, the bear ridiculously awkward. I mention these as more expressive and comprehensive than I could make definitions of my meaning; but I will apply the swan only, under whose wings I will shelter an apology for Racine, whose pieces give me an idea of that bird. The colouring of the swan is pure; his attitudes are graceful; he never displeases you when sailing on his proper element. His feet may be ugly, his notes hissing, not musical, his walk not natural; he can soar, but it is with difficulty;—still, the impression the swan leaves is that of grace. So does Racine.

Boileau may be compared to the dog, whose sagacity is remarkable, as well as its fawning on its master, and its snarling at those it dislikes. If Boileau was too austere to admit the pliability of grace, he compensates by good sense and propriety. He is like (for I will drop animals) an upright magistrate, whom you respect, but whose justice and severity leave an awe that discourages familiarity. His copies of the ancients may be too servile: but, if a good translator deserves praise, Boileau deserves more. He certainly does not fall below his originals; and, considering at what period he wrote, has greater merit still. By his imitations he held out to his countrymen models of taste, and banished totally the bad taste of his predecessors. For his "Lutrin,"[1] replete with excellent poetry, wit, humour, and satire, he certainly was not obliged to the ancients. Excepting Horace, how little idea had either Greeks or Romans of wit and humour! Aristophanes and Lucian, compared with moderns, were, the one a blackguard, and the other a buffoon. In my eyes, the "Lutrin," the "Dispensary," and the "Rape of the Lock," are standards of grace and elegance, not to be paralleled by antiquity; and eternal reproaches to Voltaire, whose indelicacy in the "Pucelle" degraded him as much, when compared with the three authors I have named, as his "Henriade" leaves Virgil, and even Lucan, whom he more resembles, by far his superiors.

[Footnote 1: The "Lutrin" is a critical poem in six cantos. Lutrin means a desk; and Hallam, who does not seem to rate it very highly, regards the plan of it as borrowed from Tassoni's "Secchia rapita," Secchia meaning a pitcher.]

"The Dunciad" is blemished by the offensive images of the games; but the poetry appears to me admirable; and, though the fourth book has obscurities, I prefer it to the three others: it has descriptions not surpassed by any poet that ever existed, and which surely a writer merely ingenious will never equal. The lines on Italy, on Venice, on Convents, have all the grace for which I contend as distinct from poetry, though united with the most beautiful; and the "Rape of the Lock," besides the originality of great part of the invention, is a standard of graceful writing.

In general, I believe that what I call grace, is denominated elegance; but by grace I mean something higher. I will explain myself by instances—Apollo is graceful, Mercury is elegant. Petrarch, perhaps, owed his whole merit to the harmony of his numbers and the graces of his style. They conceal his poverty of meaning and want of variety. His complaints, too, may have added an interest, which, had his passion been successful, and had expressed itself with equal sameness, would have made the number of his sonnets insupportable. Melancholy in poetry, I am inclined to think, contributes to grace, when it is not disgraced by pitiful lamentations, such as Ovid's and Cicero's in their banishments. We respect melancholy, because it imparts a similar affection, pity. A gay writer, who should only express satisfaction without variety, would soon be nauseous.

Madame de Sevigne shines both in grief and gaiety. There is too much of sorrow for her daughter's absence; yet it is always expressed by new terms, by new images, and often by wit, whose tenderness has a melancholy air. When she forgets her concern, and returns to her natural disposition—gaiety, every paragraph has novelty: her allusions, her applications are the happiest possible. She has the art of making you acquainted with all her acquaintance, and attaches you even to the spots she inhabited. Her language is correct, though unstudied; and, when her mind is full of any great event, she interests you with the warmth of a dramatic writer, not with the chilling impartiality of an historian. Pray read her accounts of the death of Turenne, and of the arrival of King James in

France, and tell me whether you do not know their persons as if you had lived at the time.

For my part, if you will allow me a word of digression (not that I have written with any method), I hate the cold impartiality recommended to Historians: "Si vis me flere, dolendum est Primum ipsi tibi:"[1] but, that I may not wander again, nor tire, nor contradict you any more, I will finish now, and shall be glad if you will dine at Strawberry Hill next Sunday, and take a bed there, when I will tell you how many more parts of your book have pleased me, than have startled my opinions, or, perhaps, prejudices. I have the honour to be, Sir, with regard, &c.

[Footnote 1: A quotation from Horace's "Ars Poetica," 102.]

MINISTERIAL DIFFICULTIES—THE AFFAIR OF THE NECKLACE IN PARIS—FLUCTUATING UNPOPULARITY OF STATESMEN—FALLACIES OF HISTORY.

TO SIR HORACE MANN.

STRAWBERRY HILL, *Aug.* 26, 1785.

Though I am delighted to see your handwriting, I beg you will indulge me no more with it. It fatigues you, and that gives me more pain than your letters can give me satisfaction. Dictate a few words on your health to your secretary; it will suffice. I don't care a straw about the King and Queen of Naples, nor whether they visit your little Great Duke and Duchess. I am glad when monarchs are playing with one another, instead of scratching: it is better they should be idle than mischievous. As I desire you not to write, I cannot be alarmed at a strange hand.

Your philosophic account of yourself is worthy of you. Still, I am convinced you are better than you seem to think. A cough is vexatious, but in old persons is a great preservative. It is one of the forms in which the gout appears, and exercises and clears the lungs. I know actually two persons, no chickens, who are always very ill if they have no annual cough. You may imagine that I have made observations in plenty on the gout: yes, yes, I know its ways and its jesuitic evasions. I beg its pardon, it is a better soul than it appears to be; it is we that misuse it: if it does not appear with all its credentials, we take it for something else, and attempt to cure it. Being a remedy, and not a disease, it will not be cured; and it is better to let it have its way. If it is content to act the personage of a cough, pray humour it: it will prolong your life, if you do not contradict it and fling it somewhere else.

The Administration has received a total defeat in Ireland, which has probably saved us another civil war.[1] Don't wonder that I am continually recollecting my father's *Quieta non movere*. I have never seen that maxim violated with impunity. They say, that in town a change in the Ministry is expected. I am not of that opinion; but, indeed, nobody can be more ignorant than I. I see nobody here but people attached to the Court, and who, however, know no more than I do; and if I did see any of the other side, they would not be able to give me better information; nor am I curious.

[Footnote 1: In the session of 1785 Grattan opposed a body of "resolutions" calculated to relieve the distress of the Irish manufacturers, and altogether to emancipate the trade and commerce of Ireland from many mischievous restrictions which had hitherto restrained their progress. Lord Stanhope, in his "Life of Pitt," i. 273, quotes a description of Grattan's speech as "a display of perhaps the most beautiful eloquence ever heard, but seditious and inflammatory to a degree hardly credible;" and he so far prevailed, that in the Irish House of Commons the resolutions were only carried by a majority of twenty-nine—one so small, that the Duke of Rutland, the Lord-Lieutenant, felt it safer to withdraw them.]

A stranger event than a revolution in politics has happened at Paris. The Cardinal de Rohan is committed to the Bastile for forging the Queen's hand to obtain a collar of diamonds;[1] I know no more of the story: but, as he is very gallant, it is guessed (*here* I mean) that it was a present for some woman. These circumstances are little Apostolic, and will not prop the falling Church of Rome. They used to forge donations and decretals. This is a new manoeuvre. Nor were Cardinals wont to be treated so cavalierly for peccadilloes. The House of Rohan is under a cloud: his Eminence's cousin, the Prince of Guemene,[2] was forced to fly, two or three years ago, for being the Prince of Swindlers. *Our* Nabobs are not treated so roughly; yet I doubt they collect diamonds still more criminally.

[Footnote 1: "*A collar of diamonds.*" The transaction here referred to—though, strangely enough, it is looked on as one that had a political interest—was, in fact, a scheme of a broken–down gambler to swindle a jeweller out of a diamond necklace of great value. The Court jeweller had collected a large number of unusually fine diamonds, which he had made into a necklace, in the hope that the Queen would buy it, and the Cardinal de Rohan, who was a member of one of the noblest families in France, but a man of a character so notoriously profligate, that, when he was ambassador at Vienna, Maria Teresa had insisted on his recall, was mixed up in the fraud in a manner scarcely compatible with ignorance of its character. He was brought to trial with the more evident agents in the fraud, and the whole history of the French Parliaments scarcely records any transaction more disgraceful than his acquittal. For some months the affair continued to furnish pretext to obscure libellers to calumniate the Queen with insinuations not less offensive than dangerous from their vagueness; all such writers finding a ready paymaster in the infamous Duc d'Orleans.]

[Footnote 2: The Prince de Guemenee, a very profligate and extravagant man, by 1782 had become so hopelessly embarrassed that he was compelled to leave Paris, and consequently the Princess, his wife, who ever since the birth of Louis XVI. had held the office of "Governess of the Royal Children," a life–appointment, was forced to resign it, much to the pleasure of the Queen, who disapproved of her character, and bestowed the office on Mme. de Polignac, and when, at the beginning of the Revolution, she also fled from Paris, on Mme. de Tourzel. But, in truth, under Marie Antoinette the office was almost a sinecure. She considered superintendence of the education of her children as among the most important of her duties; and how judiciously she performed it is seen in an admirable letter of hers to Mme. de Tourzel, which can hardly be surpassed for its discernment and good–feeling. (See the Editor's "Life of Marie Antoinette," iii. 55.)]

Your nephew will be sorry to hear that the Duke of Montrose's third grandson, Master William Douglas, died yesterday of a fever. These poor Montroses are most unfortunate persons! They had the comfort this spring of seeing Lord Graham marry: the Duchess said, "I thought I should die of grief, and now I am ready to die of joy." Lady Graham soon proved with child, but soon miscarried; and the Duke and Duchess may not live to have the consolation of seeing an heir—for we must hope and make visions to the last! *I am asking for samples of Ginori's porcelain at sixty–eight!* Well! are not heirs to great names and families as frail foundations of happiness? and what signifies what baubles we pursue? Philosophers make systems, and we simpletons collections: and we are as wise as they—wiser perhaps, for we know that in a few years our rarities will be dispersed at an auction; and they flatter themselves that their reveries will be immortal, which has happened to no system yet. A curiosity may rise in value; a system is exploded.

Such reflections are applicable to politics, and make me look on them as equally nugatory. Last year Mr. Fox was burnt in effigy; now Mr. Pitt is. Oh! my dear Sir, it is all a farce! On *this day*, about a hundred years ago (look at my date), was born the wisest man I have seen.[1] He kept this country in peace for twenty years, and it flourished accordingly. He injured no man; was benevolent, good-humoured, and did nothing but the common necessary business of the State. Yet was he burnt in effigy too; and so traduced, that his name is not purified yet!—Ask why his memory is not in veneration? You will be told, from libels and trash, that he was *the Grand Corruptor.*—What! did he corrupt the nation to make it happy, rich, and peaceable? Who was oppressed during his administration? Those saints Bolingbroke and Pulteney were kept out of the Paradise of the Court; ay, and the Pretender was kept out and was kept quiet. Sir Robert fell: a Rebellion ensued in four years, and the crown shook on the King's head. The nation, too, which had been tolerably corrupted before his time, and which, with all its experience and with its eyes opened, has not cured itself of being corrupt, is not quite so prosperous as in the day of that man, who, it seems, poisoned its morals. Formerly it was the most virtuous nation on the earth!

[Footnote 1: He means his own father, the Prime Minister from 1720 to 1741.]

Under Henry VIII. and his children there was no persecution, no fluctuation of religion: their Ministers shifted their faith four times, and were sincere honest men! There was no servility, no flattery, no contempt of the nation abroad, under James I. No tyranny under Charles I. and Laud; no factions, no civil war! Charles II., however, brought back all the virtues and morality, which, somehow or other, were missing! His brother's was a still more blessed reign, though in a different way! King William was disturbed and distressed by no contending factions, and did not endeavour to bribe them to let him pursue his great object of humbling France! The Duke of Marlborough was not overborne in a similar and more glorious career by a detestable Cabal!—and if Oxford and Bolingbroke did remove him, from the most patriot motives, they, good men! used no corruption! Twelve Peerages showered at once, to convert the House of Lords, were no bribes; nor was a shilling issued for secret services; nor would a member of either House have received it!

Sir R. Walpole came, and strange to tell, found the whole Parliament, and every Parliament, at least a great majority of every Parliament, ready to take his money. For what?—to undo their country!—which, however, wickedly as he meant, and ready as they were to concur, he left in every respect in the condition he found it, except in being improved in trade, wealth, and tranquillity; till *its friends* who expelled him, had dipped their poor country in a war; which was far from mending its condition. Sir Robert died, foretelling a rebellion, which happened in less than six months, and for predicting which he had been ridiculed: and in detestation of a maxim ascribed to him by his enemies, that *every man has his price*, the tariff of every Parliament since has been as well known as the price of beef and mutton; and the universal electors, who cry out against that traffic, are not a jot less vendible than their electors.—Was not Sir Robert Walpole an abominable Minister?

29th.

P.S.—The man who certainly provoked Ireland *to think*, is dead—Lord Sackville.[1]

[Footnote 1: Lord George Sackville Germaine, third son of Lionel [first] Duke of Dorset, who, when secretary to his father, when Lord-Lieutenant of Ireland, gave rise, by his haughty behaviour, to the factions that have ever since disturbed that country, and at last shaken off its submission to this country.—WALPOLE.]

30th.

I see, by the *Gazette*, that Lord Cowper's pinchbeck principality is allowed. I wonder his Highness does not desire the Pope to make one of his sons a bishop *in partibus infidelium*.

BREVITY OF MODERN ADDRESSES—THE OLD DUCHESS OF MARLBOROUGH.

TO SIR HORACE MANN.

STRAWBERRY HILL, *Oct.* 4, 1785.

I don't love to transgress my monthly regularity; yet, as you must prefer facts to words, why should I write when I have nothing to tell you? The newspapers themselves in a peaceable autumn coin wonders from Ireland, or live on the accidents of the Equinox. They, the newspapers, have been in high spirits on the prospect of a campaign in Holland; but the Dutch, without pity for the gazetteers of Europe, are said to have submitted to the Emperor's terms: however, the intelligence-merchants may trust that *he* will not starve them long!

Your neighbour, the Queen of Sardinia, it seems, is dead: but, if there was anything to say about her, you must tell it to me, not I to you; for, till she died, I scarce knew she had been alive.

Our Parliament is put off till after Christmas; so, I have no more resource from domestic politics than from foreign wars. For my own particular, I desire neither. I live here in tranquillity and idleness, can content myself with trifles, and think the world is much the happier when it has nothing to talk of. Most people ask, "Is there any news?"—How can one want to know one does not know what? when anything has happened, one hears it.

There is one subject on which I wish I had occasion to write; I think it long since I heard how you go on: I flatter myself, as I have no letter from you or your nephew, prosperously. I should prefer a letter from him, that you may not have the trouble; and I shall make this the shorter, as a precedent for his not thinking more than a line necessary. The post does not insist on a certain quantity; it is content with being paid for whatever it carries—nay, is a little unreasonable, as it doubles its price for a cover that contains nothing but a direction: and now it is the fashion to curtail the direction as much as possible. Formerly, a direction was an academy of compliments: "To the most noble and my singularly respected friend," &c., &c.—and then, "Haste! haste, for your life, haste!" Now, we have banished even the monosyllable *To*! Henry Conway,[1] Lord Hertford's son, who is very indolent, and has much humour, introduced that abridgment. Writing to a Mr. Tighe at the Temple, he directed his letter only thus: "T. Ti., Temple"[2]—and it was delivered! Dr. Bentley was mightily flattered on receiving a letter superscribed "To Dr. Bentley in England." Times are altered; postmen are now satisfied with a hint. One modern retrenchment is a blessing; one is not obliged to study for an ingenious conclusion, as if writing an epigram—oh! no; nor to send compliments that never were delivered. I had a relation who always finished his letters with "his love to all that was near and dear to us," though he did not care a straw for me or any of his family. It was said of old Sarah, Duchess of Marlborough, that she never put dots over her *i's*, to save ink: how she would have enjoyed modern economy in that article! She would have died worth a thousand farthings more than she did—nay, she would have known exactly how many; as Sir Robert Brown[3] did, who calculated what he had saved by never having an orange or lemon on his sideboard. I am surprised that no economist has retrenched second courses, which always consist of the dearest articles, though seldom touched, as the hungry at least dine on the first. Mrs. Leneve,[4] one summer at Houghton, counted thirty-six turkey-pouts[5] that had been served up without being meddled with.

[Footnote 1: Second son of Francis Seymour Conway, first Earl of Hertford.—WALPOLE.]

[Footnote 2: This address was surpassed towards the end of the reign, by a letter which arrived in London addressed to "Srumfredafi, England;" and was correctly interpreted at the Post Office as being designed for Sir Humphrey Davy.]

[Footnote 3: A noted miser, who raised a great fortune as a merchant at Venice, though his whole wealth, when he went thither, consisted in one of those vast wigs (a second-hand one, given to him) which were worn in the reign of Queen Anne, and which he sold for five guineas. He returned to England, very rich, in the reign of George II., with his wife and three daughters, who would have been great fortunes. The eldest, about eighteen, fell into a consumption, and, being ordered to ride, her father drew a map of the by-lanes about London, which he made the footman carry in his pocket and observe, that she might ride without paying a turnpike. When the poor girl was past recovery, Sir Robert sent for an undertaker, to cheapen her funeral, as she was not dead, and there was a possibility of her living. He went farther; he called his other daughters, and bade them curtsy to the undertaker, and promise to be his friends; and so they proved, for both died consumptive in two years.—WALPOLE.]

[Footnote 4: A lady who lived with Sir Robert Walpole, to take care of his youngest daughter, Lady Maria, after her mother's death. After Sir Robert's death, and Lady Mary's marriage with Mr. Churchill, she lived with Mr. H. Walpole to her death.—WALPOLE.]

[Footnote 5: As the sons of rajahs in India are called Rajah Pouts, and as turkeys came from the East, quaere if they were not called Turkey-pouts, as an Eastern diminutive?—WALPOLE.]

5th.

I had written thus far yesterday. This minute I receive your nephew's of Sept. 20th; it is not such an one by any means as I had wished for. He tells me you have had a return of your disorder—indeed, he consoles me with your recovery; but I cannot in a moment shake off the impression of a sudden alarm, though the cause was ceased, nor can a second agitation calm a first on such shattered nerves as mine. My fright is over, but I am not composed. I cannot begin a new letter, and therefore send what I had written. I will only add, what you may be sure I feel, ardent wishes for your perfect health, and grateful thanks to your nephew for his attention—he is rather your son; but indeed he is Gal.'s son, and that is the same thing. How I love him for his attendance on you! and how very kind he is in giving me accounts of you! I hope he will continue, and I ask it still more for your sake than for my own, that you may not think of writing yourself. If he says but these words, "My uncle has had no return of his complaint," I shall be satisfied—satisfied!—I shall be quite happy! Indeed, indeed, I ask no more.

LADY CRAVEN—MADAME PIOZZI—"THE ROLLIAD"—HERSCHEL'S ASTRONOMICAL DISCOVERY.

TO SIR HORACE MANN.

BERKELEY SQUARE, *Oct.* 30, 1785.

I am a contradiction, yet very naturally so; I wish you not to write yourself, and yet am delighted when I receive a letter in your own hand: however, I don't desire it should be of four pages, like this last of the 11th. When I have had the gout, I have always written by proxy. You will make me ashamed, if you don't use the precedent. Your account of yourself is quite to my satisfaction. I approve, too, of your not dining with your company. Since I must be old and have the gout, I have long turned those disadvantages to my own account, and plead them to the utmost when they will save me from doing anything I dislike. I am so lame, or have such a sudden pain, when I do not care to do what is proposed to me! Nobody can tell how rapidly the gout may be come, or be gone again; and then it is so pleasant to have had the benefit, and none of the anguish!

Letters of Horace Walpole, V2

I did send you a line last week in the cover of a letter to Lady Craven,[1] which I knew would sufficiently tell your quickness how much I shall be obliged to you for any attentions to her. I thought her at Paris, and was surprised to hear of her at Florence. She has, I fear, been *infinitamente* indiscreet; but what is that to you or me? She is very pretty, has parts, and is good-natured to the greatest degree; has not a grain of malice or mischief (almost always the associates, in women, of tender hearts), and never has been an enemy but to herself. For that ridiculous woman Madame Piozzi,[2] and t'other more impertinent one, of whom I never heard before, they are like the absurd English dames with whom we used to divert ourselves when I was at Florence. As to your little knot of poets, I do not hold the cocks higher than the hens; nor would I advise them to repatriate. We have at present here a most incomparable set, not exactly known by their names, but who, till the dead of summer, kept the town in a roar, and, I suppose, will revive by the meeting of Parliament. They have poured forth a torrent of odes, epigrams, and part of an imaginary epic poem, called the "Rolliad,"[3] with a commentary and notes, that is as good as the "Dispensary"[4] and "Dunciad," with more ease. These poems are all anti-ministerial, and the authors very young men, and little known or heard of before. I would send them, but you would want too many keys: and indeed I want some myself; for, as there are continually allusions to Parliamentary speeches and events, they are often obscure to me till I get them explained; and besides, I do not know several of the satirised heroes even by sight: however, the poetry and wit make amends, for they are superlative.

[Footnote 1: Lady Craven, *nee* Berkeley, had given abundant cause for scandal during her husband's life, which did not abate when, a month after his death, she married the Margrave of Anspach.]

[Footnote 2: Mme. Piozzi, the Mrs. Thrale of Boswell's "Life of Johnson." Mr. Thrale was a brewer, the founder of the great firm now known as Barclay and Perkins. She was many years younger than he; and, after his death, she married Signor Piozzi, a professional musician of eminence. Johnson, who had been an habitual guest of her husband and her at their villa at Streatham, set the fashion of condemning this second marriage as a disgraceful *mesalliance*; but it is not very easy to see in what respect it was so. In social position she had certainly had the advantage over Mr. Thrale, being the daughter of a Carnarvonshire baronet of ancient family. But a first-rate musician was surely the equal of a brewer. After Johnson's death she published a volume of her reminiscences of him, which may be allowed to have been worthy neither of him nor of her, and which was ridiculed by Peter Pindar in "A Town Eclogue," in which the rivals

Bozzy and Piozzi, on Virgil's principle—*Alternis dicetis, amant alterna Camaenae*—relate in turn anecdotes of Johnson's way of life, his witty sayings, &c., &c. Sir John Hawkins, as judge of the contest, gives neither a prize; tells the lady, "Sam's Life, dear ma'am, will only *damn your own*;" calls the gentleman "a chattering magpie;" and—

> Then to their pens and paper rush'd the twain,
> To kill the mangled RAMBLER o'er again.]

[Footnote 3: In 1785 the wits of Brooks's, being much disappointed at the result of the political conflict of 1784, gave some vent to their spleen in verse. For their subject they selected an imaginary epic, of which they gave fictitious extracts, and for their hero they took the Member for Devonshire, John Rolle, invoking him—

> Illustrious Rolle! oh may thy honoured name
> Roll down distinguished on the rolls of fame.

It is a little odd that they abstained from similar puns on Pitt and *pit*; but their indignation was chiefly directed at his youth as ill-suited to his powers—

> A sight to make surrounding nations stare,
> A kingdom trusted to a schoolboy's care.

The chief contributors were Burke's friend, Dr. Lawrence; Sheridan's brother-in-law, Tickell; General Fitzpatrick, Mr. G. Ellis, Lord G. Townshend, and General Burgoyne.]

[Footnote 4: "The Dispensary" was a poem by a physician named Garth, to advocate the cause of the physicians in a quarrel between them and the apothecaries about the price to be charged for medicines. Johnson, in his "Lives of the Poets," allows it the credit of smooth and free versification, but denies it that of elegance. "No passage falls below mediocrity, and few rise above it." It may be doubted whether Byron himself could have risen high "above it" on subjects so unpoetical as pills and black-doses.]

News I have none, wet or dry, to send you: politics are stagnated, and pleasure is not come to town. You may be sure I am glad that Caesar is baffled; I neither honour nor esteem him. If he is preferring his nephew to his brother, it is using the latter as ill as the rest of the world.

Mrs. Damer is again set out for the Continent to-day, to avoid the winter, which is already begun severely; we have had snow twice. Till last year, I never knew snow in October since I can remember; which is no short time. Mrs. Damer has taken with her her cousin Miss Campbell, daughter of poor Lady William, whom you knew, and who died last year. Miss Campbell has always lived with Lady Aylesbury, and is a very great favourite and a very sensible girl. I believe they will proceed to Italy, but it is not certain. If they come to Florence, the Grand Duke should beg Mrs. Damer to give him something of her statuary; and it would be a greater curiosity than anything in his Chamber of Painters. She has executed several marvels since you saw her; and has lately carved two colossal heads for the bridge at Henley, which is the most beautiful one in the world, next to the Ponte di Trinita, and was principally designed by her father, General Conway. Lady Spencer draws—incorrectly indeed, but has great expression. Italy probably will stimulate her, and improve her attention. You see we blossom in ruin! Poetry, painting, statuary, architecture, music, linger here,

   on this sea-encircled coast (GRAY),

as if they knew not whither to retreat farther for shelter, and would not trust to the despotic patronage of the Attilas, Alarics, Amalasuntas of the North! They leave such heroic scourges to be decorated by the Voltaires and D'Alemberts of the Gauls, or wait till by the improvement of balloons they may be transported to some of those millions of worlds that Herschel[1] is discovering every day; for this new Columbus has thrown open the great gates of astronomy, and neither Spanish inquisitors nor English Nabobs will be able to torture and ransack the new regions and their inhabitants. Adieu!

[Footnote 1: Herschel, having constructed the largest telescope that at that time had ever been seen, in 1781 had given proof of its value by the discovery of the *Georgium sidus*.]

MRS. YEARSLEY—MADAME PIOZZI—GIBBON—"LE MARIAGE DE FIGARO."

TO MISS HANNAH MORE.[1]

[Footnote 1: Miss H. More was a remarkable woman. She was the daughter of the village schoolmaster of Stapleton, near Bristol. But though she had no higher education than he could give her, she soon began to show a considerable literary talent. Her first compositions were dramas, one of which, "Percy," Garrick accepted for the stage, where for a season it had fair success. But she soon quitted that line for works of morality, intended to promote the religious improvement of society in her day. The most celebrated of them was "Coelebs in Search of a Wife." But some of the tales which she published in "The Cheap Repository," a series of stories for the common people, had a greater sale. One, "The Shepherd of Salisbury Plain," was so popular that it is said that a million copies of it were sold. Her talents led to her acquaintance being cultivated by such men as Johnson, Reynolds, Burke, and Bishop Porteus; and her exercise of them was so profitable, that though she gave large sums in charity, she left a fortune of L30,000.]

STRAWBERRY HILL, *Oct.* 14, 1787.

My dear Madam,—I am shocked for human nature at the repeated malevolence of this woman! [Mrs. Yearsley.] The rank soil of riches we are accustomed to see overrun with seeds and thistles; but who could expect that the kindest seeds sown on poverty and dire misfortunes should meet with nothing but a rock at bottom? Catherine de' Medici, suckled by hopes and transplanted to a throne, seems more excusable. Thank heaven, Madam, for giving you so excellent a heart; ay, and so good a head. You are not only benevolence itself, but, with fifty times the genius of a Yearsley, you are void of vanity. How strange, that vanity should expel gratitude! Does not the wretched woman owe her fame to you, as well as her affluence? I can testify your labours for both. Dame Yearsley reminds me of the Troubadours, those vagrants whom I used to admire till I knew their history; and who used to pour out trumpery verses, and flatter or abuse accordingly as they were housed and clothed, or dismissed to the next parish. Yet you did not set this person in the stocks, after procuring an annuity for her! I beg your pardon for renewing so disgusting a subject, and will never mention it again. You have better amusement; you love good works, a temper superior to revenge.

I have again seen our poor friend in Clarges Street [Mrs. Vesey]: her faculties decay rapidly, and of course she suffers less. She has not an acquaintance in town; and yet told me the town was very full, and that she had had a good deal of company. Her health is re-established, and we must now be content that her mind is not restless. My pity now feels most for Mrs. Hancock, whose patience is inexhaustible, though not insensible.

Letters of Horace Walpole, V2

Mrs. Piozzi, I hear, has two volumes of Dr. Johnson's Letters ready for publication. Bruce is printing his travels, which I suppose will prove that his narratives were fabulous, as he will scarce repeat them by the press. These, and two more volumes of Mr. Gibbon's "History," are all the literary news I know. France seems sunk indeed in all respects. What stuff are their theatrical goods, their "Richards," "Ninas," and "Tarares"! But when their "Figaro"[1] could run threescore nights, how despicable must their taste be grown! I rejoice that their political intrigues are not more creditable. I do not dislike the French from the vulgar antipathy between neighbouring nations, but for their insolent and unfounded airs of superiority. In arms, we have almost always outshone them: and till they have excelled Newton, and come near to Shakspeare, pre-eminence in genius must remain with us. I think they are most entitled to triumph over the Italians; as, with the most meagre and inharmonious of all languages, the French have made more of that poverty in tragedy and eloquence, than the Italians have done with the language the most capable of both. But I did not mean to send you a dissertation. I hope it will not be long before you remove to Hampton.—Yet why should I wish that? You will only be geographically nearer to London till February. Cannot you, now and then, sleep at the Adelphi on a visit to poor Vesey and your friends, and let one know if you do?

[Footnote 1: "Le Mariage de Figaro" was a play by a man who assumed the name of Beaumarchais (as Poquelin had taken the name of Moliere and Arouet that of Voltaire); and the histories of both the author and the play are curious. The author's real name was Caron, and he had been bred a watchmaker. But he was ambitious; he gave up his trade, and bought a place about the Court, which was among those which conferred gentility, and which enabled him afterwards on one occasion to boast that he could establish a better claim to the rank of noble than most of that body, since he could produce a stamped receipt for it. He married two rich widows. He next obtained the place of music-master on the harp to the daughters of Louis XV., and conducted some of their concerts. He became involved in a law-suit, which he conducted in person against some of the most renowned advocates of the day, and gained great applause for the talent he had exhibited in his pleadings. He crossed over to England, where he made acquaintance with Wilkes and the agents of some of the North American colonies, and became a volunteer agent for them himself at the beginning of the American war, expending, according to his own statement, 150,000 francs in the purchase of arms and stores, which he sent out, when the President of Congress contented himself with thanking him for his liberality, but refused to pay his bill. He resolved to try his skill as a dramatist. His earlier plays were not particularly successful, but in 1781 he produced "The Marriage of

Figaro," a sort of sequel to one of its predecessors, "The Barber of Seville." During the progress of its composition he had shown some of the scenes to his critical friends, who had pronounced it witty, and prophesied its success. But it had also become known that it contained sarcasms on some of the exclusive privileges of the nobles, and the officer who had charge of such matters in consequence refused to license it for performance, as a dangerous satire on the institutions of the country. He had by this time made friends enough to form a party to remonstrate against the hardship of the Censor's decision; till the King determined to judge for himself, and caused Mme. Campau to read it to himself and the Queen, when he fully agreed with the Censor, and expressed a positive determination not to permit its performance. Unluckily he was never firm in his resolutions; and Beaumarchais having secured the patronage of Louis's brother, the Comte d'Artois, and Mme. de Polignac, felt confident of carrying his point at last. His royal and noble patrons arranged parties for private readings of the play. He then declared, untruly, that he had altered all the passages which had been deemed offensive, and Louis was weak enough to believe him without further examination, and to sanction a private performance of it at the country house of the Comte de Vandreuel. After this it was impossible to exclude it from the theatre in Paris; and in April, 1784, it was acted before an audience whom the long-continued contest had brought in unprecedented numbers to hear it. If it had not been for the opposition which had been made to it, it probably would never have attracted any particular attention; for, though it was lively, and what managers call a fair "acting play," it had no remarkable merit as a composition, and depended for its attraction more on some of its surprises and discoveries than on its wit. But its performance and the reception it met with were regarded by a large political party as a triumph over the Ministry; and French historical writers, to whatever party they belong, agree in declaring that it had given a death-blow to many of the oldest institutions of the country, and that Beaumarchais proved at once the herald and the pioneer of the approaching Revolution. (See the Editor's "Life of Marie Antoinette," c. 19.)]

GENTLEMEN WRITERS—HIS OWN REASONS FOR WRITING WHEN YOUNG—VOLTAIRE—"EVELINA"—MISS SEWARD—HAYLEY.

TO MISS HANNAH MORE.

Letters of Horace Walpole, V2

Strawberry Hill, *July* 12, 1788.

Won't you repent having opened the correspondence, my dear Madam, when you find my letters come so thick upon you? In this instance, however, I am only to blame in part, for being too ready to take advice, for the sole reason for which advice ever is taken,—because it fell in with my inclination.

You said in your last that you feared you took up time of mine to the prejudice of the public; implying, I imagine, that I might employ it in composing. Waving both your compliment and my own vanity, I will speak very seriously to you on that subject, and with exact truth. My simple writings have had better fortune than they had any reason to expect; and I fairly believe, in a great degree, because gentlemen-writers, who do not write for interest, are treated with some civility if they do not write absolute nonsense. I think so, because I have not unfrequently known much better works than mine much more neglected, if the name, fortune, and situation of the authors were below mine. I wrote early from youth, spirits, and vanity; and from both the last when the first no longer existed. I now shudder when I reflect on my own boldness; and with mortification, when I compare my own writings with those of any great authors. This is so true, that I question whether it would be possible for me to summon up courage to publish anything I have written, if I could recall time past, and should yet think as I think at present. So much for what is over and out of my power. As to writing now, I have totally forsworn the profession, for two solid reasons. One I have already told you; and it is, that I know my own writings are trifling and of no depth. The other is, that, light and futile as they were, I am sensible they are better than I could compose now. I am aware of the decay of the middling parts I had, and others may be still more sensible of it. How do I know but I am superannuated? nobody will be so coarse as to tell me so; but if I published dotage, all the world would tell me so. And who but runs that risk who is an author after seventy? What happened to the greatest author of this age, and who certainly retained a very considerable portion of his abilities for ten years after my age?[1] Voltaire, at eighty-four, I think, went to Paris to receive the incense, in person, of his countrymen, and to be witness of their admiration of a tragedy he had written, at that Methusalem age. Incense he did receive till it choked him; and, at the exhibition of his play, he was actually crowned with laurel in the box where he sat. But what became of his poor play? It died as soon as he did—was buried with him; and no mortal, I dare to say, has ever read a line of it since, it was so bad.

[Footnote 1: Voltaire had for several years been in disgrace at Court, and had been living in Switzerland; but in 1778 he returned to Paris to superintend the performance of a new tragedy, "Irene." He was, however, greatly mortified at the refusal of Marie Antoinette to allow him to be presented to her, and was but partly comforted by the enthusiasm of the audience at the theatre, who crowned him on the stage after the performance. Mme. du Deffand, who, in a letter to Walpole a few days before, had said that if the tragedy did not succeed it would kill him, says in a subsequent letter that its success had been very moderate—that the enthusiasm of the audience had been for Voltaire himself; and at all events her prophecy was fulfilled, for he died a few weeks afterwards.]

As I am neither by a thousandth part so great, nor a quarter so little, I will herewith send you a fragment that an accidental *rencontre* set me upon writing, and which I find so flat, that I would not finish it. Don't believe that I am either begging praise by the stale artifice of hoping to be contradicted; or that I think there is any occasion to make you discover my caducity. No; but the fragment contains a curiosity—English verses written by a French Prince[1] of the Blood, and which at first I had a mind to add to my "Royal and Noble Authors;" but as he was not a royal author of ours, and as I could not please myself with an account of him, I shall revert to my old resolution of not exposing my pen's grey hairs.

[Footnote 1: He was the Duc d'Orleans, who was taken prisoner by Henry V. at Agincourt, and was detained in England for twenty-five years. The verses are published in "Walpole's Works," i. 564.]

Of one passage I must take notice; it is a little indirect sneer at our crowd of authoresses. My choosing to send this to *you*, is a proof that I think you an author, that is, a classic. But, in truth, I am nauseated by the Madams Piozzi, &c., and the host of novel-writers in petticoats, who think they imitate what is inimitable, "Evelina" and "Cecilia."[1] Your candour, I know, will not agree with me, when I tell you I am not at all charmed with Miss Seward[2] and Mr. Hayley[3] piping to one another: but *you* I exhort, and would encourage to write; and flatter myself you will never be royally gagged and promoted to fold muslins, as has been lately wittily said on Miss Burney, in the List of five hundred living authors. *Your* writings promote virtues; and their increasing editions prove their worth and utility. If you question my sincerity, can you doubt my admiring you, when you have gratified *my* self-love so amply in your "Bas Bleu"? Still, as much as I love your writings, I respect yet more your heart and your goodness. You are so good that I believe you would go to heaven, even though there were no Sunday, and only six *working* days in the week. Adieu, my best Madam!

[Footnote 1: "Evelina" and "Cecilia" are novels by Miss Burney, afterwards Mme. d'Arblay. The former was extravagantly praised by Johnson and the Literary Club, and is probably a favourable specimen of the style of the conversation of the day.]

[Footnote 2: Miss Seward was the authoress of that most ingenious riddle on the letter *H*, and also of some volumes of poetry.]

[Footnote 3: Mr. Hayley was the author of several works in prose and verse; in the latter, of a poem called "The Triumphs of Temper," and entitled to the name, according to Byron, since "at least they triumphed over his" ("English Bards and Scotch Reviewers").]

DIVISIONS IN THE ROYAL FAMILY—THE REGENCY—THE IRISH PARLIAMENT.

TO SIR HORACE MANN.

BERKELEY SQUARE, *Feb.* 12, 1789.

I now do believe that the King is coming to him_self: not in the language of the courtiers, to his senses—but from their proof, viz., that he is returned to his what! what! what! which he used to prefix to every sentence, and which is coming to his nonsense. I am corroborated in this opinion by his having said much more sensible things in his lunacy than he did when he was reckoned sane, which I do not believe he has been for some years.

Well! now, how will this new change of scene operate? I fancy if any one could win access to him, who would tell him the truth, he would be as little pleased with his Queen, and his or her Pitt, as they will take care he shall be with his sons. Would he admire the degradation of his family in the person of all the Princes? or with the tripartite division of Royalty between the Queen, the Prince, and Mr. Pitt, which I call a *Trinity in disunity*? Will he be charmed with the Queen's admission to power, which he never imparted to her? Will he like the discovery of his vast private hoard? Will he be quite satisfied with the codicil to his Will,[1] which she surreptitiously obtained from him in his frenzy *in the first agony of her grief*? How will he digest that discovery of his treasure, which will not diffuse great compassion when he shall next ask a payment of his pretended debts? Before his madness he was indisposed towards Pitt; will he be better pleased with him for his new dictatorial presumption?

[Footnote 1: "*His will.*" This refers to a scandal propagated by some of the opposition newspapers, for which there was not the slightest foundation.]

Turn to the next page—to Ireland. They have chosen for themselves, it is believed, a Regent without restrictions,[1] in scorn of the Parliament of England, and in order further to assert their independence. Will they recede? especially when their courtiers have flown in the face of our domineering Minister? I do not think they will. They may receive the King again on his recovery; but they have united interests with the Prince, and act in league with him, that he may pledge himself to them more deeply in future at least; they will never again acknowledge any superiority in our Parliament, but rather act in contradistinction.

[Footnote 1: "*Regent without restrictions.*" The King, in the autumn of 1788, having fallen into a state of temporary derangement, Pitt proposed that the Parliament should appoint the Prince of Wales Regent, with some temporary limitations in the exercise of the power. Fox and his followers contended that the Prince, being of full age, was as absolutely entitled to the Regency as his right, as he would have been to the Crown in the event of his father's death; and Grattan, who had a paramount influence over the Irish Parliament, adopting Fox's view, carried an address to the Prince, entreating him to take upon himself the Regency as his right—a view which, of course, was incompatible with any power of limiting his authority. Fortunately, before this address could be acted upon, the King recovered. The matter unfortunately caused great divisions in the Royal Family, to which Walpole alludes in the latter part of the letter; the Queen considering (not without grounds) that the Prince had shown unfilial eagerness to grasp at power; and indeed he had already made it known that he had intended to dismiss Pitt and to appoint Fox Prime Minister.]

[Illustration: Hand-written Letter]

Feb. 22nd.

Letters of Horace Walpole, V2

The person who was to have brought you this was prevented leaving town, and therefore I did not finish my letter; but I believe I shall have another opportunity of sending, and therefore I will make it ready.

Much has happened this last week. The Prince is Regent of Ireland without limitations—a great point for his character; for Europe will now see that it was a faction which fettered him here, and not his unpopularity, for then would not he have been as much distasted in Ireland? Indeed, their own Attorney-General made way for him by opposing on the most injudicious of all pleas, that it would be necessary before he could be Regent there, to set the *Great Seal of England* to the act! How could the fool imagine, that when that phantom had been invented here, it would not be equally easy for the Irish to invent a parallel phantom of their own? But though this compliment is most grateful to the Prince at present, he will probably find hereafter that he has in effect lost Ireland, who meant more to emancipate themselves from this country than to compliment the Prince or contradict the English ministerial faction.

What will be the consequence of that rapid turn in Ireland, even immediately, who can tell? for the King is called recovered, and the English Regency is suspended, with fresh and grievous insults to the Prince, who with the Duke of York are violently hindered by the Queen from even seeing their father, though she and their sisters play at cards with him in an evening; and that the Chancellor was with him for an hour and three quarters on the 19th.

Under colour of what new phantom her Majesty, the Chancellor,[1] and Pitt will assume the Government, we shall know in two or three days; for I do not suppose they will produce the King instantly, at the risk of oversetting his head again, though they seem half as mad as he, and capable of any violent act to maintain themselves. And so much the better: I do not wish them temperate; and it looks as if people never were so in minorities and incapacities of their kings. The Prince set out as indiscreetly as Pitt.

[Footnote 1: The Chancellor was Lord Thurlow, an able but unprincipled man. Johnson expressed a high opinion of him as an arguer "who brought his mind to bear upon yours." But Fox declared his very face "proved him an impostor, since no man could be as wise as he looked."]

Of the event I am very glad; it saves the Prince and the Opposition from the rashness of changing the Administration on so precarious and shackled a tenure, and it saves them too from the expense of re-elections. If the King recovers, they are but where they were, but with the advantage of having the Prince and Duke of York rooted in aversion to the Ministers, and most unlikely to be governed by the Queen. If the King relapses, the Opposition stock will rise; though in the mean time I do not doubt but the nation will grow drunk with the loyalty of rejoicing, for kings grow popular by whatever way they lose their heads. Still, whatever eccentricity he attempts, it will be imputed to his deranged understanding. And, however even Lord Hawkesbury[1] may meditate the darkest mischiefs under the new fund of pity and loyalty, he will *not* be for extending the prerogative, which must devolve (on any accident to the King) on the Prince, Duke of York, or some of the Princes, who will all be linked in a common cause with their brothers, who have been so grossly affronted; and Prince William, the third, particularly so by the last cause of hindering his peerage while abroad. The King's recovery before the Regency Act was passed will be another great advantage to the Prince; his hands would have been so shackled, that he could not have found places for half the expectants, who will now impute their disappointments to the King's amendment, and not to the Prince.

[Footnote 1: Lord Hawkesbury was afterwards promoted to the Earldom of Liverpool, and was the father of the sagacious, prudent, but resolute minister under whose administration the French Revolutionary War was brought to a conclusion by the final overthrow of Napoleon.]

Monday, 24th.

The King has seen the Prince [of Wales], and received him kindly, but the Queen was present. Iron Pluto (as Burke called the Chancellor) wept again when with the King; but what is much more remarkable, his Majesty has not asked for Pitt, and did abuse him constantly during his frenzy. The Chancellor certainly did not put him in mind of Pitt, whom he detests; so there is a pretty portion of hatred to be quaffed amongst them! and swallowed, if they can; yet *aurum potabile* will make it sit on their stomachs.

"THE ARABIAN NIGHTS"—THE AENEID—BOCCALINI—ORPHEUS AND EURYDICE.

TO MISS BERRY.[1]

[Footnote 1: The lady to whom this letter is addressed was the elder of two sisters who in 1787 came to reside with their father in Walpole's neighbourhood. Both the sisters, according to his description of them, were very accomplished and sufficiently good-looking. He gradually became so enthusiastic in his regard for her, that he proposed to marry her, old as he was, in order that he might have an excuse for leaving her all his fortune; and he wrote the "Reminiscences of the Courts of George I. and II.," which are among his published works, for the amusement of the two sisters.]

STRAWBERRY HILL, *June* 30, 1789.

Were there any such thing as sympathy at the distance of two hundred miles, you would have been in a mightier panic than I was; for, on Saturday se'nnight, going to open the glass case in the Tribune, my foot caught in the carpet, and I fell with my whole weight (*si* weight *y a*) against the corner of the marble altar, on my side, and bruised the muscles so badly, that for two days I could not move without screaming. I am convinced I should have broken a rib, but that I fell on the cavity whence two of my ribs were removed, that are gone to Yorkshire. I am much better both of my bruise and of my lameness, and shall be ready to dance at my own wedding when my wives return. And now to answer your letter.

If you grow tired of the "Arabian Nights," you have no more taste than Bishop Atterbury,[1] who huffed Pope for sending him them (or the "Persian Tales"), and fancied he liked Virgil better, who had no more imagination than Dr. Akenside. Read "Sinbad the Sailor's Voyages," and you will be sick of Aeneas's. What woful invention were the nasty poultry that dunged on his dinner, and ships on fire turned into Nereids! A barn metamorphosed into a cascade in a pantomime is full as sublime an effort of genius. I do not know whether the "Arabian Nights" are of Oriental origin or not: I should think not, because I never saw any other Oriental composition that was not bombast without genius, and figurative without nature; like an Indian screen, where you see little men on the foreground, and larger men hunting tigers above in the air, which they take for perspective. I do not think the Sultaness's narratives very natural or very probable, but there is a wildness in them that captivates. However, if you could wade through two octavos of Dame Piozzi's *though's* and *so's* and *I trow's*, and cannot listen to seven volumes of Scheherezade's narrations, I will sue for a divorce *in foro Parnassi*, and Boccalini shall be my proctor. The cause will be a counterpart to the sentence of the Lacedaemonian, who was condemned for breach of the peace, by saying in three words what he might have said in two.

[Footnote 1: Atterbury (Pope's "mitred Rochester") was Bishop of Rochester in the reigns of Anne and George I. He was so violent in his Jacobitism, that on the death of Queen Anne he offered to head a procession to proclaim James III. as king at Charing Cross. Afterwards Sir R. Walpole had evidence of his maintaining a treasonable correspondence with the Court of St. Germains, sufficient to have ensured his conviction, but, being always of a merciful disposition, and naturally unwilling to bring a Bishop to the block, he contented himself with passing a Bill of Pains and Penalties to deprive him of his bishopric and banish him for life.]

You are not the first Eurydice[1] that has sent her husband to the devil, as you have kindly proposed to me; but I will not undertake the jaunt, for if old Nicholas Pluto should enjoin me not to look back to you, I should certainly forget the prohibition like my predecessor. Besides, I am a little too close to take a voyage twice which I am so soon to repeat; and should be laughed at by the good folks on the other side of the water, if I proposed coming back for a twinkling only. No; I choose as long as I can

   Still with my fav'rite Berrys to remain.

So, you was not quite satisfied, though you ought to have been transported, with King's College Chapel, because it has no aisles, like every common cathedral. I suppose you would object to a bird of paradise, because it has no legs, but shoots to heaven in a trail, and does not rest on earth. Criticism and comparison spoil many tastes. You should admire all bold and unique essays that resemble nothing else; the "Botanic Garden,"[2] the "Arabian Nights," and King's Chapel are above all rules: and how preferable is what no one can imitate, to all that is imitated even from the best models! Your partiality to the pageantry of popery I do approve, and I doubt whether the world would not be a loser (in its visionary enjoyments) by the extinction of that religion, as it was by the decay of chivalry and the proscription of the heathen deities. Reason has no invention; and as plain sense will never be the legislator of human affairs, it is fortunate when taste happens to be regent.

[Footnote 1: The story of Eurydice's death and the descent of Orpheus, her husband, to hell for her recovery, with which Virgil closes the fourth Georgic, is among the most exquisite passages in all Latin poetry. Pope made it the subject of his Ode on St. Cecilia's Day; but if Pluto and Proserpine really relented at the doggerel that the English poet puts into the mouth of the half-divine minstrel, they cannot deserve the title of *illacrymabiles* which Horace gives them. Some of the pedantic scientists (to borrow a new word) have discovered in this tale of true love an allegory about the alternations of Day and Night, Sun and Moon, and what not, for which they deserve the anathema of every scholar and lover of true poetry.]

[Footnote 2: "The Botanic Garden," a poem by Dr. Darwin; chiefly remembered for Mr. Gladstone's favourite "Upas-tree," a plant which has not, and never had, any existence except in the fancy of some traveller, who hoaxed the too-scientific poet with the story, which, years afterwards, hoaxed the orator also.]

DISMISSAL OF NECKER—BARON DE BRETEUIL—THE DUC D'ORLEANS—MIRABEAU.

TO THE HON. H.S. CONWAY.

STRAWBERRY HILL, *Wednesday night, July* 15, 1789.

I write a few lines only to confirm the truth of much of what you will read in the papers from Paris. Worse may already be come, or is expected every hour.

Mr. Mackenzie and Lady Betty called on me before dinner, after the post was gone out; and he showed me a letter from Dutens, who said two couriers arrived yesterday from the Duke of Dorset and the Duchess of Devonshire, the latter of whom was leaving Paris directly. Necker had been dismissed, and was thought to be set out for Geneva.[1] Breteuil, who was at his country-house, had been sent for to succeed him. Paris was in an uproar; and, after the couriers had left it, firing of cannon was heard for four hours together. That must have been from the Bastile, as probably the *tiers etat* were not so provided. It is shocking to imagine what may have happened in such a thronged city! One of the couriers was stopped twice or thrice, as supposed to pass from the King; but redeemed himself by pretending to be despatched by the *tiers etat*. Madame de Calonne[2] told Dutens, that the newly encamped troops desert by hundreds.

[Footnote 1: The Baron de Breteuil had been the Controller of the Household, and was appointed Necker's successor; but his Ministry did not last above a fortnight, as the King found himself compelled to restore Necker.]

[Footnote 2: Mme. de Calonne's husband had been Prime Minister for some years, having succeeded Necker in 1780.]

Here seems the egg to be hatched, and imagination runs away with the idea. I may fancy I shall hear of the King and Queen leaving Versailles, like Charles the First, and then skips imagination six-and-forty years lower, and figures their fugitive Majesties taking refuge in this country. I have besides another idea. If the Bastile conquers, still is it impossible, considering the general spirit in the country, and the numerous fortified places in France, but some may be seized by the *dissidents*, and whole provinces be torn from the Crown? On the other hand, if the King prevails, what heavy despotism will the *etats*, by their want of temper and moderation, have drawn on their country! They might have obtained many capital points, and removed great oppression. No French monarch will ever summon *etats* again, if this moment has been thrown away.

Though I have stocked myself with such a set of visions for the event either way, I do not pretend to foresee what will happen. Penetration argues from reasonable probabilities; but chance and folly are apt to contradict calculation, and hitherto they seem to have full scope for action. One hears of no genius on either side, nor do symptoms of any appear. There will perhaps: such times and tempests bring forth, at least bring out, great men. I do not take the Duke of Orleans[1] or Mirabeau[2] to be built *du bois dont on les fait*; no, nor Monsieur Necker. He may be a great traitor, if he made the confusion designedly: but it is a woful evasion, if the promised financier slips into a black politician! I adore liberty, but I would bestow it as honestly as I could; and a civil war, besides being a game of chance, is paying a very dear price for it.

[Footnote 1: The Duke of Orleans, the infamous Egalite, fomented the Revolution in the hope that it might lead to the deposition of the King, and to his own election to the throne, as in England, a century before, the Prince of Orange had succeeded James II. He voted for the death of his cousin and king, and was, in just retribution, sent to the guillotine by Robespierre at the end of the same year.]

[Footnote 2: Mirabeau was the most celebrated of all the earlier leaders of the Revolution. At the time of this letter he had connected himself closely with the Duc d'Orleans, in whose pay, in fact, he was, as his profligacy and extravagance had long before dissipated all the property which had fallen to his share as a younger son. Afterwards, on discovering the cowardice and baseness of the Duke, he broke with him, and exerted himself in the cause of the King, whom, indeed, he had originally desired to support, if his advances had not been, with incredible folly, rejected by Necker. But he had no time to repair the mischief he had done, even if it had been in his power, which it probably would not have been, since he died, after a short illness, in April, 1791.]

For us, we are in most danger of a deluge; though I wonder we so frequently complain of long rains. The saying about St. Swithin is a proof of how often they recur; for proverbial sentences are the children of experience, not of prophecy. Good night! In a few days I shall send you a beautiful little poem from the Strawberry press.

BRUCE'S "TRAVELS"—VIOLENCE OF THE FRENCH JACOBINS—NECKER.

TO THE HON. H.S. CONWAY.

STRAWBERRY HILL, *Wednesday night, July* 1, 1790.

It is certainly not from having anything to tell you, that I reply so soon, but as the most agreeable thing I can do in my confinement. The gout came into my heel the night before last, perhaps from the deluge and damp. I increased it yesterday by limping about the house with a party I had to breakfast. To-day I am lying on the settee, unable to walk alone, or even to put on a slipper. However, as I am much easier this evening, I trust it will go off.

I do not love disputes, and shall not argue with you about Bruce; but, if you like him, you shall not choose an author for me. It is the most absurd, obscure, and tiresome book I know. I shall admire if you have a clear conception about most of the persons and matters in his work; but, in fact, I do not believe you have. Pray, can you distinguish between his *cock* and *hen* Heghes, and between all Yasouses and Ozoros? and do you firmly believe that an old man and his son were sent for and put to death, because the King had run into a thorn-bush, and was forced to leave his clothes behind him! Is it your faith, that one of their Abyssinian Majesties pleaded not being able to contribute towards sending for a new Abuna, because he had spent all his money at Venice in looking-glasses? And do you really think that Peter Paez was a Jack-of-all-trades, and built palaces and convents without assistance, and furnished them with his own hands? You, who are a little apt to contest most assertions, must have strangely let out your credulity! I could put forty questions to you as wonderful; and, for my part, could as soon credit ——.

I am tired of railing at French barbarity and folly. They are more puerile now serious, than when in the long paroxysm of gay levity. Legislators, a senate, to neglect laws, in order to annihilate coats of arms and liveries! to pull down a King, and set up an Emperor! They are hastening to establish the tribunal of the praetorian guards; for the sovereignty, it seems, is not to be hereditary. One view of their Fete of the 14th,[1] I suppose, is to draw money to Paris; and the consequence will be, that the deputies will return to the provinces drunk with independence and self-importance, and will commit fifty times more excesses, massacres, and devastations, than last year. George Selwyn says, that *Monsieur*, the King's brother, is the only man of rank from whom they cannot take a title.

[Footnote 1: The grand federation in the Champ de Mars, on the anniversary of the taking of the Bastile.]

How franticly have the French acted, and how rationally the Americans! But Franklin and Washington were great men. None have appeared yet in France; and Necker has only returned to make a wretched figure! He is become as insignificant as his King; his name is never mentioned, but now and then as disapproving something that is done. Why then does he stay? Does he wait to strike some great stroke, when everything is demolished? His glory, which consisted in being Minister though a Protestant, is vanished by the destruction of Popery; the honour of which, I suppose, he will scarce assume to himself. I have vented my budget, and now good night! I feel almost as if I could walk up to bed.

THE PRINCE OF WALES—GROWTH OF LONDON AND OTHER TOWNS.

TO THE MISS BERRYS.

BERKELEY SQUARE, *June* 8, 1791.

Your No. 34, that was interrupted, and of which the last date was of May 24th, I received on the 6th, and if I could find fault, it would be in the length; for I do not approve of your writing so much in hot weather, for, be it known to you ladies, that from the first of the month, June is not more June at Florence. My hay is crumbling away; and I have ordered it to be cut, as a sure way of bringing rain. I have a selfish reason, too, for remonstrating against long letters. I feel the season advancing, when mine will be piteous short; for what can I tell you from Twickenham in the next three or four months? Scandal from Richmond and Hampton Court, or robberies at my own door? The latter, indeed, are blown already. I went to Strawberry on Saturday, to avoid the Birthday [4th June] crowd and squibs and crackers. At six I drove to Lord Strafford's, where his goods are to be sold by auction; his sister, Lady Anne [Conolly], intending to pull down the house and rebuild it. I returned a quarter before seven; and in the interim between my Gothic gate and Ashe's Nursery, a gentleman and gentlewoman, in a one-horse chair and in the broad face of the sun, had been robbed by a single highwayman, *sans* mask. Ashe's mother and sister stood and saw it; but having no notion of a robbery at such an hour in the high-road, and before their men had left work, concluded it was an acquaintance of the robber's. I suppose Lady Cecilia Johnstone will not descend from her bedchamber to the drawing-room without life-guard men.

The Duke of Bedford eclipsed the whole birthday by his clothes, equipage, and servants: six of the latter walked on the side of the coach to keep off the crowd—or to tempt it; for their liveries were worth an argosie. The Prince [of Wales] was gorgeous too: the latter is to give Madame d'Albany[1] a dinner. She has been introduced to Mrs. Fitzherbert.[2] You know I used to call Mrs. Cosway's concerts Charon's boat: now, methinks, London is so. I am glad Mrs. C. [osway] is with you; she is pleasing—but surely it is odd to drop a child and her husband and country all in a breath!

[Footnote 1: Mme. d'Albany was the widow of Prince Charles Edward, who had died in 1788 in Italy. She was presented at Court, and was graciously received by the Queen. She was generally believed to be married to the great Italian tragic poet, Alfieri. Since her husband's death she had been living in Paris, but had now fled to England for safety.]

[Footnote 2: Mrs. Fitzherbert, the Roman Catholic lady whom the Prince of Wales had married.]

I am glad you are dis_franchised of the exiles. We have several, I am told, here; but I strictly confine myself to those I knew formerly at Paris, and who all are quartered on Richmond-green. I went to them on Sunday evening, but found them gone to Lord Fitzwilliam's, the next house to Madame de Boufflers', to hear his organ; whither I followed them, and returned with them. The Comtesse Emilie played on her harp; then we all united at loto. I went home at twelve, unrobbed; and Lord Fitzwilliam, who asked much after you both, was to set out the next morning for Dublin, though intending to stay there but four days, and be back in three weeks.

I am sorry you did not hear all Monsieur de Lally Tollendal's[1] Tragedy, of which I have had a good account. I like his tribute to his father's memory. Of French politics you must be tired; and so am I. Nothing appears to me to promise their chaos duration; consequently I expect more chaos, the sediment of which is commonly despotism. Poland ought to make the French blush; but that, they are not apt to do on any occasion....

[Footnote 1: M. de Lally Tollendal was the son of that unfortunate Count Lally, so iniquitously condemned for his conduct in the government of India, as is mentioned in a former note.]

The Duke of St. Albans has cut down all the brave old trees at Hanworth, and consequently reduced his park to what it issued from—Hounslow-heath: nay, he has hired a meadow next to mine, for the benefit of embarkation; and there lie all the good old corpses of oaks, ashes, and chestnuts, directly before *your* windows, and blocking up one of my views of the river! but so impetuous is the rage for building, that his Grace's timber will, I trust, not annoy us long. There will soon be one street from London to Brentford; ay, and from London to every village ten miles round! Lord Camden has just let ground at Kentish Town for building fourteen hundred houses—nor do I wonder; London is, I am certain, much fuller than ever I saw it. I have twice this spring been going to stop my coach in Piccadilly, to inquire what was the matter, thinking there was a mob—not at all; it was only passengers. Nor is there any complaint of depopulation from the country: Bath shoots out into new crescents, circuses, and squares every year: Birmingham, Manchester, Hull, and Liverpool would serve any King in Europe for a capital, and would make the Empress of Russia's mouth water. Of the war with Catherine Slay–Czar I hear not a breath, and thence conjecture it is dozing into peace.

Mr. Dundas[1] has kissed hands for Secretary of State; and Bishop Barrington, of Salisbury, is transferred to Durham, which he affected not to desire, having large estates by his wife in the south—but from the triple mitre downwards, it is almost always true, what I said some years ago, that *"nolo episcopari* is Latin for *I lie.*" Tell it not in Gath that I say so; for I am to dine to–morrow at the Bishop of London's at Fulham, with Hannah *Bonner*, my *imprimee*.[2] This morning I went with Lysons the Reverend to see Dulwich College, founded in 1619 by Alleyn, a player, which I had never seen in my many days. We were received by a smart divine, *tres bien poudre*, and with black satin breeches—but they are giving new wings and red satin breeches to the good old hostel too, and destroying a gallery with a very rich ceiling; and nothing will remain of ancient but the front, and an hundred mouldy portraits, among apostles, sibyls, and Kings of England. On Sunday I shall settle at Strawberry; and then woe betide you on post–days! I cannot make news without straw. The Johnstones are going to Bath, for the healths of both; so Richmond will be my only staple. Adieu, all three!

[Footnote 1: Mr. Dundas, President of the Board of Control, subsequently raised to the peerage as Lord Melville. In Pitt's second administration he became First Lord of the Admiralty, but in 1805 was impeached by the House of Commons on a charge of malversation while Treasurer of the Navy in Pitt's first Ministry. Of that he was acquitted; but it was proved that some of the subordinate officers of the department had misapplied large sums of the public money, which they could not have done if he had not been grossly negligent of his duties as head of the department, and he was consequently removed from the Privy Council.]

[Footnote 2: Miss Hannah More is meant; but I do not know what peculiar cruelty of temper or practice entitled her to the name of Mary's persecuting and pitiless Bishop.]

SIR W. AND LADY HAMILTON—A BOAT-RACE—THE MARGRAVINE OF ANSPACH.

TO THE MISS BERRYS.

BERKELEY SQUARE, *Tuesday, Aug.* 23, 1791.

I am come to town to meet Mr. Conway and Lady Aylesbury; and, as I have no letter from you yet to answer, I will tell you how agreeably I have passed the last three days; though they might have been improved had you shared them, as I wished, and as I *sometimes* do wish. On Saturday evening I was at the Duke of Queensberry's (at Richmond, *s'entend*) with a small company: and there were Sir William Hamilton and Mrs. Harte[1]; who, on the 3rd of next month, previous to their departure, is to be made Madame l'Envoyee a Naples, the Neapolitan Queen having promised to receive her in that quality. Here she cannot be presented, where only such over-virtuous wives as the Duchess of Kingston and Mrs. Hastings[2]—who could go with a husband in each hand—are admitted. Why the Margravine of Anspach, with the same pretensions, was not, I do not understand; perhaps she did not attempt it. But I forget to retract, and make *amende honorable* to Mrs. Harte. I had only heard of her attitudes; and those, in dumb show, I have not yet seen. Oh! but she sings admirably; has a very fine, strong voice; is an excellent buffa, and an astonishing tragedian. She sung Nina in the highest perfection; and there her attitudes were a whole theatre of grace and various expressions.

[Footnote 1: Mrs. Harte, the celebrated Lady Hamilton, with whom Nelson was so intimately acquainted, though old Lord St. Vincent always maintained that it had never been more than a purely Platonic attachment. Her previous life, however, had been notoriously such as rendered her inadmissible at our Court, though that of Naples was less particular.]

[Footnote 2: Mrs. Hastings, the wife of the great Governor-General, had previously been married to Baron Imhoff, a German miniature painter; but she had obtained a divorce from him, and, as the Baron returned to Germany with an amount of riches that he could hardly have earned by skill in his profession, the scandalous tongues of some of Hastings's enemies imputed to him that he had, in fact, bought her of her husband.]

Letters of Horace Walpole, V2

The next evening I was again at Queensberry House, where the Comtesse Emilie de Boufflers played on her harp, and the Princesse di Castelcigala, the Neapolitan minister's wife, danced one of her country dances, with castanets, very prettily, with her husband. Madame du Barry was there too, and I had a good deal of frank conversation with her about Monsieur de Choiseul; having been at Paris at the end of his reign and the beginning of hers, and of which I knew so much by my intimacy with the Duchesse de Choiseul.

On Monday was the boat-race [at Richmond]. I was in the great room at the Castle, with the Duke of Clarence, Lady Di., Lord Robert Spencer, and the House of Bouverie, to see the boats start from the bridge to Thistleworth, and back to a tent erected on Lord Dysart's meadow, just before Lady Di.'s windows; whither we went to see them arrive, and where we had breakfast. For the second heat, I sat in my coach on the bridge; and did not stay for the third. The day had been coined on purpose, with my favourite south-east wind. The scene, both up the river and down, was what only Richmond upon earth can exhibit. The crowds on those green velvet meadows and on the shores, the yachts, barges, pleasure and small boats, and the windows and gardens lined with spectators, were so delightful, that when I came home from that vivid show, I thought Strawberry looked as dull and solitary as a hermitage. At night there was a ball at the Castle, and illuminations, with the Duke's cypher, &c. in coloured lamps, as were the houses of his Royal Highness's tradesmen. I went again in the evening to the French ladies on the Green, where there was a bonfire; but, you may believe, not to the ball.

Well! but you, who have had a fever with *fetes*, had rather hear the history of the new *soi-disante* Margravine. She has been in England with her foolish Prince, and not only notified their marriage to the Earl [of Berkeley] her brother, who did not receive it propitiously, but his Highness informed his Lordship by a letter, that they have an usage in his country of taking a wife with the left hand; that he had espoused his Lordship's sister in that manner; and intends, as soon as she shall be a widow, to marry her with his right hand also. The Earl replied, that he knew she was married to an English peer [Lord Craven], a most respectable man, and can know nothing of her marrying any other man; and so they are gone to Lisbon. Adieu!

ARREST OF THE DUCHESSE DE BIRON—THE QUEEN OF FRANCE—PYTHAGORAS.

TO THE MISS BERRYS.

STRAWBERRY HILL, *Tuesday evening, eight o'clock, Oct.* 15, 1793.

Though I do not know when it will have its whole lading, I must begin my letter this very moment, to tell you what I have just heard. I called on the Princesse d'Hennin, who has been in town a week. I found her quite alone, and I thought she did not answer quite clearly about her two knights: the Prince de Poix has taken a lodging in town, and she talks of letting her house here, if she can. In short, I thought she had a little of an Ariadne-air—but this was not what I was in such a hurry to tell you. She showed me several pieces of letters, I think from the Duchesse de Bouillon: one says, the poor Duchesse de Biron is again arrested[1] and at the Jacobins, and with her "une jeune etourdie, qui ne fait que chanter toute la journee;" and who, think you, may that be?—only our pretty little wicked Duchesse de Fleury! by her singing and not sobbing, I suppose she was weary of her *Tircis*, and is glad to be rid of him. This new blow, I fear, will overset Madame de Biron again. The rage at Paris seems to increase daily or hourly; they either despair, or are now avowed banditti. I tremble so much for the great and most suffering victim of all, the Queen,[2] that one cannot feel so much for many, as several perhaps deserve: but her tortures have been of far longer duration than any martyrs, and more various; and her courage and patience equal to her woes!

[Footnote 1: The Duchess, with scores of other noble ladies, was put to death in the course of these two horrible years, 1793-94.]

[Footnote 2: Marie Antoinette was put to death the very next day. And I cannot more fitly close the allusions to the Revolution so frequent in the letters of the past four years than by Burke's description of this pure and noble Queen in her youth: "It is now sixteen or seventeen years since I saw the Queen of France, then the Dauphiness of Versailles; and surely never lighted on this orb, which she hardly seemed to touch, a more delightful vision. I saw her, just above the horizon, glittering like the morning star, full of life and splendour and joy. Oh! what a revolution! and what a heart must I have to contemplate without emotion that elevation and that fall! Little did I dream, when she added titles of veneration to those of enthusiastic, distant, respectful love, that she should ever be obliged to carry the sharp antidote against disgrace concealed in that bosom; little did I dream that I should have lived to see such disasters fallen upon her in a nation of gallant men and cavaliers. I thought ten thousand swords must have leaped from their scabbards to avenge even a look that threatened her with insult" ("Reflections on the French Revolution ").]

My poor old friend, the Duchesse de la Valiere, past ninety and stone-deaf, has a guard set upon her, but in her own house; her daughter, the Duchesse de Chatillon, mother of the Duchesse de la Tremouille, is arrested; and thus the last, with her attachment to the Queen, must be miserable indeed!—but one would think I feel for nothing but Duchesses: the crisis has crowded them together into my letter, and into a prison;—and to be a prisoner among cannibals is pitiable indeed!

Thursday morning, 17th, past ten.

I this moment receive the very comfortable twin-letter. I am so conjugal, and so much in earnest upon the article of recovery, that I cannot think of *a pretty thing* to say to very pretty Mrs. Stanhope; nor do I know what would be a pretty thing in these days. I might come out with some old-fashioned compliment, that would have been very genteel

In good Queen Bess's golden day, when I was a dame of honour.

Let Mrs. Stanhope imagine that I have said all she deserves: I certainly think it, and will ratify it, when I have learnt the language of the nineteenth century; but I really am so ancient, that as Pythagoras imagined he had been Panthoides Euphorbus[1] in the Trojan war, I am not sure that I did not ride upon a pillion behind a Gentleman-Usher, when her Majesty Elizabeth went into procession to St. Paul's on the defeat of the Armada! Adieu! the postman puts an end to my idle speculations—but, Scarborough for ever! with three huzzas!

[Footnote 1: "*Euphorbus.*" This is an allusion to the doctrine of metempsychosis taught by the ancient philosopher Pythagoras of Samos, according to which when a man died his soul remained in the shades below suffering any punishment which the man had deserved, till after a certain lapse of time all the taint of the former existence had been worn away, when the soul returned to earth to animate some other body. The passage referred to here by Walpole occurs in Ovid's "Metamorphoses," xvi. 160, where Pythagoras is expounding his theory, which is also explained to Aeneas by Anchises in the shades below (Aeneid, vi. 745). But the two poets differ in more points than one. According to Anchises, one thousand years are required between the two existences; according to Pythagoras, not above four hundred or five hundred. According to Anchises, before the soul revives in another body it must have forgotten all that happened to it in the body of its former owner. As Dryden translates Virgil—

> Whole droves of minds are by the driving God
> Compell'd to drink the deep Lethaean flood,
> In large forgetful draughts to steep the cares
> Of their past labours, and their irksome years;
> That unremembering of its former pain
> The soul may suffer mortal flesh again.

(Aeneid, vi. 1020).

Pythagoras, on the other hand, professes a distinct recollection of who he was and what he suffered in his former life. He remembers that in the time of the Trojan war (at the outside not five hundred years before his time) he was a Trojan—Euphorbus, the son of Panthous—and that in the war he was killed by Menelaus; and his memory is so accurate, that not long before he had recognised the very shield which he had borne in the conflict hanging up as a trophy in the temple of Juno at Argos.]

EXPECTATIONS OF A VISIT TO STRAWBERRY BY THE QUEEN.

TO THE HON. H.S. CONWAY.

STRAWBERRY HILL, *July* 2, 1795.

I will write a word to you, though scarce time to write one, to thank you for your great kindness about the soldier, who shall get a substitute if he can. As you are, or have been in town, your daughter will have told you in what a bustle I am, preparing—not to resist, but to receive an invasion of royalties to-morrow; and cannot even escape them like

Admiral Cornwallis, though seeming to make a semblance; for I am to wear a sword, and have appointed two aides–de–camp, my nephews, George and Horace Churchill. If I *fall*, as ten to one but I do, to be sure it will be a superb tumble, at the feet of a Queen and eight daughters of Kings; for, besides the six Princesses, I am to have the Duchess of York and the Princess of Orange! Woe is me, at seventy–eight, and with scarce a hand and foot to my back! Adieu! Yours, &c.

A POOR OLD REMNANT.

REPORT OF THE VISIT.

July 7, 1795.

I am not dead of fatigue with my Royal visitors, as I expected to be, though I was on my poor lame feet three whole hours. Your daughter [Mrs. Damer], who kindly assisted me in doing the honours, will tell you the particulars, and how prosperously I succeeded. The Queen was uncommonly condescending and gracious, and deigned to drink my health when I presented her with the last glass, and to thank me for all my attentions.[1] Indeed my memory *de la vieille cour* was but once in default. As I had been assured that her Majesty would be attended by her Chamberlain, yet was not, I had no glove ready when I received her at the step of her coach: yet she honoured me with her hand to lead her up stairs; nor did I recollect my omission when I led her down again. Still, though gloveless, I did not squeeze the royal hand, as Vice–chamberlain Smith[2] did to Queen Mary.

[Footnote 1: There cannot be a more fitting conclusion than this letter recording the greatest honour conferred on the writer and his Strawberry by the visit of the Queen of the realm and her condescending proposal of his health at his own table.]

[Footnote 2: "*Vice–Chamberlain Smith.*" An allusion to a gossiping story of King William's time, that when Queen Mary came back to England she asked one of her ladies what a squeeze of the hand was supposed to intimate; and when the reply was, "Love," "Then," said Her Majesty, "my Vice–Chancellor must be in love with me; for he always squeezes my hand."]

You will have stared, as I did, at the Elector of Hanover deserting his ally the King of

Great Britain, and making peace with the monsters. But Mr. Fawkener, whom I saw at my sister's [Churchill's] on Sunday, laughs at the article in the newspapers, and says it is not an unknown practice for stock-jobbers to hire an emissary at the rate of five hundred pounds, and dispatch to Franckfort, whence he brings forged attestations of some marvellous political event, and spreads it on 'Change, which produces such a fluctuation in the stocks as amply overpays the expense of his mission.

This was all I learnt in the single night I was in town. I have not read the new French constitution, which seems longer than probably its reign will be. The five sovereigns will, I suppose, be the first guillotined. Adieu! Yours ever.

UNWIN BROTHERS, THE GRESHAM PRESS, CHILWORTH AND LONDON.

Printed in the United Kingdom
by Lightning Source UK Ltd.
102174UKS00001B/13